Advance praise for
**The
Community
Planning
Handbook**

*"This publication is a major step towards a better
understanding of the processes whereby people can learn
from each other in helping to determine better planning for
our future built environments. It brings together experience
that exists in Britain with international experience from
across the globe. The layout brings a new standard of design
excellence to the art of communication in this field. I highly
recommend it as a practical tool for communities and their
activists. It has a truly international perspective."*
Michael Parkes, Expert on Urban Policy to the European
Commission, Directorate General Development,
Brussels, Belgium

*"The clear and concise copy as well as the very appealing
graphic formatting of the material make this an excellent
handbook which will be useful to so many different users in
so many ways."*
Tony Costello, Professor of Architecture,
Ball State University, USA

*"Community planning is set to become part of the
mainstream planning process. Whether you are a developer,
a planning professional or an active member of your
community,* The Community Planning Handbook *will be an
invaluable guide in helping you choose and plan the
participatory events and structures to meet your needs."*
John Thompson, architect and community planner

*"I like it and I like the format. It should be a useful tool
in the toolbox."*
Simon Croxton, International Institute for
Environment and Development

*"An excellent book and well worth while."*
Rod Hackney, community architect

*"Comprehensive and useful."*
Sonia Khan, Freeform Arts Trust

*"A really useful document – I like the approach, layout
and methodology."*
Babar Mumtaz, Development Planning Unit, London

# THE
# **COMMUNITY PLANNING**
# HANDBOOK

*"If you want to know how the shoe fits, ask the person who is wearing it, not the one who made it."*

# THE
# **COMMUNITY**
# **PLANNING**
# HANDBOOK

## How people can shape their cities, towns and villages in any part of the world

Compiled and edited by
**Nick Wates**

Designed by
**Jeremy Brook**

Published in association with
The Urban Design Group
The Prince's Foundation
South Bank University, London

With the generous support of
Department of the Environment, Transport
and the Regions, England
Department for International Development, UK
European Commission Humanitarian Office

Earthscan Publications Ltd, London

# The Community Planning Handbook

How people can shape their cities, towns and villages in any part of the world.

Compiler and Editor: Nick Wates.
Design and production: Jeremy Brook, Graphic Ideas, Hastings.
Cover design: Declan Buckley.
Advisory Group: Roger Bellers, John Billingham, Roger Evans, Nick Hall, Birgit Laue, Arnold Linden, Jenneth Parker, David Lunts, Michael Mutter, Renate Ruether-Greaves, Jon Rowland, Ros Tennyson, John Thompson, John F C Turner.

First published in the UK in 2000 by Earthscan Publications Ltd.

A catalogue record for this book is available from the British Library.

ISBN: 1 85383 654 0.

Published in association with:
The Urban Design Group;
The Prince's Foundation;
South Bank University, London.

With the generous support of:
Department of the Environment, Transport and the Regions, England;
Department for International Development, UK;
European Commission Humanitarian Office.

Printed and bound by Thanet Press, Margate, Kent.

Individual pages may be freely copied for use for community planning activity providing the source is visible on all copies.

This document is an output from a project partially funded by the UK Department for International Development (DFID) for the benefit of developing countries. The views expressed are not necessarily those of the DFID or any of the other supporting organisations.

This book is printed on elemental chlorine free paper.

*Freestanding quotations are from interviews by the editor unless otherwise indicated.*

For a full list of Earthscan publications please contact:

**Earthscan Publications Ltd**
120 Pentonville Road
London, N1 9JN, UK
Tel:  +44 (0)20 7278 0433
Fax: +44 (0)20 7278 1142
Email: earthinfo@earthscan.co.uk
http://www.earthscan.co.uk

Earthscan is an editorially independent subsidiary of Kogan Page Ltd and publishes in association with WWF-UK and the International Institute for Environment and Development.

Cover photographs:
Mapping in Yellamanchilli, Adrapradesh, India, 1996
Design workshop in Berlin, Germany, 1996
Design fest in Hong Kong, 1998
Architecture centre in London, UK, 1999

Frontispiece:
Design workshops at a planning weekend in Liverpool, UK, 1997

"I know of no safe depository of the ultimate powers of society, but the people themselves; and if we think them not enlightened enough to exercise their control with a wholesome discretion, the remedy is not take it from them, but to inform their discretion."

**Thomas Jefferson, architect and President of the United States, 1820**
Letter to William Charles Jarvis

"When dwellers control the major decisions and are free to make their own contribution to the design, construction or management of their housing, both the process and the environment produced stimulate individual and social well-being."

**John F C Turner, *Freedom to Build*, 1972**

"Public participation should be an indispensable element in human settlements, especially in planning strategies and in their formulation, implementation and management; it should influence all levels of government in the decision-making process to further the political and economic growth of human settlements."

**Delegate communiqué, United Nations Habitat 1 conference, Vancouver, 1976**

"The professionals need to consult the users of their buildings more closely. The inhabitants have the local knowledge: they must not be despised. People are not there to be planned for; they are to be worked with... There must be one golden rule – we all need to be involved together – planning and architecture are much too important to be left to the professionals."

**HRH The Prince of Wales, *A Vision of Britain*, 1989**

"Community designers draw out of people their heroic insights and find ways to implement them."

**Richard Meier, Architect, *Community Design Primer*, 1990**

"When people feel they 'belong' to a neighbourhood which is theirs through their own efforts, then it will become a place which is worth struggling to retain and develop. People will safeguard what they have helped to create."

**Lord Scarman and Tony Gibson, *The Guardian*, 11 December 1991**

"Environmental issues are best handled with the participation of all concerned citizens, at the relevant level. At the national level, each individual shall have appropriate access to information... and the opportunity to participate in decision making processes. States shall facilitate and encourage public awareness and participation by making information widely available."

**United Nations Rio Declaration, Principle 10, 1992**

"Community planning is a vehicle through which we can hope to re-engage people with their community and with society."

**Charmian Marshall, Campaign Director, Urban Villages Forum, 1993**

"Community involvement has been shown to make a positive contribution to planning and development processes. At its best, community involvement can enable: processes to be speeded up; resources to be used more effectively; product quality and feelings of local ownership to improve; added value to emerge; confidence and skills to increase – for all; conflicts to be more readily resolved."

**Department of the Environment England, Summary of planning research programme, 1994**

"Design participation is the best education a community can get. The people here have been involved down to the last nail and screw. People round here know more about architecture than anywhere else in the country! It's helped us to get what we want and to get it right."

**Tony McGann, Chair, Eldonian Community-based Housing Association, Liverpool, *Building homes people want*, 1994**

"Putting cities back on the political agenda is now fundamental. What's needed is greater emphasis on citizens' participation in city design and planning. We must put communal objectives centre-stage."

**Sir Richard Rogers, Architect, Reith Lecture, 1995**

"This is a good time to be alive as a development professional. For we seem to be in the middle of a quiet but hugely exciting revolution in learning and action."

**Robert Chambers, *Whose Reality counts?*, 1997**

"Experience shows that success depends on communities themselves having the power and taking the responsibility to make things better. A new approach is long overdue. It has to be comprehensive, long-term and founded on what works."

**Tony Blair, Prime Minister, *Bringing Britain Together; a national strategy for Neighbourhood Renewal*, 1998**

"Community planning gave us the opportunity to work alongside the powers that be, have our say and feel, for the first time, that we were really being listened to. Residents now feel much more connected with decision-making and things are really beginning to improve around here."

**Sydoney Massop, Resident, South Acton Estate, Ealing, UK, 1999**

"Community participation lies right at the heart of sustainable development. Sustainable communities will take different forms from place to place, but one thing that none of them will be able to do without is a broad and deep level of participation."

**Action Towards Local Sustainability, website introduction, 1999**

# Contents

# Introduction

All over the world there is increasing demand from all sides for more local involvement in the planning and management of the environment.

It is widely recognised that this is the only way that people will get the surroundings they want. And it is now seen as the best way of ensuring that communities become safer, stronger, wealthier and more sustainable.

But how should it be done? How can local people – wherever they live – best involve themselves in the complexities of architecture, planning and urban design? How can professionals best build on local knowledge and resources?

Over the past few decades, a wide range of methods has been pioneered in different countries. They include new ways of people interacting, new types of event, new types of organisation, new services and new support frameworks.

This handbook provides an overview of these new methods of community planning for the first time in one volume. It is written for everyone concerned with the built environment. Jargon is avoided and material is presented in a universally applicable, how-to-do-it style. Whether you are a resident wanting to improve the place where you live, a policy maker interested in improving general practice, or a development professional working on a specific project, you should quickly be able to find what you need.

The methods described here can each be effective in their own right. But it is when they are combined together creatively that community planning becomes a truly powerful force for positive and sustainable change. Just a few of the many possibilities are featured in the scenarios section towards the end of the book.

In years to come it is possible to imagine that every human settlement will have its own architecture centre and neighbourhood planning offices; that all development professionals will be equipped to organise ideas competitions and planning weekends; that everyone will have access to planning aid and feasibility funds; that all architecture schools will have urban design studios helping surrounding communities; and that everyone will be familiar with design workshops, mapping, participatory editing, interactive displays and other methods described in this book.

When that happens, there will be more chance of being able to create and maintain built environments that satisfy both individual and community needs, and that are enjoyable to live and work in.

In the meantime the art of community planning is evolving rapidly. Methods continue to be refined and new ones invented. There is a growing network of experienced practitioners. This handbook will hopefully help with the evolution of community planning by allowing people to benefit from the experience gained so far and by facilitating international exchange of good practice.

# Why get involved?

**When people are involved in shaping their local surroundings, the benefits can include:**

**1 Additional resources**

Governments rarely have sufficient means to solve all the problems in an area. Local people can bring additional resources which are often essential if their needs are to be met and dreams fulfilled.

**2 Better decisions**

Local people are invariably the best source of knowledge and wisdom about their surroundings. Better decision-making results if this is harnessed.

**3 Building community**

The process of working together and achieving things together creates a sense of community.

**4 Compliance with legislation**

Community involvement is often, and increasingly, a statutory requirement.

**5 Democratic credibility**

Community involvement in planning accords with people's right to participate in decisions that affect their lives. It is an important part of the trend towards democratisation of all aspects of society.

**6 Easier fundraising**

Many grant-making organisations prefer, or even require, community involvement to have occurred before handing out financial assistance.

**7 Empowerment**

Involvement builds local people's confidence, capabilities, skills and ability to co-operate. This enables them to tackle other challenges, both individually and collectively.

## 8 More appropriate results

Design solutions are more likely to be in tune with what is needed and wanted. Involvement allows proposals to be tested and refined before adoption, resulting in better use of resources.

## 9 Professional education

Working closely with local people helps professionals gain a greater insight into the communities they seek to serve. So they work more effectively and produce better results.

## 10 Responsive environment

The environment can more easily be constantly tuned and refined to cater for people's changing requirements.

## 11 Satisfying public demand

People want to be involved in shaping their environment and mostly seem to enjoy it.

## 12 Speedier development

People gain a better understanding of the options realistically available and are likely to start thinking positively rather than negatively. Time-wasting conflicts can often be avoided.

## 13 Sustainability

People feel more attached to an environment they have helped create. They will therefore manage and maintain it better, reducing the likelihood of vandalism, neglect and subsequent need for costly replacement.

# Getting started

**How do you get started with community planning? How do you decide which methods to use, and when? How do you design an overall strategy geared to your own circumstances?**

The approach adopted will be different for every community. There is rarely a quick fix or blueprint. Each place needs to carefully devise its own community planning strategy to suit local conditions and needs.

But there are principles, methods and scenarios which appear to be universally relevant, and can be drawn on for inspiration and guidance. These are set out in this handbook. They are based on pioneering projects and experience from many countries over the past few decades.

It is unlikely that you will be able to draw up a complete strategy at the outset. Flexibility is important, in any case, to be able to respond to new circumstances and opportunities. But planning a *provisional* overall strategy is a useful discipline so that everyone understands the context in which the chosen methods are being used and the purpose of each stage.

First, define the goal or purpose. Then devise a strategy to achieve it. Try doing some or all of the following:

- Look through the General principles A–Z (pp11–21) to understand the basic philosophy of community planning;

- Skim through the Methods A–Z (pp23–129) to get a feel for the range of options available;

**Features**
The method's main characteristics

**Sample formats**
Timetables, procedures, forms, other detailed information

**Layouts**
Room layouts, physical arrangements

**Timescale**
Rough timing of activities

**Activities**
Sequence and brief description

METHODS **C**

### Sample Community Planning Forum Format

**1 Interactive displays**
As people arrive they are guided towards a variety of interactive displays where they are encouraged to make comments using Post-its, marker pens or stickers (☞ Interactive display). General mingling and discussion. Refreshments. (45 mins)

**2 Open Forum**
People are seated in a horseshoe shape, perhaps with model, plan or drawing on a table in the centre. Introductions by organisers. Feed back on interactive displays by pre-warned rapporteurs. Open debate chaired by organiser. (45 mins)

**3 Workshop groups**
People are divided into groups and work around tables on various topics/areas, either pre-selected or agreed during the Open Forum. (45 mins)

**4 Networking**
Informal mingling and discussion. Refreshments. (45 mins)

**5 Feedback (optional)**
Reports from workshop groups to plenary. (Or separate presentation session later.)

**Total running time: 3 hours minimum**
**Ideal numbers 30 – 150**

### Key roles at a planning forum

☐ Chairperson for Open Forum
☐ Facilitator/stage manager
☐ Hosts as people arrive
☐ Photographer
☐ Reporters for each interactive display
☐ Workshop and forum recorders
☐ Workshop facilitators

THE **COMMUNITY PLANNING** HANDBOOK

*Ideal layout in a large hall*

**Open forum**
*Debate in a horseshoe arrangement following a warm-up interactive display and before dividing up into workshop groups.*

---

**FURTHER INFORMATION**

☞ Methods: *Interactive display. Table scheme display. Elevation montage. Task force. Scenarios: Community centre. Village revival.*

☆ Richard John

**41**

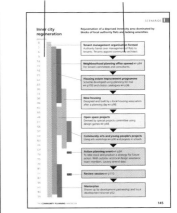

**Scenario layout**
Possible strategy for a particular development situation

**Images**
Explanatory photos from case studies. Locations are identified on page 220

**Where to find more details**

☞ *Method or scenario* pages with related information

☉ *Publication or film title.* Refer to pages 203–208 for further details

✉ *Contact organisation.* Refer to pages 209–217 for further details

☆ Contributors to this page. Special thanks

**Checklists**
Roles, equipment lists, things to remember

# Project stages

| | Initiate ▶ | Plan ▶ | Implement ▶ | Maintain |
|---|---|---|---|---|
| **Self Help** Community control | Community initiates action alone | Community plans alone | Community implements alone | Community maintains alone |
| **Partnership** Shared working and decision-making | Authorities & community jointly initiate action | **Authorities & community jointly plan and design** | Authorities & community jointly implement | Authorities & community jointly maintain |
| **Consultation** Authorities ask community for opinions | Authorities initiate action after consulting community | Authorities plan after consulting community | Authorities implement with community consultation | Authorities maintain with community consultation |
| **Information** One way flow of information Public relations | Authorities initiate action | Authorities plan and design alone | Authorities implement alone | Authorities maintain alone |

*Level of community involvement* (vertical axis label)

**Participation matrix**
A simple illustration of how different levels of participation are appropriate at different stages of a project. Most community planning operates in the shaded areas. Any party may initiate action but the crucial ingredient is joint planning and design, shown in the dark square. Implementation and maintenance will either be carried out jointly or by the authorities after consulting the community. (☞ 'Ladder of Participation' in the Glossary.)

# General principles A–Z

Whatever community planning approach you choose, there are general principles which apply to most situations. This section summarises some of the most important. Adopt and adapt as appropriate.

### Accept different agendas
People will want to be involved for a variety of reasons, for instance: academic enquiry, altruism, curiosity, fear of change, financial gain, neighbourliness, professional duty, protection of interests, socialising. This need not be a problem but it helps to be aware of people's different agendas.

### Accept limitations
No community planning activity can solve all the world's problems. But that is not a reason for holding back. Limited practical improvements will almost always result, and community planning activity can often act as a catalyst for more fundamental change.

### Accept varied commitment
Far too much energy is wasted complaining that certain people do not participate when the opportunity is provided. All of us could spend our lives many times over working to improve the local environment. Everyone has their own priorities in life and these should be respected. If people do not participate it is likely to be because they are happy to let others get on with it, they are busy with things which are more important to them or the process has not been made sufficiently interesting.

### Agree rules and boundaries
There should be a common understanding by all main interest groups of the approach adopted. Particularly in communities where there is fear – for instance that others may be trying to gain territorial advantage – it is vital that the rules and boundaries are clearly understood and agreed.

**Be visionary yet realistic**
As the proverb says: 'Where there is no vision, the people perish'.

## Avoid jargon

Use plain language. Jargon prevents people from engaging and is usually a smokescreen to hide incompetence, ignorance or arrogance.

## Be honest

Be open and straightforward about the nature of any activity. People will generally participate more enthusiastically if they know that something can be achieved through their participation (eg if there is a budget for a capital project). But they may be quite prepared to participate 'at risk' providing they know the odds. If there is only a small chance of positive change as a result of people participating, say so. Avoid hidden agendas.

## Be transparent

The objectives and people's roles should be clear and transparent at events. For instance, it may seem trivial but the importance of name badges to prevent events being the preserve of the 'in-crowd' can never be stressed enough.

## Be visionary yet realistic

Nothing much is likely to be achieved without raising expectations. Yet dwelling entirely on the utopian can be frustrating. Strike a balance between setting visionary utopian goals and being realistic about the practical options available.

## Build local capacity

Long-term community sustainability depends on developing human and social capital. Take every opportunity to develop local skills and capacity. Involve local people in surveying their own situation, running their own programmes and managing local assets.

---

### JOB VACANCY

**Project worker
4 months part-time**

**To coordinate community planning event in June**

**Applications from local residents especially welcome**

Details from: PO Box 5
Anytown 2246987

---

*Build local capacity*
*Employing residents to organise community planning activity is invariably worthwhile.*

### Communicate

Use all available media to let people know what you are doing and how they can get involved. Community newspapers or broadsheets in particular are invaluable.

### Encourage collaboration

Create partnerships wherever possible between the various interest groups involved and with potential contributors such as financial institutions.

### Flexibility

Be prepared to modify processes as circumstances dictate. Avoid inflexible methods and strategies.

### Focus on attitudes

Behaviour and attitude are just as, if not more, important than methods. Encourage self-critical awareness, handing over control, personal responsibility and sharing.

### Follow up

Lack of follow-up is the most common failing, usually due to a failure to plan and budget for it. Make sure you set aside time and resources for documenting, publicising and acting on the results of any community planning initiative.

### Go at the right pace

Rushing can lead to problems. On the other hand, without deadlines things can drift. Using experienced external advisors may speed up the process but often at the expense of developing local capacity. Get the balance right.

***Communicate***
*Let people know what you are doing and how they can get involved.*

## Go for it

This is the phrase used most by people who have experienced community planning when asked what their advice would be to others. You are bound to have doubts, it is usually a leap in the dark. But you are unlikely to regret taking the plunge.

## Have fun

Getting involved in creating and managing the environment should not be a chore. It can be a great opportunity to meet people and have fun. The most interesting and sustainable environments have been produced where people have enjoyed creating them. Community planning requires humour. Use cartoons, jokes and games whenever possible.

## Human scale

Work in communities of a manageable scale. This is usually where people at least recognise each other. Where possible, break up larger areas into a series of smaller ones.

## Involve all those affected

Community planning works best if all parties are committed to it. Involve all the main interested parties as early as possible, preferably in the planning of the process. Activities in which key players (such as landowners or planners) sit on the sidelines are all too common and rarely achieve their objectives completely. Time spent winning over cynics before you start is well worthwhile. If there are people or groups who cannot be convinced at the outset, keep them informed and give them the option of joining in later on.

*Have fun*
*Planning your environment can be enjoyable. Community planning in the Philippines (top) and in the UK (bottom).*

### Involve all sections of the community
People of different ages, gender, backgrounds and cultures almost invariably have different perspectives. Ensure that a full spectrum of the community is involved. This is usually far more important than involving large numbers.

### Learn from others
There is no need to re-invent the wheel. One of the best sources of information is people who have done it before. Don't think you know it all. No one does. Be open to new approaches. Get in touch with people from elsewhere who have relevant experience. Go and visit them and see their projects; seeing is believing. Do not be afraid of experienced 'consultants' but choose and brief them carefully.

### Local ownership of the process
The community planning process should be 'owned' by local people. Even though consultants or national organisations may be providing advice and taking responsibility for certain activities, the local community should take responsibility for the overall process.

### Maintain momentum
Regularly monitor progress to ensure that initiatives are built on and objectives achieved. Development processes are invariably lengthy, the participation process needs to stay the course. If there has to be a break, start again from where you left off, not from the beginning. Periodic review sessions can be very valuable to maintain momentum and community involvement.

*Involve all sections of the community*
*Non-literate women draw a systems diagram, Pakistan (top). Children present ideas for the future of their community, UK (bottom).*

## Mixture of methods

Use a variety of involvement methods as different people will want to take part in different ways. For instance, some will be happy to write letters, others will prefer to make comments at an exhibition or take part in workshop sessions.

## Now is the right time

The best time to start involving people is at the beginning of any programme. The earlier the better. But if programmes have already begun, participation should be introduced as soon as possible. Start now.

## Personal initiative

Virtually all community planning initiatives have happened only because an individual has taken the initiative. Don't wait for others. That individual could be you!

## Plan your own process carefully

Careful planning of the process is vital. Avoid rushing into any one approach. Look at alternatives. Design a process to suit the circumstances. This may well involve combining a range of methods or devising new ones.

## Plan for the local context

Develop unique strategies for each neighbourhood. Understand local characteristics and vernacular traditions and use them as a starting point for planning. Encourage regional and local diversity.

## Prepare properly

The most successful activities are invariably those on which sufficient time and effort have been given to preliminary organisation and engaging those who may be interested.

***Learn from others***
*Seeing is believing. Group of farmers visit a farm where innovation is taking place, Honduras (top). Group of residents visit a housing scheme before designing their own new homes, UK (bottom).*

## Process as important as product

The way that things are done is often as important as the end result. But remember that the aim is implementation. Participation is important but is not an end in itself.

## Professional enablers

Professionals and administrators should see themselves as enablers, helping local people achieve their goals, rather than as providers of services and solutions.

## Quality not quantity

There is no such thing as a perfect participation process. The search for one is healthy only if this fact is accepted. Generally, the maximum participation by the maximum number of people is worth aiming at. But any participation is better than none and the quality of participation is more important than the numbers involved. A well organised event for a small number of people can often be more fruitful than a less well organised event for larger numbers.

## Record and document

Make sure participation activities are properly recorded and documented so that it can be clearly seen who has been involved and how. Easily forgotten, such records can be invaluable at a later stage.

## Respect cultural context

Make sure that your approach is suitable for the cultural context in which you are working. Consider local attitudes to gender, informal livelihoods, social groupings, speaking out in public and so on.

Attendance:
Exhibition of plans
Monday 27 May 2000

| Name | Organisation (if any) | Contact details | Comments |
|---|---|---|---|
| | | | |

**Record and document**
*So easily forgotten.*

## Respect local knowledge

All people, whether literate or not, whether rich or poor, whether children, women or men, have a remarkable understanding of their surroundings and are capable of analysing and assessing their situation, often better than trained professionals. Respect local perceptions, choices and abilities and involve local people in setting goals and strategies.

## Shared control

The extent of public participation in any activity can vary from very little to a great deal. Different levels are appropriate at different stages of the planning process but shared control at the planning and design stage is the crucial ingredient (☞ participation matrix, page 10).

## Spend money

Effective participation processes take time and energy. There are methods to suit a range of budgets and much can be achieved using only people's time and energy. But over-tight budgets usually lead to cutting corners and poor results. Remember that community planning is an important activity, the success or failure of which may have dramatic implications for future generations as well as your own resources. The costs of building the wrong thing in the wrong place can be astronomical and make the cost of proper community planning pale into insignificance. Budget generously.

*Spend money*
*Demolition of perfectly sound buildings because people do not want them; an all too frequent occurrence. The cost of failing to involve people properly in planning and design can be astronomical.*

## Think on your feet

Once the basic principles and language of participatory planning are understood, experienced practitioners will find it easy to improvise. Avoid feeling constrained by rules or guidance (such as this handbook)!

**Visualise**
*Venn diagram of village institutions, Sri Lanka (above). Before and after of proposed changes to a public square, Czech Republic (below).*

### Train

Training is invaluable at all levels. Encourage visits to other projects and attendance on courses. Build in training to all your activities.

### Trust in others' honesty

Start from a position of trusting others and generally this will be reciprocated. Lack of trust is usually due to lack of information.

### Use experts appropriately

The best results emerge when local people work closely and intensively with experts from all the necessary disciplines. Creating and managing the environment is very complicated and requires a variety of expertise and experience to do it well. Do not be afraid of expertise, embrace it. But avoid dependency on, or hijacking by, professionals. Keep control local. Use experts 'little and often' to allow local participants time to develop capability, even if it means they sometimes make mistakes.

### Use facilitators

Orchestrating group activities is a real skill. Without good facilitation the most articulate and powerful may dominate. Particularly if large numbers of people are involved, ensure that the person (or people) directing events has good facilitation skills. If not, hire someone who has.

### Use local talent

Make use of local skills and professionalism within the community before supplementing them with outside assistance. This will help develop capability within the community and help achieve long-term sustainability.

## Use outsiders, but carefully

A central principle of community planning is that local people know best. But outsiders, if well briefed, can provide a fresh perspective which can be invigorating. Getting the right balance between locals and outsiders is important; avoid locals feeling swamped or intimidated by 'foreigners'.

## Visualise

People can participate far more effectively if information is presented visually rather than in words, A great deal of poor development, and hostility to good development, is due to people not understanding what it will look like. Use graphics, maps, illustrations, cartoons, drawings, photomontages and models wherever possible. And make the process itself visible by using flipcharts, Post-it notes, coloured dots and banners.

## Walk before you run

Developing a participatory culture takes time. Start by using simple participation methods and work up to using more complex ones as experience and confidence grow.

## Work on location

Wherever possible, base community planning activities physically in the area being planned. This makes it much easier for everyone to bridge the gap from concept to reality.

**Work on location**
*Village improvement consultations, Kenya (top). Community garden design workshop, UK (bottom).*

# Methods A–Z

**A selection of the most effective methods for helping people to get involved in physical planning and design.**

*People's wall at a design fest,*
*Hong Kong, 1998*

You are
invited to an

# Action planning event

Community
Planning Forum

Design Workshop

Microplanning
Workshop

Planning for Real
Session

**Action planning events allow people to produce plans of action at carefully structured sessions at which all those affected work creatively together. They can be used at any stage of the development process and provide an alternative to reliance on bureaucratic planning.**

■ The nature of the action planning event is decided on and agreed by the main parties involved. There are many common types (see left) and the scope for inventing new formats is unlimited. Events may last for an afternoon, a weekend, a week or a month.

■ Preparation takes place including arranging timetables, venues, publicity, equipment, technical support, background information.

■ The event is held, often assisted by a facilitator or team of facilitators from elsewhere. Proposals for action result.

■ The event is followed up to ensure that proposals are put into action.

✎ Careful planning and preparation are essential. Try and get some documented research and preliminary consultation input from key interested parties prior to an event. The creative burst is always part of – albeit a key part of – a longer process.

✎ Imaginative timetabling is crucial. Try linking up with other activities such as local festivals, anniversaries, conferences, etc.

$ Costs vary immensely from virtually nothing to tens of thousands of dollars. There is usually an event suited to most budgets, and scope for securing support in kind from interested parties.

PLÁNOVACÍ VÍKEND PRO VÁCLAVSKÉ NÁMĚSTÍ
25.–29. dubna, 1996 - Palác Lucerna, Praha

***Working together***
Local residents, business people, professionals, officials and politicians all work creatively together for an intensive period. Conventional boundaries tend to break down, releasing spirit, humour, imagination, positive thinking and collective creativity. Photos such as this are often taken to celebrate this energy.

## Action planning event timetable structure
Common for many events, regardless of length.

1 **Introduction**
Tours, briefings, icebreakers, launch.
2 **Problems/Issues**
Workshops, plenaries, individual and group working.
3 **Solutions/Options**
Workshops, plenaries, design sessions, individual and group working.
4 **Synthesis/Analysis**
Individual and group working.
5 **Production**
Report writing, photo selection, drawing, model-making.
6 **Presentation**
Slide show, film, public meeting, symposium.

---

### FURTHER INFORMATION

☞ Methods: *Community planning forum. Design fest. Design workshop. Future search conference. Microplanning workshop. Open space workshop. Planning day. Planning for Real. Planning weekend. Roadshow. Task force.* Scenarios: *Inner city regeneration. Local neighbourhood initiative.*

⊘ *Action Planning. Plan for Action.*

# Activity week

**Activity weeks are a way of focusing energy and attention on the local environment and initiatives to improve it. They are particularly effective if they become an annual event and even more so if part of a national programme.**

- A programme of events and activities is produced on a suitable theme. One week is a good length for making an impact but it can be longer or shorter.

- Organisations and individuals are invited to organise activities and events during the week and have them advertised in the programme.

- The programme is promoted by a coordinating body which may be a partnership, preferably including local media.

**Public focus**
*Local newspaper promotes an 'Environment Week' programme. Other common themes are 'Architecture Week', 'Urban Design Week', 'Preservation Week'.*

✎ Organising a first activity week will take a lot of effort. Once established as an annual event, they become relatively easy to organise as participating organisations know what is expected of them. The main coordinating task then involves compiling the programme.

✎ Make sure the programme is produced well in advance and widely publicised. Get it printed in the local paper in full, preferably as a pull-out.

✎ It helps if national organisations can provide an overall framework and get local organisations to co-ordinate local programmes.

✎ If you have an event longer than a week (one month, one year), make sure you have the stamina to maintain the momentum.

**Fact**: Over half a million pieces of publicity were printed by the Civic Trust for 'Environment Week 1991' which included 350,000 leaflets, 50,000 ideas for action booklets, 250,000 badges, 40,000 window stickers, 65,000 posters, 500 balloons and 100 banners. Over 3,000 events were held throughout the UK. Interviews were screened on 13 national TV programmes and at least 2,200 items published in newspapers.

$ Core costs: printing programme, co-ordination (several person weeks), launch event. Costs of individual activities should be covered by participating organisations. Plenty of scope for securing sponsorship.

# Activity week activities

☐ **Award ceremony**
For most imaginative local project, group or individual.

☐ **Competition**
For best kept gardens or shopfronts, best improvement ideas, best kids' drawings, etc.

☐ **Exhibition**
Exhibitions on week theme by local businesses, voluntary groups, artists, etc.

☐ **Guided tour**
Around area of interest. Or for birdwatching, looking at wild flowers, etc.

☐ **Launch reception**
Pre-week gathering for organisers, exhibitors, sponsors, the media, etc.

☐ **Lecture or film show**
On subject of interest.

☐ **Litter-pick**
Help clear up an eyesore. Bags provided.

☐ **Open day**
For projects, organisations, professional offices, etc.

☑ **Open building or garden**
See round fine local buildings or gardens.

☐ **Opening ceremony**
Formal event for press, dignatories, etc.

☐ **Party**
End of week celebration for organisers, etc.

☐ **Project opening or launch**
Unveil a plaque for a recently completed project or launch a new initiative.

☐ **Public meeting**
On a theme of current interest, inaugural meeting of new group, new initiative, etc.

☐ **Reception or 'coffee morning'**
Refreshments with a relevant theme.

☐ **Self build project**
Create a garden, build a play structure, dig a ditch, paint a mural, clear a pond, etc.

☐ **Street party**
Clear out the cars for an evening.

☐ **Workshop, Forum, Symposium, Debate**
On relevant subjects.

Plus normal festival activities: facepainting, music, dancing, juggling, theatre, poetry readings, sculptures, races, and lots more.

---

## ANYTOWN URBAN DESIGN WEEK
### 2 to 9 April 2004

### *Making places work better*

**Co-ordinated by Anytown Urban Forum**
**Sponsored by Viz Inc and The Herald**

| Day | Time | Event details | Organiser |
|---|---|---|---|
| Mon | 2.30 | **Town Centre Walk.** See the latest plans with the City Planner. Meet in Town Square. | Planning Dept. |
| | All day | **Exhibition.** Competition entries for Broadway. At Space Gallery. | Old Town Trust |
| | 18.00 | **Prize giving and party.** For Broadway competition. At Space Gallery | *The Herald* |
| Tues | 10.00 | **Rubbish clearance.** Downs Park. Sacks and refreshments provided. | Down residents |
| | 12.00 | etc etc | |

**ON ALL WEEK**

| | |
|---|---|
| Open House | See how the Duke Street project office works, 7 Duke Street, 10.00 to 17.00 |
| Gardening | Help Love Lane residents create a community garden on the derelict sidings land. Tools provided. 11.00 to 18.00 daily. |

**Further information: 446488**

*Sample programme format*
*Key ingredients: Theme; dates; timetable of activities; map with location of activities; credits; further info contact. A way of suggesting ideas for next year's programme could also be added.*

---

### FURTHER INFORMATION

☞ Scenario: *Urban conservation.*

✉ Civic Trust (Environment Week). Royal Institute of British Architects (Architecture Week). Urban Design Group (Urban Design Week).

# Architecture centre

Architecture centres are places set up to help people understand, and engage in, the design of local buildings and the built environment. They can become focal points for local environmental initiatives and a shop window and meeting place for all those involved in shaping the future of their surroundings.

- A suitable building is found with space for exhibitions, seminars, and social activities. It will normally be a building of architectural or historic interest.

- Permanent and temporary exhibits are mounted relating to the local built environment.

- A programme of activities is organised designed to stimulate interest, start initiatives and provide educational experiences for young people.

*Sample promotional poster*

*"You just want to reach out and touch and play with all the displays. I never knew buildings could be so exciting."*
**Janet Ullman, resident, London,** on Hackney Building Exploratory, London, 1998.

*"The number of visitors we've had in our first two years – 30,000 – shows there is a real public demand for what we have to offer."*
**Sasha Lubetkin, Director, Bristol Architecture Centre,** '98.

"These organisations are the key to greater public participation and access to the wider debates on architecture and related social and political issues."
**Marjorie Allthorpe-Guyton Director of Visual Arts, Arts Council of England,** Report, '99.

✎ Lots of space is needed in order to be able to house models and exhibits.

✎ Centres need time to generate momentum. At least a three-year set up timetable is advisable.

✎ Centres can be themed depending on the needs of the locality. A historic area might be better off calling it a 'Conservation Centre' or 'Heritage Centre' and focusing the exhibits and activities accordingly. Where the emphasis is entirely on education, it might be called an 'Urban Studies Centre'.

✎ Centres can be set up by local authorities, education institutes or local amenity societies. They are likely to work best if they are independent, perhaps starting off as a partnership venture.

$ Main costs: building and running costs, staff, exhibits. Scope for sponsorship from the building industry and educational grants.

# Architecture centre exhibit ideas

☐ **Aerial photo.** Of local area (people love aerial photos of where they live).

☐ **Building date maps.** Showing what was built when.

☐ **Building models and plans.** For typical or interesting local buildings.

☐ **Conservation map.** Showing location of historic buildings and landscapes.

☐ **Construction models.** Models of vernacular building methods, brick bonds, window details, etc.

☐ **Development proposals and ideas.** Drawings and models of proposed new construction in the local area with comment facilities.

☐ **Electronic or digital map.** Computer terminal (☞ p 56).

☐ **Geological model.** Showing rock strata. 'What is beneath your home?'

☐ **Historical maps.** Showing development of the area, war damage, etc.

☐ **House-type photos.** 'Put a sticker on the house you would most like to live in' (distinguish between adults, children, visitors).

☐ **Local area map.** 'Stick in a pin to show where you live.'

☐ **Local area model.** Accurate and detailed or conceptual (see photo right).

☐ **Neighbourhood jigsaw.** Lift up pieces based on district boundaries to reveal street plans, transport links, sewage systems, etc.

☐ **Site models.** Block models of a range of different styles of development in the area. 'Guess which is which?'

☐ **Space photo.** The view from a satellite. Good crowd puller.

☐ **Technical services.** Displays showing how things work; plumbing, insulation, electrics.

☐ **Tracing paper ideas.** 'Sketch your ideas on overlays of maps or drawings'.

☐ **World map.** Stick in pins to show where your parents come from.

☐ ...................................................................
...................................................................

**Bringing the built environment alive**
*Discussion takes place around a model of the local area built from recycled materials over 6 months by 350 school children.*

---

**FURTHER INFORMATION**

☞   Methods: *Community design centre. Environment shop.* Scenarios: *New neighbourhood. Regeneration infrastructure. Urban conservation.*

✉   Architecture Centres Network. Hackney Building Exploratory.

☆   Polly Hudson. Barry Shaw.

# Art workshop

**Art workshops allow local people to help design and construct artworks to improve their environment. This can be an end in itself or part of a wider regeneration effort. Community arts projects are particularly useful for helping people express their creativity and develop skills, a sense of identity and community pride.**

**Community art**
*Street lights designed by local residents with community artists.*

■ Ideas are generated by local people working closely with community artists and sculptors in studio workshop sessions. People of all ages, backgrounds and abilities can be involved.

■ Architects, landscape designers and other technical experts ensure that the designs are buildable.

■ The community chooses which of the design options generated should be built, usually through some form of voting at an exhibition.

■ The artworks are manufactured and installed, often with the assistance of local residents.

■ A celebration is held to mark completion.

✎ Good way of involving people in development who might not be attracted by more conventional consultation methods. Can break down social barriers and help communities form a common vision.

✎ Finding artists willing and able to work with community groups is essential. Providing leadership without dominating is a vital skill.

*"Community arts was a way of communicating more easily and excitingly and to get real ideas from people."*
**Waheed Saleem, Chair, Caldmore-Palfrey Youth Forum, Walsall, UK**
*Free Form Update, 1998.*

$ Can be relatively expensive in professional input and project costs. Needs to be seen as a cultural and educational initiative as well as a way of achieving environmental improvements. In this way costs can be partially covered by education or other budgets. Using recycled or scrap materials can reduce costs.

**30**

**Designing**
School children work with artists in studio workshops developing designs for a pavement mosaic using poster paints, cardboard and scissors.

**Making**
The mosaic is made by local people with no previous experience under the supervision of artists and architects.

**Celebration**
Local people celebrate an attractive improvement to the street scene which has been designed and made with their help. In contrast to much corporate artworks, such initiatives provide a visible sign of local communities' participation in the environment and can help create places which are successful, safe and respected.

## Community arts opportunities

- [ ] Bicycle paths
- [ ] Bridge decoration
- [ ] Community gardens and parks
- [ ] Fountains
- [ ] Murals
- [ ] Paving
- [ ] Play areas
- [ ] Railings and gateways
- [ ] School buildings
- [ ] Sculptures and statues
- [ ] Street lighting
- [ ] ...............................................................

### FURTHER INFORMATION

☞ Scenarios: *Derelict site re-use. Environmental art project. Inner city regeneration.*

✉ Free Form Arts Trust. Candid Arts Trust.

☆ Sonia Kahn.

# Award scheme

Award schemes provide a way to stimulate activity and spread good practice at a local, national or even international level. They can be set up by any organisation from a local community group to an international agency.

■ The organisers establish the purpose of the scheme and assemble partners and sponsors.

■ An entry form is drafted setting out the themes, categories (if any), entry criteria, judging procedure and prizes and the scheme is widely publicised to attract entries.

■ Entries are judged and an award ceremony is held to focus publicity on the winning entry and the themes behind the awards.

■ Procedures are refined and the awards held on a regular, often annual, basis.

✎ Financial incentives are not usually necessary. People will enter for the prestige. But a good plaque or framed certificate which can be publicly displayed will be highly valued.

✎ High profile patrons are very helpful in attracting entries and getting publicity. eg Royalty or local mayor.

✎ Use schemes to develop a catalogue of case studies for information exchange.

✎ Judging can be highly educational. Have as many judges as possible and get them to visit short-listed schemes. Such visits can be valuable for both the judges and local projects.

$ Local schemes: few costs involved. National schemes can be complex and involve considerable administration. The more successful they become, the more administration is required to ensure fairness and impartiality. Great scope for sponsorship.

---

**Do you know of a community planning project worthy of an award?**

Entry forms from:
**Community Planning Awards**
PO Box 7, Anytown

Organised by Environment Agency
Sponsored by Glass Ltd, Big Land and Grassroots Foundation

Closing date for entries:
**7 May 2002**

---

"The awards are an uplifting experience. They raise the spirits of those of us who are fortunate enough to be short-listed. They raise the horizons of those who miss out this time but look on and think 'we could do that' and have a crack next time. And they raise the profile of our kind of work amongst a much wider audience than we might ever otherwise hope to address."
**David Robinson, Director, Community Links, London**
Acceptance speech, 1.3.94.

"All over the country there are remarkable groups of people working incredibly hard to make a real difference to their communities. The whole object of these awards is to reward and recognise all these unsung heroes."
**HRH The Prince of Wales, Chairman, UK Community Enterprise Awards, 1995**

---

## *Anytown Shopfront award*

presented to

................................................

by

................................................

dated

................................................

**An annual award for the best shopfront improvements in Anytown.**

Sponsored by the Anytown Trust and Anytown Chamber of Commerce

*Local award certificate*

---

# National community enterprise award

Category **Community buildings**

presented to _____

by _____

dated _____

**An annual award for the most enterprising and sustainable community projects in Anycountry.**

**Patrons:** Princess Mary, Sir John Knevitt. Organised by the Housing Institute and Planners Network. Sponsored by Glass Ltd, Big Land and Grassroots Foundation.

*National award certificate*

CITY'S DIY HOME-BUILDERS IN LINE FOR A TOP AWARD

Centre of excellence in a stark estate

Centre brings hope to estate facing anarchy

**Park's action group wins award**

## Sample judging criteria

For community projects

☐ **Need or value**
The project's value to the community for which it is designed.

☐ **Community involvement**
The quality of community involvement in the project's initiation and development.

☐ **Design**
The appropriateness of the design solution adopted.

☐ **Sustainability**
The ability for the project to be maintained over time.

### Spreading the word
*Securing an award, or even just being considered for an award, can generate publicity for a project which can help with funding and other support.*

---

### FURTHER INFORMATION

☞ Scenarios: *Regeneration infrastructure. Urban conservation.*

✉ Business in the Community.

---

# Briefing workshop

**Briefing workshops are simple, easy-to-organise working sessions held to establish a project agenda or brief. Simultaneously they can:**
- **introduce people to the project;**
- **help establish the key issues;**
- **get people involved and motivated;**
- **identify useful talent and experience;**
- **identify the next steps needed.**

**They are useful at the start of a project or action planning event and can act as a public launch.**

■ Potential users of the project are invited to attend a workshop, usually lasting around 1.5 hours. Similar workshops may be held with different interest groups (eg: staff, leaders, young people, etc) or on different topics (eg: housing, jobs, open space, etc).

■ The workshop is facilitated by one or more individuals who will have planned a format to suit the context  (☞ example, right).

■ A record is kept of those who attend, the points made and key issues identified.

■ People's contributions are unattributable unless agreed otherwise.

### Main steps
1 Individual brainstorm on Post-it notes or cards;
2 Categorising in small groups sitting round a table or on the floor;
3 Presenting the results;
4 General discussion and planning the next steps.

✎ If people find it hard to get started, say "Just write down the first thing that comes into your head, however big or small."

✎ The record should ideally include typing up all Post-it notes and flip-chart sheets as well as key points from all debate.

✎ Follow up by circulating a summary to all participants.

$ Core costs: Facilitator's fees; venue hire; typing up workshop notes (allow one person day per workshop).

# Briefing workshop format

Sample covering most contexts.

**1  Introduction**

Purpose of event explained by facilitator. Everyone introduces themselves and explains briefly their interest. Notetaker and flipcharter identified. (15 mins)

**2  Individual brainstorm**

Everyone is given Post-it notes or cards of 3 different colours and asked to write down their responses, in relation to any given topic, to 3 questions:

| What is wrong? | What is your dream? | How can it happen? |
|---|---|---|

Each Post-it note should contain only one response. A limit can be set for the number of responses per person to make the total manageable. Symbols can be used if people are illiterate. (15 mins)

**3  Categorising**

People divide into three sub-groups. Each sub-group categorises Post-its of one colour by arranging them on large sheets of paper and making headings. Graphics can be added if helpful. (20 mins)

**4  Presenting**

Each sub-group explains its findings to the whole group. (20mins)

**5  Discussion**

On the results and next stage in the process. Strategic recommendations and immediate action identified. (20 mins)

If the workshop is part of a larger action planning event, a report back will then be made to a plenary session.

**Running time: 1.5 hours**.
Ideal numbers: **9 – 24**. With larger numbers, split up into more subgroups for categorising **or** have a facilitating team doing the categorising (see right).

**Facilitated categorising**

*A team of facilitators (who may be volunteers) read out responses one by one and place them in categories on wall sheets. An alternative to the procedure outlined left, useful when there are large numbers.*

# Briefing workshop props

☐  Attendance sheets
☐  Banners with workshop title
☐  Display material, eg maps, photos, plans
☐  Flip-chart (or paper on wall)
☐  Felt-tip markers (or chalk)
☐  Pens or pencils
☐  Post-it notes (or small pieces of paper or card) in three colours
☐  Tape (or drawing pins or Blu-tack)

### FURTHER INFORMATION

☞  Method: *Design workshop.*
Scenarios: *Community centre. Housing development.*

# Choice catalogues

**Choice catalogues provide a way to make design choices within a predetermined structure. They are particularly useful for helping people understand the range of options available and provide a way for making choices where large numbers of people are involved.**

***Fixtures and fittings options***
*Catalogues used by future occupants of a large housing development. Standard choices can be made which have no real cost effect. Residents can choose up to 400 points-worth of other items.*

■ Choice catalogues can be used to make design choices at a range of levels; from housing layouts to sanitary fittings.

■ Options available are worked out by the experts in consultation with a small group of residents.

■ The options are presented in the form of a simple menu made as visual as possible, using photographs or simple sketches. Choices can be costed using a simple points system if necessary.

■ People make choices based on the catalogue. This may be done individually or in groups using workshop procedures.

✎ Makes it possible to give residents of large housing developments individual choice, particularly using computers to log people's selections.

✎ Can be used as a way of generally finding out people's attitudes to design issues as well as for making specific selection.

$ Dependant on scale of consultation. Main costs: graphics; printing; distribution. If well managed and planned at an early stage, providing choice on large housing schemes need not add to overall capital costs. Indeed savings can be made by avoiding the provision of items that some people do not want.

## What would you like your housing to look like?

### Instructions

1 Select the images you like most and least.
2 Discuss your selection in a group.
3 Make a group decision on the group's most and least liked images.

***House image options***

*Choice menu format for use by future residents of a housing scheme in a group. Useful for briefing an architect. Images are selected which reflect locally available options.*

## Uses for choice menus

- ☐ Bathroom fittings
- ☐ Front entrance
- ☐ House image
- ☐ House type
- ☐ Light fittings
- ☐ Room layout
- ☐ Security equipment

## What room arrangement do you want?

### Instructions

1 Select the options you prefer.
2 Fill in the points score and add up.
3 Revise until the total score is less than 41
   **OR**
3 The cost of your home will be roughly the number of points multiplied by $..,......

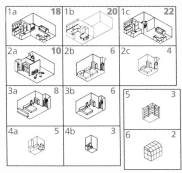

| Options | Score |
|---|---|
| 1a  Living/dining & kitchen | ☐☐ |
| 1b  Living & dining/kitchen | 2 0 |
| 1c  Living & dining & kitchen | ☐☐ |
| 2a  Large children's bedroom/play area | ☐☐ |
| 2b  Large children's bedroom | ☐ |
| 2c  Small children's bedroom | 4 |
| 3a  Large parents' bedroom | ☐ |
| 3b  Small parents' bedroom | 6 |
| 4a  Bathroom | 5 |
| 4b  Half bathroom | ☐ |
| 5    Storage room | 3 |
| 6    Greenhouse | ☐ |
| **Total** | 3 8 |

***Room layout options***

*Choice menu for selecting alternative room layouts.*

### FURTHER INFORMATION

☞ Scenario: *Housing development.*

@ *Building Homes People Want.
Participatory Design.*

✉ North Carolina State University.
Wilkinson Hindle Hallsall Lloyd.

☆ Bill Hallsall. Henry Sanoff.

# Community design centre

**Community design centres are places where communities can get affordable technical help to plan and manage their environment. They are the environmental equivalent of health centres and are invaluable for helping local people design and implement environmental projects, particularly in poor communities.**

■ Community design centres are staffed by people with a range of the technical skills needed for environmental management. They are also known as 'community *technical aid* centres'.

■ Centres provide services to local voluntary groups – and sometimes individuals – covering all aspects of environmental management. Services will normally be free unless groups are able to afford to pay for them or fees can be built into capital project bids.

■ Centres will normally be independent charitable agencies funded by governments, local authorities, universities, charities or private sponsors. Sometimes they are controlled by the groups to whom they provide services. Independent consultants may also provide the same service, subsidised by other work.

✎ Securing funding is a constant headache. Centres are most likely to be sustainable if they carry out fee earning work as well as providing free services.

$ Dependent on the number of paid staff and cost of premises. For instance a well equipped centre with 5 full-time technical staff could cost US$200,000 per annum. A centre run by volunteers or secondees using free accommodation could cost very little.

---

**Are you**
- a community organisation?
- a tenants' association?
- a residents' association?
- an ethnic organisation?
- a women's group?

**Do you want to**
- Clear up an eyesore?
- Build a community hall?
- Build a women's refuge?
- Develop a play area?
- Landscape a derelict site?

**We can provide**
- Architects
- Planners
- Surveyors
- Ecologists
- Project management
- Help with fundraising and constitutions
- Publications and videos

Contact
**Anytown Community Technical Aid Centre**
01234 666444

A free service to community groups funded by Anytown City Council, Ministry for Environment and Jet plc

---

*"What makes the community architect different from the traditional architect is that he's available, he's there – seven days a week, twenty-four hours a day to feel the vibration and pulse of the community. The architect's presence on site is essential. That very presence is wealth – not just for the architect but for the whole community."*
**Rod Hackney, Community architect**
*Architects Journal, 20.2.1985.*

# Community design centre services

Customise to satisfy local needs.

- [ ] Action planning
- [ ] Art and graphics
- [ ] Community arts
- [ ] Competition management
- [ ] Construction work supervision
- [ ] Design of buildings and landscape
- [ ] Employment generation
- [ ] Feasibility studies; buildings and landscape
- [ ] Fundraising
- [ ] Maintenance of buildings and landscape
- [ ] Organisation formation and development
- [ ] Planning advice and advocacy
- [ ] Plant nursery development and maintenance
- [ ] Property management and development
- [ ] Rectifying building defects
- [ ] Strategic planning
- [ ] Training in environmental management and design
- [ ] ................................................................

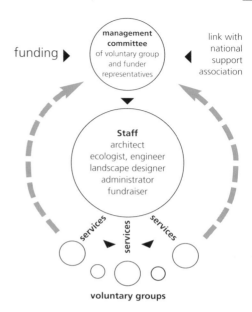

*Organisation chart for a community design centre managed by a committee of representatives of groups that use it and funders.*

**Technical expertise**
*A community-based nerve centre providing skills and experience on environmental management.*

## FURTHER INFORMATION

☞ Methods: *Environment shop. Neighbourhood planning office. Urban design studio.* Scenarios: *Derelict site re-use. Regeneration infrastructure. Shanty settlement. Urban conservation.*
✉ Association for Community Design. Association of Community Technical Aid.

# Community planning forum

Community planning forums are open, multipurpose events lasting several hours. The three-stage format is designed to secure information, generate ideas and create interaction between interest groups with a minimum of advance planning.

**Sample advertising leaflet.**
*Key components: Slogan summarising overall purpose; venue; time; date; statement of immediate objectives and perhaps some background information; map of area with venue marked; name of organisers.*

- Community planning forums can be organised at any time but are particularly useful at an early stage in a participation or development process.

- Forums can be organised by any interested party and can be organised at short notice.

- The format combines interactive displays, an open forum, workshop groups and informal networking.

- Key ingredients are a leaflet advertising the event, a means of distributing it, a venue and a facilitator.

✎ Keep the atmosphere informal to get best results. Good refreshments worthwhile.

✎ Particularly useful events for students engaged in urban design projects because they do not necessarily need to relate to any 'real' development timetable or be organised by local people. They can be organised by anyone at any time (though they will normally work better if locals assist).

✎ Getting students to organise the format themselves can be highly educational, particularly if linked with a process planning session (☞ Process planning session). Providing a framework may be helpful (ie arranging publicity and venue in advance).

*"It was a very effective formula. It allowed us, as a group, to find out what the inhabitants expected of their place for the future. And it didn't impose too much on people's time. In fact I think everyone had a very enjoyable evening."*
**Laura Dotson**
*Interior designer*
Student organiser of a community planning forum at Richmond, Virginia, USA, 1996.

$ Main costs: Venue hire; advertising leaflet production.

# Sample Community Planning Forum Format

### 1 Interactive displays
As people arrive they are guided towards a variety of interactive displays where they are encouraged to make comments using Post-its, marker pens or stickers (☞ Interactive display). General mingling and discussion. Refreshments. (45 mins)

### 2 Open forum
People are seated in a horseshoe shape, perhaps with model, plan or drawing on a table in the centre. Introductions by organisers. Feed back on interactive displays by pre-warned rapporteurs. Open debate chaired by organiser. (45 mins)

### 3 Workshop groups
People are divided into groups and work around tables on various topics/areas, either pre-selected or agreed during the open forum. (45 mins)

### 4 Networking
Informal mingling and discussion. Refreshments. (45 mins)

### 5 Feedback (optional)
Reports from workshop groups to plenary. (Or separate presentation session later.)

**Total running time: 3 hours minimum
Ideal numbers 30 – 150**

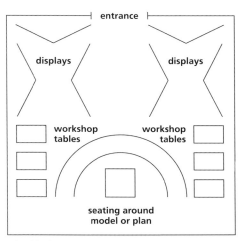

*Ideal layout in a large hall*

**Open forum**
*Debate in a horseshoe arrangement following a warm-up interactive display and before dividing up into workshop groups.*

# Key roles at a planning forum

☐ Chairperson for open forum

☐ Facilitator/stage manager

☐ Hosts as people arrive

☐ Photographer

☐ Reporters for each interactive display

☐ Workshop and forum recorders

☐ Workshop facilitators

---

### FURTHER INFORMATION

☞ Methods: *Elevation montage. Interactive display. Table scheme display. Task force.* Scenarios: *Community centre. Village revival.*

☆ Richard John

# Community profiling

**Community profiling involves building up a picture of the nature, needs and resources of a community with the active participation of that community. It is a useful first stage in any community planning process to establish a context which is widely agreed.**

**Taking stock**
*Government officials analysing information gained from the community analysing itself using a variety of profiling methods.*

- A range of methods are used to enable the community to develop an understanding of itself.

- The methods combine group working and group interaction techniques with data collection and presentation techniques.

- The focus is on methods which are visual in order to generate interest and make the process accessible to the illiterate and those unused to verbal communication.

- The results are in the public realm. Reports include as many of the words, writings and pictures of local people as possible.

✎ Good facilitation is particularly important to avoid manipulated or simply poor results. A strategy is often needed to prevent domination by the more powerful or aggressive. Facilitators should listen and learn at all times. Even when relaxing, insights into local dynamics can be gained.

✎ Closer attention and differing sessions may be needed to obtain the views of women and any under-represented groups.

✎ Informal observation is a powerful source of information on local dynamics.

*"The benefit of using this method is the diverse number of people who can work together and still achieve an outcome which involves everyone."*
**Pat Jefferson, Carlisle City Council**
*Tidelines* newsletter, Solway Firth Partnership, 1997.

$ Cost effective compared with conventional analysis by outside consultants. Main cost: facilitators' fees.

# Community profiling methods

- [ ] **Activity chart.** Plotting people's activities each day, or each week. Useful for understanding divisions of labour, roles and responsibilities in a community.

- [ ] **Building survey.** Recording the state of repair of buildings.

- [ ] **External relationship profiling.** Examining the roles and impact of external organisations.

- [ ] **Gender workshop.** Separate sessions for women (or sometimes men) to analyse their situation, needs and priorities.

- [ ] **Historical profile.** Identifying and listing key events, beliefs and trends in a community's past and their importance for the present.

- [ ] **Household livelihood analysis.** Comparing sources of income and support with expenditure patterns and looking at coping strategies for times of hardship.

- [ ] **Informal walk.** Walking in a group without a definite route, stopping to chat and discuss issues as they arise. (☞ *Reconnaissance trip*)

- [ ] **Mapping.** Making maps showing various characteristics, eg resources. (☞ *Mapping*)

- [ ] **Organisation review.** Review of existing groups and organisations to assess their roles, membership, plans and potential.

- [ ] **Personal history.** Recording detailed oral accounts of individuals' lives, perhaps asking them to emphasise specific issues.

- [ ] **Problem tree.** Analysing the inter-relationships among community issues and problems using a graphic based on a tree. (☞ *Glossary*, and illustration, below)

- [ ] **Role play.** Adopting the role of others and acting out scenarios. (☞ *Gaming*)

- [ ] **Seasonal calendar.** Exploring changes taking place throughout the year, eg in work patterns, production. (☞ *Diagrams*)

- [ ] **Semi-structured interview.** Conversational open discussion using a checklist of questions as a flexible guide instead of a formal questionnaire. Different types include; individual, group, focus group, and key informant. (☞ *Glossary*)

- [ ] **Simulation.** Acting out a real event or activity in order to understand its effect. (☞ *Simulation*)

- [ ] **Skills survey.** Assessing skills and talent in a community. (☞ *Glossary*, and p175)

- [ ] **Transect walk.** Systematic walk through an area to observe and record key features, for instance land use zones. (See also *Reconnaissance trip*)

- [ ] **Well-being or wealth ranking.** Assessing levels of well-being of different households using pile sorting. (☞ *Glossary*)

- [ ] ........................................................

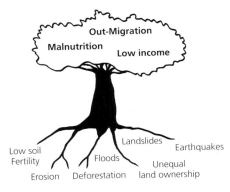

**Problem tree**
*Simple graphic used to analyse complex issues.*

---

### FURTHER INFORMATION

☞ Methods: *Diagrams. Gaming. Mapping. Reconnaissance trip. Simulation.* Scenarios: *Community centre. Village revival.*

⊘ *Participatory Learning & Action. 4B.*

☆ Roger Bellers. Nick Hall.

---

# Design assistance team

## Team members' luggage

- ☐ Camera.
- ☐ Clothes with lots of pockets for camera, notebook, pens, etc.
- ☐ Favourite drawing pens.
- ☐ Material for special presentation if required.
- ☐ Pocket notebook.
- ☐ Useful general facts and figures or illustrative material likely to be relevant.
- ☐ .........................
- ☐ .........................

**Independent expertise**
*Team members discuss options with a local landowner.*

"We owe thanks to all our 'outsiders'. They were so friendly from the start. It was like one big happy family."
**Local resident, Ore Valley Action Planning Weekend**, 1997.

**Assistance teams comprise a number of specialists from a variety of relevant disciplines who visit an area and take part in a participation process (for instance, a planning weekend). They are particularly useful for providing a fresh and independent viewpoint.**

- Assistance teams are invited in by local people or agencies and provided with a brief. This may be simply to listen and advise, or to act as facilitators.

- Teams will normally be multidisciplinary and be led by a team chairperson.

- Team members are often paid expenses only, to ensure independence. If they are paid a fee, this needs to be made clear.

- The team will usually prepare a report with their recommendations before leaving.

✎ Good briefing beforehand is essential; on both content and process.

✎ Strong leadership is vital to keep events moving forward. Give team members roles (see box, right) to focus people's energy.

✎ Get each team member to supply quotes (soundbites) and recommendations to standard bullet point format, in 3 categories: Background; issues; recommendations (to make sure they listen and provide evidence of their contribution).

✎ Ensure that team members commit themselves to attending for the whole event.

$ Main costs for team: Travel; accommodation; meals; film; equipment and supplies.

# Assistance team roles

For large action planning events where the team is facilitating and preparing a report. Several compatible roles may be taken by one individual. Not all roles will be needed in every event. Customise.

- ☐ **Contacts person.** Keep names and phone numbers of useful resource people.
- ☐ **Diplomats.** Liaise between different workshops to create linkages.
- ☐ **Follow-up co-ordinator.** Ensure follow-up takes place and publicise.
- ☐ **Photographer.** Ensure key events are photographed (slides and prints).
- ☐ **Report editor.** Commission, gather and edit copy and illustrations.
- ☐ **Report subeditor.** Subedit copy. Assist editor.
- ☐ **Report production manager.** Liaise with printer and photo lab.
- ☐ **Slide show editor.** Select slides for presentation.
- ☐ **Sound recorder.** Tape key sessions and index tapes.
- ☐ **Stage manager.** Co-ordinate pool of people for errands etc.
- ☐ **Team chairperson.** Provide leadership, orchestrate event, take responsibility.
- ☐ **Team facilitator.** Keep roving eye on group dynamics, reporting back to team chairperson.
- ☐ **Workshop facilitators.** Steer workshop sessions (one per workshop).
- ☐ **Workshop note-takers.** Prepare notes of workshops in format for final report.
- ☐ ..................................................

# Team synthesis process

Sample process for drawing up proposals after public workshops or planning day.

1 **Roles and responsibilities meeting**
Team only. Determine tasks, report structure and division of roles.

2 **Individual team working**
All workshops analysed to standard format summarising points made and identifying key themes. Proposals drawn up to standard format (heading plus one summary paragraph).

3 **Team participatory editing**
Text and graphics displayed on wall for comment (using pens and Post-its).

4 **General participatory editing**
Non team members return (eg local enthusiasts) to make comments.

5 **Review session**
Open workshop session to discuss any major omissions or controversial issues.

6 **Final editing and production**
Team only

**Total running time: 1 day**

**FURTHER INFORMATION**

☞ Methods: *Participatory editing. Planning day. Planning weekend.* Scenarios: *Industrial heritage. Local neighbourhood.*

➋ *Action Planning. Creating a Design Assistance Team for Your Community.*

# Expertise needed on design assistance team

Checklist of skills and professional backgrounds likely to be useful. Customise for each event.

- ☐ Architecture
- ☐ Community development
- ☐ Ecology
- ☐ Economics and finance
- ☐ Historic preservation
- ☐ Journalism
- ☐ Landscape design
- ☐ Law
- ☐ Management
- ☐ Planning
- ☐ Property development
- ☐ Sociology
- ☐ Urban design
- ☐ .....................
- ☐ .....................

It helps if people are also good at writing, drawing, organising, analysing and working as a team.

# Design fest

**Design fests produce creative concepts for the future of an area by getting multidisciplinary design teams to develop and present their ideas in public. They are a good way to stimulate debate and develop imaginative solutions, particularly on controversial issues.**

*Sample poster*
*Key ingredients: Theme; logo; visual image; details of activities; organisers; sponsors; further information.*

- Organisers decide on a theme that needs exploring and determine a brief. A specific, challenging site will normally be selected to focus creativity towards practical solutions.

- Multidisciplinary design teams are selected and briefed. The teams are likely to comprise architecture or planning students as well as practising professionals from a range of disciplines.

- The teams hold an intensive design workshop (or 'charrette') in public, coinciding with a public exhibition on the theme. The public are encouraged to respond to the theme and the team's ideas as they emerge and to develop their own.

- A high profile public symposium is held immediately after the workshops when the ideas generated are presented and debated by a prominent panel.

- The results are published and widely distributed.

*"As the Saturday night deadline drew near, the pace was frenzied. Some drawings were coloured by up to six people at a time, models were being glued together, slides being taken for presentation at the Sunday symposium."*
**Designing Hong Kong report poster,** 1998.

✎ Ideally suited to being organised by university architecture and planning schools. Students learn a lot by taking part in teams, organising exhibition material, doing surveys of the public and helping the public to engage in design issues.

$ A well organised, high profile design fest could cost US$40,000. But there is a great deal of scope for securing sponsorship.

### Designing in public

*Multidisciplinary design teams develop ideas in three small cubicles erected inside a large shopping centre. Members of the public view the teams at work from the balconies above, explore exhibition material and interactive displays pinned to the outside of the screens, are interviewed by team members and develop and pin up their own ideas in a fourth cubicle (shown left above). The teams also have the use of a private resource room (not shown) with photocopying and other facilities. They are told to produce simple, straightforward and graphic presentation material to capture the attention of the viewing public on the balcony. The workshop may last for one or several days. Then, slides are made of the drawings and all the ideas emerging are presented and debated at a public symposium.*

### FURTHER INFORMATION

☞ Methods: *Design workshop. Interactive display.*

✉ Chinese University of Hong Kong (Department of Architecture)

☆ Jack Sidener

# Design game

**Movable pieces**
*Residents move pieces around until they are happy with their design.*

**Design games are like jigsaw puzzles. They are a highly visual way of allowing people to explore physical design options for a site or internal space. They are particularly useful for designing parks and room layouts and can also be used for land-use planning. They can be used in isolation or as part of a broader participation process.**

- A base map of a site or room is prepared.

- Cut-out pieces representing items that could be incorporated are made to the same scale. Materials for making pieces are kept at hand to allow new items to be made as desired.

- Individuals or groups move pieces around until they are happy with the design, which is then photographed.

- Layouts produced by different individuals or groups are discussed and analysed as a basis for drawing up sketch designs and costings.

"The most vital aspect of our approach was the design game: it was intended to be, and was, fun; this made it less threatening, and thus more accessible.... Playing the game illustrated far better than words spoken by either side ever could, both the urban design principles discussed and residents' own preferences for the site."
**Robert Brown, Architect**
*Urban Design Quarterly,*
January 1998.

✎ Cut-outs are normally simple two-dimensional, hand-drawn illustrations, using coloured felt-tip on cardboard. Three-dimensional cut-outs are even better but take more time.

✎ Putting capital and revenue costings on pieces can make the design process more realistic.

✎ Make sure the pieces are visually explanatory so that photographs of the designs will make sense. Exhibiting or publishing photos of the designs of different groups can be a useful next step.

$ Depends on standard of design. Can be done very simply.

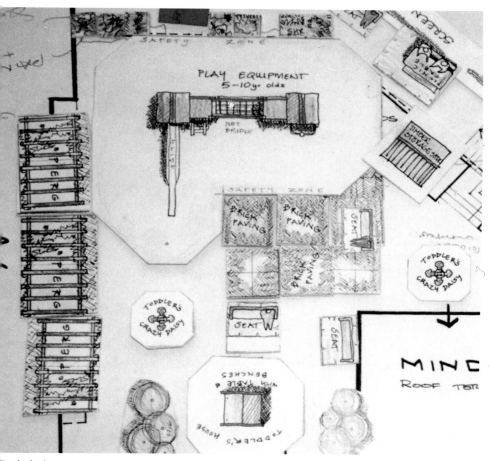

**Park design**
One resident group's design for a park showing layout of fencing, children's play facilities and planting.

**Comparing options**
Discussion of layouts prepared by different groups.

**FURTHER INFORMATION**

☞ Method: *Planning for Real.*
Scenario: *Inner city regeneration.*

⊘ *Good Practice Guide to Community Planning and Development. Participatory Design.*

☆ Alexandra Rook. Dee Stamp. Michael Parkes. Henry Sanoff.

# Design workshop

**Design workshops are hands-on sessions allowing small groups of professionals and non-professionals to work creatively together developing planning and design ideas. They will normally be held as part of a planning day or other action planning event.**

**Hands-on**
*Residents and architects devise improvements to a housing estate together.*

**Report back**
*Participant explains design workshop outcome to a plenary session.*

*"Brief intensive brainstorming workshops can be enormously productive – people of mixed backgrounds, grouped together for the first time, with clear challenges, find that they can focus their minds and tap hidden reservoirs of creativity."*
**Jack Sidener, Professor of Architecture, Chinese University of Hong Kong** workshop brief, 1998.

- People work in groups around a table with plans or a flexible model. Different groups can deal with different areas or the same area at different scales. Groups can be allocated a topic such as transport, open spaces or housing. Groups can vary in size (8 – 10 is a good average to aim at).

- Everyone is encouraged to develop their ideas by drawing or making adjustments to the model. Each group usually needs a facilitator, a note-taker and a mapper (who marks points on a map or plan).

- A structured workshop procedure is often followed, especially if people have not worked together before (☞ sample format opposite).

✎ Using plans is often more suitable than models because little preparation is needed. People generally find it surprisingly easy to read plans once they have started working with them. It helps though if the facilitator has previous experience of design workshops and urban design expertise.

✎ Design workshops often work best if people have done a briefing workshop first (☞ Briefing workshop).

✎ Get people going by telling them that "no idea is too big, no idea too small". At the end everyone should sign drawings and it is often useful to draw up a tidy version for presentation.

$ Main costs: Planning and preparation; facilitator's fees; supplies (see box, right).

*Creative working*
*Participants use tracing paper over a plan, mini Post-it notes and felt-tip pens to explore options for an inner city neighbourhood. Most have no previous design experience.*

## Design workshop format
Sample to suit most contexts.

**1  Arrangements**
People choose a workshop group and sit round tables with plan or model. (5 mins)

**2  Introductions**
People briefly introduce themselves. (10 mins)

**3  Getting started**
Facilitator asks people to write ideas on mini Post-it notes or cards and place them on the plan. Responses to questions such as:
• Where are the problems?
• Where are the opportunities?
• Where do you want things to happen?
(15 mins)

**4  Design ideas**
People use coloured pens to sketch ideas, discussing things as they do so. Different options can be drawn on separate sheets of tracing paper. (50 mins)

**5  Prepare summary**
Summary drawings prepared of main suggestions. (10 mins)

**Running time: 90 mins.**
**Ideal numbers: 8-10 per workshop.**

## Design workshop supplies

**On table**
☐ Base plan of area.
☐ Tracing paper overlays (large sheets and A4 pads) taped with masking tape.
☐ Felt-tip coloured pens. Different colours.
☐ Mini Post-it notes or small cards.
☐ Ball point pens or pencils (one per person)
☐ Lined A4 writing pads (2 per group)

**To one side**
☐ Flipchart and marker pens.
☐ Pin-up space (Blu-tack or pins needed).
☐ Attendance sheets.
☐ Site photographs.

**If using model**
☐ Base model with movable parts.
☐ Spare cardboard or polystyrene.
☐ Scissors.
☐ Post-it notes and cocktail sticks.

**FURTHER INFORMATION**

☞  Methods: *Action planning event. Briefing workshop. Planning day. Planning weekend. Planning for Real.*

METHODS

# Development trust

**Development trusts provide a mechanism for communities to undertake regeneration and development projects themselves. They make it possible to achieve the long-term sustained effort that is needed to evolve a community's own plans and put them into action.**

- Development trusts are community-based organisations working for the regeneration of their areas. They may undertake a specific project or, more likely, a range of economic, environmental, cultural or social initiatives.

- Development trusts are independent bodies with management structures ensuring accountability to local people. They are not-for-profit bodies, often with charitable status, making it possible to attract resources from public, private and charitable sectors.

- Administrative structures are designed to allow development trusts to own and manage property, employ staff and develop efficient project management capability.

✎ Funding is easiest to secure at the outset in the form of grants from government and local authority regeneration budgets. The challenge is to build up a secure asset base, some committed sponsors and income generating capacity before grants expire. Having a linked trading company is often useful to make it possible to earn income without losing charity status.

✎ Having a clear focus, based on local priorities, is important to attract support. Select a name, slogan and style to reflect this.

$ Essential core costs: Manager's wages, premises, office running. Desirable to have several staff and a project seed fund. Aim at £100,000 per annum but be prepared to start with volunteers.

---

## Anytown Environment Trust

- **Become a member**
- **Become a volunteer**
- **Start a local project**
- **Offer your expertise**
- **Donate equipment**
- **Lend premises**
- **Second a staff member**
- **Sponsor a project**
- **Leave a bequest in your Will**

Environmental improvements
Property management
Community facilities
Regeneration expertise
Environmental education

**HELPING PEOPLE IMPROVE THEIR ENVIRONMENT**

*Sample promotion leaflet*
*Key components: Name of organisation; what it can do; how people can get involved; slogan summarising aim.*

*"The strength of development trusts is that they can demonstrate the creativity and added competence that comes from bringing together expertise and enthusiasm from public, private, voluntary and community sectors."*
**David Wilcox**
*The Guide to Development Trusts and Partnerships*, 1998.

**52**

THE **COMMUNITY PLANNING** HANDBOOK

# Typical development trust activities

- ☐ Administering grant schemes
- ☐ Building and managing workspace
- ☐ Developing community plans
- ☐ Environmental education programmes
- ☐ Holding training programmes
- ☐ Organising competitions
- ☐ Organising events
- ☐ Preserving historic buildings
- ☐ Promoting community development
- ☐ Providing sports and recreational facilities
- ☐ Running childcare centres
- ☐ Running award schemes
- ☐ Running resource centres
- ☐ Setting up and managing arts facilities
- ☐ Setting up community enterprises
- ☐ Supporting community groups
- ☐ Supporting small businesses

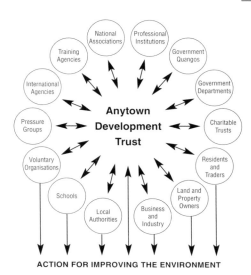

**ACTION FOR IMPROVING THE ENVIRONMENT**

### Concept
*Bringing together national, regional and local agencies – in the public, private and voluntary sectors – to promote action by local people to improve the environment.*

### Typical democratic management structure
*Elected local members have a majority on the Board to ensure local accountability. Elections are usually held annually with members serving two years each.*

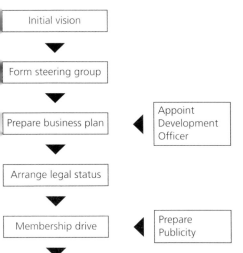

### Setting up
*The main steps. Likely to take at least one year.*

### FURTHER INFORMATION

- ☞ Scenarios: *Inner city regeneration. Local neighbourhood initiative. Urban conservation*
- ✉ Development Trusts Association.
- ⊘ *The Guide to Development Trusts and Partnerships.*

# Diagrams

**Diagrams and charts are a highly effective visual way to collect, discuss and display information at all stages of the planning process.**

***Venn diagram***
*Showing relationships between village institutions.*

***Mind map***
*Showing perceptions of trends and linkages.*

- Individuals or groups use the construction of diagrams as a basis for gathering and analysing information. Fairly complex issues or processes can be represented simply if the right type of diagram is chosen.

- The diagrams provide a focus for discussing issues – by both literate and non-literate people – and help stimulate creative thinking.

- The diagrams are used for ordering and presenting information, prioritising issues, decision making and monitoring.

- Making diagrams can form part of a workshop or be undertaken as an activity in its own right. A group diagramming process is similar to a group mapping process (☞ Mapping).

✎If diagrams are made on the ground, photograph or draw them to keep a record.

✎ Involve people who are particularly knowledgeable, and involve as many others as possible. Facilitators should sit back and watch, not interfere too much.

✎ Minimise text. Use colour coding, symbols and local materials wherever possible.

$ Few expenses necessary. Main cost: facilitators' fees. May be worth spending money on materials to improve presentation.

**Calendar**
*Showing seasonal changes in work patterns by plotting people's activities on a monthly basis.*

**Matrix**
*Assessing the value of different tree species by placing stones to score various attributes.*

**Network diagram**
*Identifying institutional changes needed by plotting flows and links between villages.*

# Common diagram types and their uses

- **Calendar.** For understanding seasonal patterns, eg planting, tourism or rainfall.

- **Flow diagram.** Showing the components of any activity and the linkages between them. For understanding the impact of an initiative.

- **Matrix.** Grid allowing comparison of two variables. Used for assessing options and prioritising.

- **Mind map.** Showing people's perceptions of trends and linkages. Used for collective brainstorming to develop common outlook.

- **Network diagram.** Showing flows and linkages between people, organisations or places. Used for highlighting strengths and weaknesses in institutional relationships.

- **Organisation chart.** Showing who is responsible for what. Used for understanding how organisations work.

- **Pie chart.** Dividing a circle into different sized segments. For showing population structure, distances to work and so on.

- **Time-line.** List of events over time. For understanding historical trends.

- **Timetable.** For analysing daily routines, street activity and so on.

- **Venn diagram.** Using circles of different sizes to indicate roles of different organisations and the relationships between them.

---

**FURTHER INFORMATION**

☞ Methods: *Community profiling. Mapping.*

❧ *Participatory Learning & Action.*

---

# Electronic map

**Electronic maps allow people to explore an area and make comments at computer terminals with specially created software. They have immense potential for helping people to visualise proposals and make their views known.**

***Digital age participation***
*Finding out what is going on in your neighbourhood and making your views known at a computer terminal.*

- Electronic maps are created as software which can be run on desk-top computers or touch screen monitors.

- Aerial photography, maps, video clips, sounds, photos and 3-dimensional visualisations can all be incorporated to build up a series of images of an area from a variety of perspectives.

- People can explore the map at computer terminals in libraries, cafes and cultural centres and add their own comments.

- The maps can be continually adapted to provide an ongoing information service and consultation process.

## Technical data

Based on a custom geo-location database engine with SQL interface. Scaleable and modular design allows limitless adaptation and infinite extension of map area. Performs on low spec machines due to low memory overheads with no more than 1.5MB on screen at any time. Works on ordinary desk-top machines, both mac and pc formats.

✎ Great potential for linking up with maps in different areas and for accessing via the Internet.

✎ Gathering the content for maps is itself a part of the exploration and participation process.

$ Developing software from scratch could cost as much as US$80,000. But it should soon be possible to purchase software under license for a few hundred pounds. Then cost is reduced to gathering the raw material for your map. This could cost around US$15,000 or much less if you use material already available.

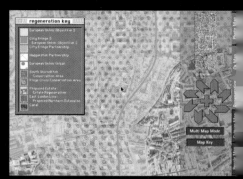

**1 Bird's eye view.** Start with an aerial photo on screen. Use cursor keys to move about and to zoom in to the place you are interested in.

**2 Map layers.** Superimpose maps on the aerial photo or view them separately. Maps might include: regeneration initiatives (as shown), cultural facilities, proposed new buildings.

**3 Street level walkabout.** Click on a place you want to view and it fills the screen. It may be a photograph, drawing, photomontage or model of how it could be. Click arrows to move about.

**4 Video clips.** See live action through video clips. This might include presentations, art works, interviews with people (as shown), street scenes, performances.

**5 Comment.** See and hear what other people think. Add your own comment by typing or speaking.

### FURTHER INFORMATION

☞  Scenario: *New neighbourhood.*

✉  Architecture Foundation.

☆  Example based on a map of Hackney, London by Muf Architects and ShoeVegas for Hackney Council.

# Elevation montage

**Elevation montages show the facade of a street by assembling photos of individual buildings. They can be useful for helping people gain an understanding of the building fabric and devise improvements.**

■ An elevation of a street is created by assembling a series of individual photographs. Both sides of a street can be done and pasted either side of a plan.

■ Simple instructions ask people to make comments on Post-it notes or cards and place them underneath the relevant section (what they like/don't like/would like to see).

■ The build up of Post-it notes or cards generates a dialogue amongst participants and useful data for later discussion and analysis.

**Wall-mounted**
*Residents pasting Post-it notes on a wall-mounted montage.*

*Detail of above with comment.*

✎ Table-mounted displays make it possible to have both sides of a street opposite each other on a plan. Wall mounted displays only work if it does not matter treating both sides separately.

✎ Useful debates can take place around the exhibit. Keep a notepad or tape recorder handy.

✎ Very useful as an ice-breaker at the beginning of a workshop, and as a visual prompt for all participants during a workshop. Also useful as part of an open house event.

$ Main costs: Film processing and purchase. Preparation time (2 person days).

## Advantages of elevation montages

- Good icebreaker at the beginning of workshop sessions

- Helps participants and design professionals gain a visual understanding of the environment they are dealing with.

- Secures the views of people lacking the confidence to speak in group discussions.

- Can be left as part of an unmanned exhibition over a period of time.

## Disadvantages

- Can be costly to prepare and may not be cost-effective compared with other methods.

## Tips on montage making

- Stand the same distance from the building line when taking all photos unless there are setbacks in the buildings, when you should move closer.

- If relating to a plan, then it is best to mount the montage on a long table. If on a wall, then one elevation will be upside down.

- Digital mapping which can be re-scaled is useful for adjusting the plan to fit the elevation.

- The plan is more understandable if photos are placed directly on the building line.

- Elevations are more understandable if photos are stuck together so that shop signs are readable even if there is some mismatch at roof level.

**Table-mounted**
*Photomontages as part of a workshop aimed at generating urban design proposals.*

---

### FURTHER INFORMATION

☞ Methods: *Interactive display. Open house event. Photo survey.*

☆ Julie Withers, Kathryn Anderson, Roger Evans Associates.

# Environment shop

**Local environment shops provide a permanent way to disseminate information and create dialogue. They can be independent outfits or part of a local regeneration agency or community centre.**

- Ideally, a shop premises in a prominent location with a large window area is chosen, perhaps with offices behind or above. Alternatively, an open air stall or spare space in a building is used.

- The shop combines the sale of useful material on environmental improvement with displays and information on local initiatives and projects.

- The shop provides a first port of call for local people on how they can improve their environment, and perhaps a public face and reception area for a local regeneration agency or community centre as well.

Visit our
## Environment Shop

**For information and advice on how to improve your environment**

*Books • T-shirts*
*Leaflets • Posters • Gifts*
*Noticeboards • Postcards*
*Guides • Window stickers*
*Resource packs • Videos*
*Education packs*

**20 High Street, Anytown**
**Open Mon to Sat, 10am to 5pm**

### Mobile shop
*We can arrange a stall at your local event.*
*Call for details.*

**Sample promotion leaflet**

✎ Setting up can take time and be complicated but, once established, shops can easily be manned by volunteers. Start with a small range of stock and build up slowly.

✎ Once up and running, shop material can easily be taken out to local festivals, markets and conferences.

✎ If 'Environment shop' is not the right name for your area try 'Regeneration shop', 'Conservation shop', etc

$ Main need is for capital to purchase stock and display fittings. 'Sale or return' terms can be arranged for many items but requires more administration. Don't expect environment shops to make large profits although they can bring in useful income. Their value is as a local resource and in helping an agency get its act together (by putting it on show). If well organised they can ultimately relieve pressure on agency staff by allowing people to help themselves.

**Shop interior**
*Bird's eye view photo
of neighbourhood;
display boards on
local projects;
publications for loan
or sale; somewhere
to sit. (Not all shops
need to be as smart
and tidy as this one.)*

## Environment shop stock

Books, pamphlets, videos, manuals, postcards,
models, T-shirts relating to:
☐ **Building** – how-to-do-it information on
local vernacular building and architecture.
☐ **General merchandise** – to attract people
in (eg environmental T-shirts, local crafts).
☐ **Local interest** – items on past, present
and future of local environment.
☐ **Regeneration generally** – how-to-do-it
material on community regeneration.
☐ **Visitor information** – items specifically
for visitors to the area.
☐ ...............................................................

## Benefits of shops

- Addition to local trading environment.
- Helps agencies to become user friendly by
displaying what they can offer.
- Helps people to help themself rather than
be dependent on development workers.
- Provides outlet for local publishers.
- Raises profile of local environmental issues
and projects.
- Source of revenue for community
development organisations (long-term).

## Environment shop features

☐ **Bird's-eye view photograph** of local
area (very useful for discussing issues and
always a popular attraction, especially if lit
up at night and visible from the street).
☐ **Community noticeboard** for job ads,
competitions, events.
☐ **Magazine rack** for periodicals.
☐ **Model** of local area and developments.
☐ **Project information board** for info on
local regeneration projects.
☐ **Reception desk** for info, access to project,
purchasing items.
☐ **Reference library** for items not for sale.
☐ **Seating area** for reading and chatting.
☐ **Window display** promoting merchandise.
☐ **Window noticeboard** with constantly
changing posters on local activities.
☐ ...............................................................

### FURTHER INFORMATION

☞ Methods. *Architecture centre.
Community design centre.
Neighbourhood planning office.*
Scenario: *Urban conservation.*

☆ Photo: Edinburgh World Heritage Trust.

# Feasibility fund

Feasibility funds provide money to community organisations for paying experts to undertake feasibility studies on possible projects. They are a highly effective way of kick-starting local initiatives, by getting projects to a stage where they can attract capital funding and support.

- A Fund is established by a professional institute or other suitable local, regional or national organisation. Sponsors might include companies, local authorities, government departments or charities.

- The scheme is advertised and community groups invited to apply for funding.

- Grants are awarded and feasibility studies undertaken. The study will establish whether the ideas are workable, the best options and the costs.

- If projects succeed in attracting capital funding, the grant money is repaid to the organising body.

✎ Grants need not be large to be effective. Depending on the nature of the project, US$1,500 – 5,000 is usually enough to enable a group to produce a highly professional study. The Fund can offer the total amount or a proportion.

✎ Money is not the only benefit. The award of a grant can also be a tremendous boost to community organisations, providing confidence and credibility.

✎ Award schemes are a good way of generating case study material for exchanging good practice.

$ An initial tranche of funding is required to establish the fund and operate it for a few years. Once up and running, quite a high proportion may eventually be paid back.

---

*If you need professional advice to get started on a community project*

**BUT**

*Can't afford the fees*

**THEN CONTACT**

The Community
Projects Fund
Institute of Architects
High Street, Anytown
000 111 22222

---

"A helping hand at the initial stage has been to us what the first steps are to a child, and today we are walking tall."
**Celeste Nre, Wandsworth Black Elderly Project, UK**
RIBA Report, 1995.

"The Fund satisfies a growing demand for communities to get involved and have a say in generating something for themselves."
**Ian Finlay, Chair, RIBA Community Projects Fund**
Report 1986.

**Fact**: A feasibility fund run by the Royal Institute of British Architects triggered US$160 million for 150 projects over 12 years from an outlay of less than $2.4 million.

# Feasibility fund
# Types of projects funded

☐ **Community centres.** New build, or improvements. In urban and rural areas.
☐ **Community plans.** Plans for a site or neighbourhood, perhaps as alternatives to those existing.
☐ **Education facilities.** Schools, creches, heritage centres, art centres.
☐ **Employment initiatives.** Creating workspace or improved facilities.
☐ **Housing.** Renovations or improvements on estates, self build schemes, new housing for rent.
☐ **Landscaping.** Improvements to public areas: play areas, parks, streetscape, city farms, artworks.
☐ **Leisure facilities.** Sports halls, youth clubs, cultural centres.

## **Feasibility study**
## A Cultural Centre for Anytown

Prepared for the Anytown Forum
by Hope Architects and Planners

**Contents**
Summary
Background history
The proposal
Site conditions
Design options
Legal and planning
Organisation
Timetable of activity
Costings
Funding sources
Appendices
  *Press cuttings*
  *Survey results*

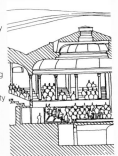

Study supported by the National Feasibility Fund
for Community Projects

**Sample cover**
*Good feasibility studies are one of the most effective ingredients for getting projects to happen.*

## **Application form**

Please read the Fund Guidelines before completing.

Name of organisation _____

Legal status (community group, charity, etc)  .

_____

Contact details _____

_____

Do you have a constitution? (if so attach copy)

_____

Brief description of organisation and activities

_____

How is the community involved in the organisation _____

How many people are involved?  Employed ☐
Management committee ☐  Voluntary ☐
Other (specify) _____

Project title _____

Description of project _____

Why do you want to undertake the project?

_____

Who will benefit from the project?_____

What will the feasibility study cover?

_____

How much will the study cost?  £ _____

Who will do it? (name and contact details)

_____

Other possible sources of income for the study

_____

Please submit a photo of the building or site and a copy of your latest annual report and accounts.

### **FURTHER INFORMATION**

☞  Scenarios: *Community centre, Regeneration infrastructure.*

✉  Community Architecture Group.

# Field workshop

**Field workshops are a way for local communities to draw up plans of action where there is little data available to start with. They are particularly suited to disaster prevention work in developing countries.**

*Evolving a common view*
*Group working. Informal walk.*
*Model making. Mapping.*

■ Field workshops involve a team of technical experts working closely with a handful of local facilitators, local officials and many local residents of all ages, backgrounds and interests.

■ A programme of activities lasting several days or even weeks is prepared in advance involving community profiling, risk assessment and plan making methods. The programme is agreed in advance by all parties but may be varied at any point to allow for results to be built on and developed.

■ The aim is to develop a common understanding of the nature of the community, the issues faced and possible solutions.

■ The technical team presents its recommendations to the whole community a few days after the main activity sessions.

✎ Technical team members need to be sensitive to local cultures. Ask permission before taking photos or taping interviews.

$ Planning a field workshop carefully in advance is essential if money is to be spent effectively. Materials need not cost much. The main costs will be people's time and accommodation and travel for the team.

# Sample field workshop format

Example: Village suffering from typhoons.

**DAY 1**

| | |
|---|---|
| 08.00 - 08.10 | **Ice breaker.** Music. Dance. |
| 08.10 - 10.00 | **Introductions.** Participants introduce themselves. Aims and process explained. |
| 10.00 - 12.00 | **Personal history.** A few participants tell their history. |
| 12.00 - 13.00 | **Historical profile.** Key events listed in date order. |
| 14.00 - 16.00 | **Map drawing.** Large map of village drawn on paper. |
| 16.00 - 17.00 | **Photo game.** Photos of all buildings (taken previously) located on map. Discussion. |
| 18.30 - 21.00 | **Social.** Music and dinner. |
| 21.00 - 23.00 | **Review session.** Day's activities reviewed. Plans revised if necessary. |

**DAY 2**

| | |
|---|---|
| 07.00 - 08.00 | **Review** of Day 1. |
| 09.30 - 12.00 | **Interviews.** Key public figures explain their roles and are questioned. |
| 09.00 - 13.00 Group A | **Model making.** Model made of village showing hills, rivers, valleys and other main features. |
| 09.00 - 13.00 Group B | **Map making.** Map made showing different house types (eg concrete, bamboo, mud, timber). |
| 14.00 - 16.00 | **Simulation exercise.** Disaster simulated to understand people's reactions. (eg to typhoon) |
| 16.30 - 17.30 | **Damage classification.** Models and maps used to classify extent of damage (total destruction, damage to roof, partial damage etc) |
| 19.00 - 21.00 | **Review and planning.** Review of activities and process. Schedule revised. |

**DAY 3**

| | |
|---|---|
| 08.30 - 12.00 | **Reconnaissance.** Of buildings and sites identified in previous day's review. |
| 09.00 - 12.00 | **Interviews.** With key officials |

and politicians (by some).

| | |
|---|---|
| 13.00 - 16.00 | **Review session.** For research team and facilitators. Information gathered so far structured using a matrix. Process reviewed. |
| 13.00 - 20.00 | **Construction workshop.** Scale models of houses built by local carpenters to identify structural problems. Queries by research team. Discussion. |
| 15.00 - 19.00 | **Gender workshop.** Participants divide into male and female groups. Analysis of different roles and responsibilities. |
| 19.00 - 19.30 | **Informal walk.** For research team and facilitators. |

**DAY 4**

| | |
|---|---|
| 09.00 - 13.00 | **Interviews.** Further questions to key figures. |
| 09.00 - 13.00 | **Construction workshop.** Continued. |
| 09.00 - 13.00 | **Gender workshop.** (cont.) |
| 14.30 - 16.00 | **Summary session.** Review of activities by research team. |
| 14.30 - 16.00 | **Next steps.** Workshop groups prepare list of recommendations. |
| 19.00 - 24.00 | **Social.** Dinner and music. |

**DAYS 5-9**

| | |
|---|---|
| All day | **Research and analysis.** Research team prepares report and presentation. |

**DAY 10**

| | |
|---|---|
| 20.00 - 22.00 | **Presentation.** Research team presents proposals to open community meeting. |

**Ideal numbers:**
research team 4;
facilitators 2; locals 20-50.

---

**FURTHER INFORMATION**

☞ Method: *Simulation*. Scenario: *Shanty settlement upgrading*.
ⓐ *Reducing Risk*.
☆ Roger Bellers, Nick Hall.

# Future search conference

**Future search conferences are highly structured events, usually lasting 2.5 days, at which a cross-section of community members or 'stakeholders' create a shared vision for the future. They are more suited for dealing with general issues than specific sites.**

**Time lines**
*Participants create personal, community and global histories by writing key events on large strips of paper on the walls. This helps to make history visible, discover patterns and understand what the past means.*

*"I've not heard so many great ideas expressed in such a variety of clever and articulate ways… I don't know what benchmarks you use but by my lights this is the most useful, tangible, actionable output that I've ever seen."*
**Dennis Alter, Chairman & CEO, Advanta Corporation**
Future Search Website intro, '99.

*"Staging a future search means changing our assumptions about large, diverse groups. In these meetings we learn that most people can bridge lines of culture, class, gender, ethnicity, power, status and hierarchy if they will work as peers on tasks of mutual concern."*
**Marvin Weisbord and Sandra Janoff**
Future Search Website intro, '99.

■ People representing the widest possible range of interests, or 'stakeholder' groups, are brought together in one room, usually for 2.5 days. The ideal number is considered to be 64 since this breaks down into 8 groups of 8. For larger groups, conferences can be run in parallel. The agenda is: 'The Future of _____ 5 to 20 years on'.

■ A highly structured 5-step procedure is adopted (as summarised in the sample timetable, right). This is designed to encourage people to think globally, focus on the future, identify common ground and make public commitments to action.

■ People carry out tasks individually, in small self-managed workshops and as a whole group.

■ The results are recorded openly on flipcharts.

✎ At least one experienced facilitator is essential plus a committed group to plan the event in advance and follow it up afterwards. The conference must be part of a wider and longer process.

✎ Discourage non-participating observers. All those present should take an active part.

$ Main costs: Venue, meals and facilitation fees. Can range from US$4,000 to $60,000. $8,000 – $16,000 is common.

# Future Search Conference Timetable

Sample to use as a basis for designing your own.

## DAY 1

13.00–18.00 Introduction.

**Review the past**
Participants explore key events in the histories of themselves, their community and the world, and present them on three time-lines.

**Explore the present**
Trends affecting the community are explored and illustrated by creating a mind map. Groups share what they are proud of and sorry about.

## DAY 2

9.00–12.00 Continue with exploring the present.

12.00–18.00 **Create ideal futures**
Visions developed in small groups and acted out to everyone. Barriers to the visions identified.

**Identify common ground**
Shared vision identified, first by small groups and then by everyone. Projects to achieve it identified.

## DAY 3

9.00–13.00 **Make action plans**
Projects planned by self-selected action groups. Public commitments to action.

**Ideal numbers**
64 (8 tables of 8).

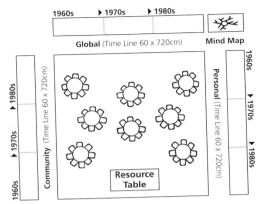

**Global** (Time Line 60 x 720cm)    **Mind Map**

**Ideal room layout**
*Eight tables with eight chairs per table; a resource table (for marker pens, notepads, etc); large sheets of paper on the walls for drawing three time-lines and a mind map.*

**Mind mapping**
*A large 'map' of present trends and linkages is created on the wall with coloured marker pens. Participants then fix sticky coloured dots onto those they think most important. This helps everybody focus on talking about the same issues. (☞p54 for mind map detail.)*

### FURTHER INFORMATION

☞ Scenario: *Whole settlement strategy.*

🖉 *Future Search* (contains sample worksheets and checklists which are highly recommended).

✉ New Economics Foundation. Future Search Network.

# Gaming

Games are a good way to help people understand the planning process and other people's viewpoints. They are also an enjoyable way to get people working together. They are particularly useful at an early stage of any community planning activity or to prepare people for a specific challenge ahead.

**Board game**
*One way of discovering about the housing development process. The game uses hurdles, gates and tradeoffs which players negotiate as they proceed through the planning process. Designed to be played at the start of a planning workshop to inform and "break the ice" between participants (see the book* Action Planning for Cities *for details.)*

- Games are devised to mirror real life planning scenarios or to teach specific skills.

- The games are mostly played in groups, usually helped by a facilitator or someone who has played them before. Many games involve role play; people acting as if they were someone else.

- There is usually no specific output other than increased awareness but they may produce preliminary design proposals or an agenda for future initiatives needed.

**Theatre**
*Powerful architect on stilts confronts a determined tenant in a performance on a housing estate designed to engage residents in conversation about their environment.*

✎ When role playing, wearing badges with the name or title of the person being imitated and even suitable hats can help people feel at ease.

✎ Make people play someone with a very different role to themselves. For example, a planner could play being a poor child; a female tenant could play a male housing officer.

✎ Sometimes it can be interesting to have the person playing a role being advised by the real thing; ie the resident playing at being a planner being advised by a real planner.

✎ Games are good energisers and help overcome shyness.

$ Main costs in use: Facilitator's fees. Developing and producing some games can be expensive in time and artwork.

# Urban design role play game format

Format for a role play game allowing people to explore planning issues that may arise in the coming years.

**1 Pick an issue**
Facilitator introduces game and helps people to agree on an issue or site as the focus of the game (eg local transport improvements). (10 mins)

**2 List interests**
All the parties with an interest in, or affected by, the issue are listed on a flipchart (eg pedestrians, bus drivers, transport planners, cyclists, etc). (5 mins)

**3 Give out roles**
Everyone is given a role which is written on their name badge. (5 mins)

**4 List desires and concerns**
People think about what someone in the role they have been given would want. (10 mins)

**5 Presentation**
Everyone in turn presents their points to the whole group with visual explanation if possible. (20 mins)

**6 Dealing**
People mingle freely and attempt to make deals with each other. (30 mins)

**7 Report back**
Everyone reports back to the whole group on what they have achieved. (15 mins)

**8 Next steps**
General debate on how to take things forward. (15 mins)

**Running time:   100 mins**
**Ideal numbers:  10-20 per workshop**

# Game types

**Board games**
Adaptations of popular board games to simulate planning and design scenarios.

**Picture analysis**
Getting people to say what they see in a picture and comparing notes.

**Role play**
Acting out being in someone else's shoes.

**Storytelling**
Reciting real or imaginary tales as a way of exploring hidden perceptions.

**Theatre**
Performing plays to characterise real life and stimulate debate.

*Acting someone else's role*
*Local resident pretending to be a public official speaking at a planning hearing. Exercise designed to help residents deal better with a forthcoming hearing about their area.*

| FURTHER INFORMATION |
| --- |

☞   Method: *Simulation.*

๑   *Action Planning for Cities. Participatory Learning and Action.*

☆   Urban design game format devised by Drew Mackie.

# Ideas competition

**Ideas competitions are a good way of stimulating creative thinking and generating interest and momentum. They can be designed to allow everyone a chance to put forward their ideas or be just for professionals.**

- Ideas competitions are normally held at the start of the development process or when there is opposition to a proposed scheme. They can be simple and immediate or highly complex.

- A brief is produced, clearly setting out the task, entry format and deadline, judging procedure, eligibility and relevant background. The task can be to produce general ideas for improving an area or proposals for a specific site, building or problem.

- Judging can done by a panel or through using a public voting system (see box, right). Alternatively different organisations can make separate awards.

- Winning entries are widely publicised and published to secure momentum for implementation.

✎ Getting the public to judge entries encourages people to present better and provides credibility for the winning entries. If you have a judging panel, make sure it is not dominated by professionals.

✎ Specify a format which is accessible to non-professionals and easy to store and copy, eg A4 or A3 maximum. Models or large panels are good for exhibitions but difficult to keep, so photograph them properly. Think about publication from the outset.

**$** Simple competitions for local sites can be organised very simply and cheaply. High profile competitions will involve considerable time and expense. Main costs: Administration; publicity; prizes; publishing end results. Plenty of scope for sponsorship.

---

## ANYTOWN 2050

### *Visions for Anytown Competition*

**Open competition for the best ideas for improving the environment of Anytown**

*What could be done to make your street, your neighbourhood, your town centre fit for the year 2050?*

*How can we create a new sense of vision to give our town a much needed boost?*

**Over £1000 in prizes to be won**

Categories:
Under 8, 8-11, 12-17, 18-24, 25 and over.

Words, drawings, or photos on one sheet of A3 paper. Name, address and age on reverse. As many entries as you want.

**Entries by 6 May to:
Jumbo, 20 High Street.**

Exhibition and judging by the general public all weekend on 7 and 8 May at the Hexagon.

The best ideas will be published in a special supplement of the local paper.

Organised by Anytown Forum in association with Darwin plc

---

**Open ideas competition**
*Sample promotion leaflet.*

## Simple public judging rules

Register at the desk and get your sticky dots. Each person has three votes in each age category.

● Red = first choice (3 points)

○ yellow = second choice (2 points)

● green = third choice (1 point)

Stick your dots on the entries.

The entries with the most points by 7pm win. Prizes to be presented by the Mayor at 7.30pm

### *Judging in public, by the public, on site*
*Passers-by use sticky dots to register their preferences for proposals for a derelict site which are pinned up on the site hoarding.*

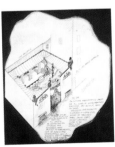

69 George Street Ideas Competition

### *Standard format*
*Asking entrants to draw their proposals on prepared bird's eye view site outlines can help people make comparisons but may restrict creativity.*

## Two-stage competition format

Sample timetable for a fairly elaborate 2-stage competition combining an open competition for the public with a closed competition for professional teams.

**Jan  Preparation**
Formation of co-ordinating body. Planning.

**Mar  Printing**
Brief and publicity material.

**April  Launch**
Widespread publicity. Detailed brief and conditions sent to those who respond.

**July  Stage 1 deadline**
Stage 1 open to all with separate categories for professionals as well as for children.

**Aug  Public exhibition**
Judging by public or panel. Small prizes.

**Sept  Stage 2 announced**
Limited number of winning entrants provided with a budget to develop their schemes further.

**Nov  Stage 2 deadline**

**Dec  Public exhibition**
Judging by public or panel. Winners announced.

**May  Publication**
Winning entries published.

### FURTHER INFORMATION

☞  Scenarios: *Derelict site re-use. Regeneration infrastructure.*

✉  Architecture Foundation. Royal Institute of British Architects.

**71**

# Interactive display

**Interactive displays allow people to engage in the issues and debate, on their own and in an enjoyable way, by making additions or alterations to pre-prepared exhibits.**

**Tools for participants**
*Post-it notes, sticky dots (several colours), coloured felt-tip pens and ballpoint pens.*

- Interactive displays can be used as part of a forum, workshop, exhibition, conference or other event.

- The displays can range from blank sheets with simple one-line questions to drawings or models of complex development proposals.

- A dynamic develops as people's comments build up on the displays over time.

- Thoughtful design is required to ensure that the information is presented simply and clearly and that people's responses are recorded in such a way that they can be used afterwards.

**Flip chart comment sheet**
*More visible than a book.*

**Cumulative comments**
*Adding points to those typed up from a workshop.*

✎ Have facilitators on hand to help people get going. Once responses start to build up, the process develops its own momentum.

✎ Shop front or on-the-street venues work well as people are attracted by others taking part (☞ Street Stall).

✎ Photograph displays – or use other ways or recording them – before dismantling them.

$ Main costs: artwork and materials. Simple displays can be designed and prepared within a few minutes and need little equipment. Employing graphic or exhibition designers improves effectiveness immensely, particularly for getting responses to complex design ideas but will normally cost a considerable amount in fees.

***Sticky dot display*** *Voting for liked and disliked buildings and spaces.*

## Post-it board ideas

Headings for four blank boards which people can stick Post-it notes on (or use scraps of paper and drawing pins):

- What do you LIKE about the area?
- What do you DISLIKE about the area?
- What IMPROVEMENTS could be made?
- What can YOU do to help?

***Post-it board*** *Comments build up in response to a simple question.*

## Interactive display ideas

### Verbal likes, dislikes and ideas
Put up large sheets of blank paper with suitable headings (see box, left) and get people to put their responses on Post-its.

### Visual likes, dislikes and ideas
Ask people to mark their most and least favourite buildings and spaces on maps or photos using Post-its or sticky dots.

### Comments on proposals
Get people's views on development proposals or options by placing sticky dots or Post-its on prepared cards linked to plans or drawings. ☞ *Table scheme display.*

### General thoughts
Use flipcharts or comment books to get general comments.

---

**FURTHER INFORMATION**

☞ Methods: *Community planning forum. Elevation montage. Open house event. Street stall. Table scheme display.* Scenarios: *Community centre. Whole settlement strategy.*

---

# Local design statement

**Sample report cover**
*Contents and style can vary*
*according to local needs.*

*"You saw the village in a*
*completely different way than*
*you ever had before. You really*
*started to look at every single*
*gable end, bit of tarmac and*
*cobblestone. That was the*
*most exciting thing, you learnt*
*so much. It was an all round*
*good exercise."*
**David Unsworth, Cartmel**
**Village Design Group**
*Village Views video, 1996.*

**Local design statements are a way for local people to provide guidelines for new development in their area. They can be incorporated in local planning policy and provide a valuable way for local people to make a positive input into the planning process at an early stage. They are particularly useful in areas where local character is threatened by insensitive development.**

■ A local design statement is drawn up by a specially formed team of local volunteers, preferably supported by local planners and national agencies.

■ The team secures the views of as many people as possible through publicity, holding workshops and circulating draft statements for comment.

■ The statement will include guidance for future developers based on the character of the landscape setting, settlement patterns, building forms and transport networks.

■ The statement is adopted by the local planning authority (as 'supplementary planning guidance' in the UK) and can be used to approve or reject planning applications from developers.

✎ The area covered by a statement can vary but the process works best at a village or neighbourhood level where people recognise each other. Break larger areas up and, if possible, combine with a Countryside Design Summary (☞ Glossary).

$ Direct costs likely to be around US$5,000 if local skills and services used. More if elaborate printing involved. Need to have a budget for reprints, especially in areas of development pressure.

**Reviewing progress**
*Villagers review pages with photographs and captions prepared during a local character workshop.*

# Sample local design statement process

**1 Establish design team**
Small group of local people. Read handbooks. Discuss with planning authority. Prepare publicity. (1 month)

**2 Go public**
Launch publicity. Draw in more participants. Prepare for workshop. (1 month)

**3 Local character workshop**
One-day event open to all. Main stages:

**A Mapping** in groups to identify key walks, areas and landmarks on base maps. (☞ *Mapping*).

**B Photographic survey** in groups taking photos which capture the character of the area (☞ *Photo survey*). Lunch while photos are developed.

**C Character assessment.** Each group prepares presentation on character of the area using photos and maps.

**D Presentation and discussion.** Groups present their work. General discussion on local character and the next steps.

**4 Prepare design statement report**
Expand design team. Refine and complete survey. Draft report. Consult on draft (☞ *Participatory editing*). (3 months)

**5 Consult with local planning authority**
Agree draft with planners and planning committee. (2 months)

**6 Print report**
Print report and distribute widely. Keep it in print and available. (2 months)

**Total running time: 9 months minimum. Can take up to 18 months.**

---

### FURTHER INFORMATION

☞ Methods: *Mapping. Photo survey. Participatory editing.* Scenario: *Village revival.*

⊘ *Village Design. Village Views.*

✉ Countryside Agency.

# Mapping

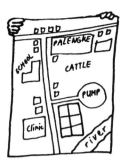

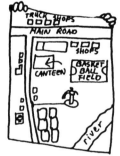

**Different perspectives**
*Two maps of the same place, one drawn by a woman, one by a man. Guess which is which. (Maps redrawn from originals.)*

**Using symbols and colour**
*Mapping various aspects of a community's capacity to cope with natural disasters helps planning to reduce their impact.*

**Mapping is an effective non-verbal way of finding out how people view their area. It is a good way to gather and present site-specific data, understand differences in perception and stimulate debate as a basis for joint planning.**

- Individuals or groups create physical maps of their neighbourhood or city using pen and paper, lines in the sand, cloth, chalk or other materials to hand.

- A framework or theme is normally provided to focus people's thoughts, eg places you visit frequently, landmarks, boundaries, places you dislike, things you would like to see.

- The maps are discussed and analysed as a basis for understanding differing viewpoints and planning what should be done.

- Records of maps and debates are made for future reference.

✎ Use symbols rather than words if participants are unable to read.

✎ Using tracing paper to build up layers can be useful, getting different information on each layer.

✎ Mapping the same thing at different times is a good way of monitoring progress.

✎ Maps made or left in a public place provide a good focus for discussion. Particularly good in schools – children love maps.

✎ Maps can be very attractive. With some thought they can become permanent exhibits or even made into postcards!

$ Depends on materials used and cost of facilitation. Need not cost anything.

# Group mapping process

**1 Purpose**
Decide what the map or maps should show (eg land use, hazards, resources, mobility, social facilities) and the best display method.

**2 People**
Gather people who know the area and are willing to share their knowledge. Decide whether to work individually or in groups.

**3 Place and materials**
Choose a suitable place (ground, table, wall) and materials (sticks, stones, seeds, pencils, felt-tips, chalk).

**4 Map making**
Facilitators might help people get started but then withdraw.

**5 Discussion**
Presentation of maps. Discussion on comparisons and lessons drawn. Notes of discussion made on flipchart or in notebook.

**6 Record**
Make a record of the maps on A4 paper for later use and/or take photos.

**7 Planning**
Use the maps to start developing proposals.

**Running time: 1-2 hours**
Process also works for diagramming. Replace word 'map' with 'diagram'.
☞ *Diagrams.*

# Map types and uses

**Activity map**
Shows where people do things, which places they visit. Useful for planning future facilities.

**Art map**
Aims to be a work of art for displaying at exhibitions, making into postcards and so on.

**Hazard map**
Shows vulnerability to natural or environmental hazards and identifies risks and capacities. Useful for disaster mitigation.

**Land use and resources map**
Shows what happens where.

**Mental map**
Shows how people perceive their area (as opposed to being geographically accurate). Useful insight into perceptions.

*Community mapping*
Making a village map on the ground using powder. Community mapping allows the less articulate to express their views.

| FURTHER INFORMATION |
| --- |

☞  Methods: *Local design statement. Risk assessment.* Scenario: *Village revival.*

𝚑  *Reducing Risk. 4B. From Place to Place.*

✉  Common Ground.

☆  Drawings taken from 4B.

*Art map*
Part of a 'parish map' used as a postcard
(☞ 'Parish mapping' in glossary).

# Microplanning workshop

**Microplanning is a comprehensive action planning procedure for producing development plans for upgrading settlements. Originally designed for use in developing countries, it is based on regular intensive workshops which involve a minimum of preparation, materials and training.**

**Structured group working**
*Participants complete charts on large sheets of paper which are then displayed on the walls.*

- The microplanning procedure involves 8 to 12 community representatives working closely with a small team of experts and facilitators for several days.

- A sequence of activities (see example in box, right) is worked through to arrive at a development plan and work programme.

- The process is structured by charts on large sheets of paper which are completed and kept as a record.

- The workshops are repeated every year or so to monitor progress and plan the next stages.

## People needed

☐ **Community representatives**
Cross-section of local population. 8 – 12 people.
☐ **Logistics officer**
Provides training materials. Government officer.
☐ **Projects Officer**
Responsible for implementing results. Local government officer.
☐ **Specialists**
Technical experts (eg health, engineering, social development). As many as appropriate.
☐ **Team facilitator**
Directs procedure. Practitioner or academic.
☐ **Workshop facilitators**
Conduct small workshop groups (usually 3 needed). Selected from participants.

✎ Facilitators must have the confidence of all participants and should participate in a workshop to understand its dynamics before running one themselves.

✎ Hold workshops in the community rather than in government offices to make local people feel more in control.

✎ Do not treat the chart format as a straitjacket. If the one you planned does not seem to work, revise it as you go along.

$ Costs are minimal apart from organisers' and participants' time.

# Sample Microplanning Process

## STAGE 1: IDENTIFY PROBLEMS

a) Reconnaissance. Survey of locality.
b) Prepare list of problems.

| Problem | Why? | To who? | Where? |
|---|---|---|---|
| _____ | _____ | _____ | _____ |
| _____ | _____ | _____ | _____ |

c) Prioritise problems

**Agreed summary list of problems**
1 _____
2 _____

## STAGE 2: IDENTIFY STRATEGY OPTIONS

a) List possible strategies (perhaps in small groups).

| Problem | Short-term Strategy | Long-term Strategy |
|---|---|---|
| _____ | _____ | _____ |
| _____ | _____ | _____ |

b) Compare different groups' priorities.

| Strategy | All agree | 2 teams agree | 1 team agrees |
|---|---|---|---|
| _____ | ☐ | ☐ | ☐ |
| _____ | ☐ | ☐ | ☐ |

c) Agree strategy priorities.

**Agreed summary list**

| Problem | Strategy |
|---|---|
| 1 _____ | _____ |
| 2 _____ | _____ |

## STAGE 3: PLAN ACTIONS NEEDED

a) List actions needed to achieve each strategy.
Consider options, eg high and low cost.

**Strategy**

| Actions needed | high cost | low cost |
|---|---|---|
| _____ | ☐ | ☐ |
| _____ | ☐ | ☐ |

b) Negotiate and select agreed options.

**Strategy**

**Agreed actions needed**
1 _____
2 _____

## STAGE 4: ALLOCATE TASKS

a) List tasks required to achieve each action.

**Action**

| Tasks | Who | What | When | How |
|---|---|---|---|---|
| 1 _____ | ____ | ____ | ____ | ____ |
| 2 _____ | ____ | ____ | ____ | ____ |

b) Locate improvements
Make plans, sections, sketches.

## STAGE 5: MONITOR AND EVALUATE

This stage takes place weeks, months or years later. Also perhaps at the beginning to review any previously planned actions.

a) Describe the status of each action.

| Action Planned | Progress |
|---|---|
| _____ | _____ |
| _____ | _____ |

b) Draw lessons.

| Action Planned | Corrective action needed | Lessons learned |
|---|---|---|
| _____ | _____ | _____ |
| _____ | _____ | _____ |

**Running time: 2-5 days**

### FURTHER INFORMATION

☞ Scenario: *Shanty settlement upgrading.*
☺ *Community Action Planning.*
 *Action Planning for Cities.*
✉ Oxford Brookes University.
☆ Nabeel Hamdi

# Mobile unit

**Mobile units can make it easier to provide the technical support necessary for community planning activity. They are particularly useful for working in communities lacking facilities or where a series of similar events are planned in several locations.**

***Mobile planning aid***
*Volkswagen van used for transporting exhibition material and model-making equipment to communities as part of a planning aid service.*

■ Mobile units can range from a van used to transport an exhibition to a mobile home or trailer converted into a fully equipped design studio.

■ The choice of vehicle is determined by its intended use, the size required and whether it needs off-road capability.

■ The units are fitted out with facilities and equipment necessary for the activities planned (see box, right).

■ Suitable graphics are applied to the outside to create the desired image.

✎ Can create a sense of presence and credibility as well as being a useful technical resource.

✎ New technologies in document production may reduce the need for such a facility or at any rate change the requirements. Could end up as an expensive toy. Plan carefully.

$ Costs of conversion can vary. Running costs of maintenance and insurance need to be considered. Savings can include costs of hiring premises and travel costs.

# Mobile studio facilities

- ☐ Computer (for word processing and layout, perhaps with modem via mobile phone).
- ☐ Dark room (for printing slides and prints).
- ☐ Drawing boards.
- ☐ Exhibition panels (perhaps for display on the outside of the unit).
- ☐ Flipcharts.
- ☐ Library of technical literature.

- ☐ Light box.
- ☐ Paper cutter or guillotine.
- ☐ Photocopier.
- ☐ Print machine (for large drawings).
- ☐ Stationery cupboard (notepads, Post-its etc).
- ☐ Storage for drawings and photos.
- ☐ Toilet and washroom.
- ☐ Video player.
- ☐ .................................................................

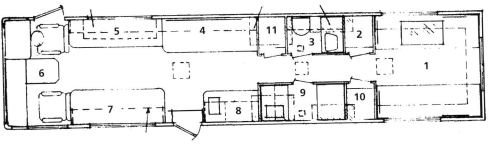

**1** Drawing Centre
**2** Storage cupboard
**3** Bathroom
**4** Reproduction area
**5** Computer centre
**6** Cockpit
**7** Typing area
**8** Kitchen
**9** Darkroom
**10** Storage cupboard
**11** Equipment cupboard

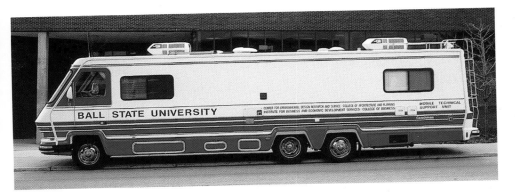

### Mobile design studio
*Custom converted 38-foot recreation vehicle used as a design studio for community planning workshops in rural areas. The internal layout is shown in the drawing above.*

**FURTHER INFORMATION**

☞ Scenario: *New neighbourhood.*
✉ Ball State University.
☆ Tony Costello

# Models

**Models are one of the most effective tools for getting people involved in planning and design. They are particularly useful for generating interest, presenting ideas and helping people think in three dimensions.**

**Making models**
*A very good way to gain an understanding of how a building or city is put together.*

- Models can be made from a wide variety of materials. They can be highly elaborate, aiming to be as realistic as possible, or simple and illustrative. The choice will depend on the purpose of the model and the resources and time available.

- Models are often adaptable so that alternative proposals or options can easily be shown by moving parts around.

- The construction of models is highly educational and enjoyable and is often done in groups as part of the planning and design process.

✎ Slick presentation models are good for presenting proposals but are usually hard to adapt and so inhibit creativity. Think through the options for construction carefully at the outset. Generally, use materials that are easily available and simple to cut up, shape, fix, colour and move about. Pasting base-maps or plans onto a rigid board is a good way to get started, and it ensures that you get the scale right.

✎ Models are an ideal centrepiece for exhibitions, workshops and venues such as architecture centres.

$ Models can cost very little if scrap materials are used. Presentation models can be extremely expensive. The main cost involved though is time. One innovative way of paying for detailed models of a neighbourhood is to get building owners to pay for the cost of having their own buildings upgraded from simple blocks or cut-outs to being fully detailed and painted.

**Neighbourhood model**
Buildings made from wood blocks and glued onto a wooden baseboard. Good for displaying outside and generating attention. Very durable. Need a workshop to make one.

**Street model**
Buildings made out of folded cardboard and glued onto a cardboard base board. Very flexible but not durable. Good focal point for design workshops and interactive exhibitions.

**House model**
Large-scale model using cardboard, allowing people to be involved in designing their homes to a high level of detail.

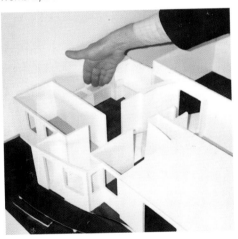

**Room layout model**
Simple cardboard model scaled to help people design room layouts. The one shown was used by blind people designing a new centre for the blind.

---

### FURTHER INFORMATION

☞ Method: *Planning for Real.* Scenarios: *Community centre. Housing development.*

# Neighbourhood planning office

**Neighbourhood planning offices provide an important local focal point for community planning activity and make it easier to follow up and sustain initiatives. Ideally every neighbourhood should have one, but they are particularly valuable in rundown areas or where there is a lot of building activity.**

**Local presence**
*Architects set up office in a flat on a housing estate which they are rehabilitating.*

■ Neighbourhood offices should be in a prominent location, preferably with a shop frontage.

■ They provide a working base for all professionals dealing with an area, a venue for meetings and workshops and a first point of contact for local people on planning and building issues.

■ They should be staffed by people with project management skills able to take a pro-active role in pursuing improvement initiatives.

✎ Neighbourhood planning offices often work best if managed by an independent body or partnership. Avoid total community control or total local authority control.

✎ Useful to base an office in a rundown building which can be renovated as a pilot project to stimulate other local improvements. Great scope for volunteers and trainees to run an office once it is set up.

**Demonstration project**
*Before and after of a shop used as a neighbourhood planning office and as a demonstration for improving street frontages.*

✎ Combining a neighbourhood planning office with an environment shop, community design centre or architecture centre can be a powerful combination.

$ Main costs: salaries, rent, heating, lighting, furniture and equipment. Costs can be reduced by seconding professional and technical staff and using volunteers to handle general enquiries and administration. From US$15,000 to $150,000 per annum.

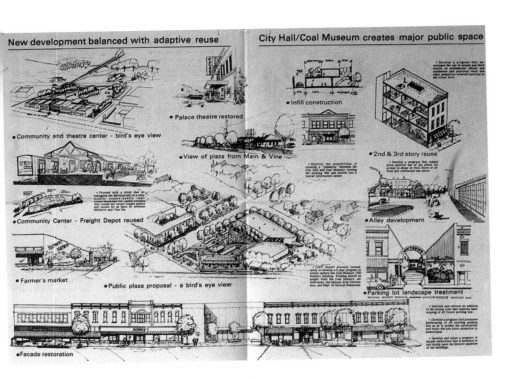

New development balanced with adaptive reuse

City Hall/Coal Museum creates major public space

- Community and theatre center - bird's eye view
- Palace theatre restored
- Infill construction
- View of plaza from Main & Vine
- Community Center - Freight Depot reused
- 2nd & 3rd story reuse
- Farmer's market
- Public plaza proposal - a bird's eye view
- Alley development
- Parking lot landscape treatment
- Facade restoration

## Advantages of a supplement

**Cheap.** Inexpensive compared with producing and distributing a special report.

**Coverage.** Reaches a very high proportion of the population (in most areas).

**Credibility.** Has greater credibility than a report produced by consultants.

**Familiarity.** Feels less threatening than most specially produced planning reports.

**Format.** Large format allows drawings to be published at a reasonable scale.

**Immediacy.** Very quick publication and distribution. The results of one day's workshop can be distributed the next day.

**Skills.** Brings expert journalistic skills to bear.

### Clear graphics

*Double-page spread from a special 8-page supplement produced during a 3-day planning weekend. Published and distributed with the local paper on the final day of the weekend, a few hours before a public presentation by the design team. Key features: concise writing; clear and understandable drawings; simple sequence.*

---

**FURTHER INFORMATION**

- ☞ Methods: *Design assistance team. Participatory editing. Planning weekend.* Scenario: *New neighbourhood.*
- ✉ Ball State University.
- ☆ Anthony Costello.

# Open house event

**Open house events allow those promoting development initiatives to present them to a wider public and secure reactions in an informal manner. They are less structured than a workshop and more informal than a traditional exhibition.**

**Inviting people in**
*Pavement sign encouraging passers-by to visit an open house event in a vacant shop on the future of the area.*

- Open house events can be organised at any stage of the design and development process by any of the parties. They can last from a few hours to several weeks.

- The venue will be arranged with a number of displays on the proposals and options using a variety of interactive display techniques (see plan, right). Organisers will be present to deal with queries and engage in informal debate.

- Material collected will be analysed afterwards and used to further develop the initiative.

✎ Good way to gauge initial public reaction to development proposals or options. Particularly useful for getting public involvement in proposals from a design workshop or planning day.

✎ There is no need to present drawings in an elaborate way, but careful thought needs to be given to highlighting the main points and on determining how reactions are obtained. Well worth engaging professional exhibition design skills if available.

✎ Prominent on-site venues work best, for instance an empty shop.

$ Main costs: Hire of venue and exhibition material; staff time; design time (3 person days).

*"I've been a councillor for 12 years and I've never been involved in an exercise like this before. We should be doing this for all of our towns instead of development control which is awful."*
**Leader of Waverley Borough Council**
*after a design workshop and open house event, 1997.*

### Relaxed atmosphere
*People move freely from display to display and hold discussions with the organisers.*

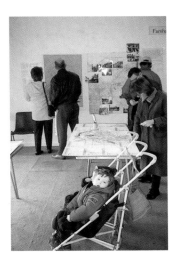

**Sample layout in shop unit**

1  **Entry desk.** Take Post-its, pens, sticky dots (Red=Dislike. Green=Like. Yellow=Not sure).

2  **Welcome panel.** Read about history and aim of present initiative.

3  **Participant data.** Stick dots on panels to show where you live/work, age group and other relevant statistics.

4  **Issues, goals and action needed.** Use Post-its to make additional points to those listed.

5  **Likes and dislikes.** Put stickers on map to show favourite and least favourite buildings/spaces.

6  **Visions.** Add Post-it comments to sketches of area visions (preferably before and after).

7  **Table scheme displays.** Use sticky dots to make your views known on proposals already drawn up. ☞ *Table scheme display.*

8  **Draw your own.** Sketch your own ideas with felt-tips on tracing paper laid over base plans.

9  **What next.** Read about it.

10  **Help.** Sign up if you can offer any assistance.

11  **Comments.** Write on flipcharts any comments not already covered.

12  **Further information.** Write your name and address if you want to receive further information as things develop.

# Open space workshop

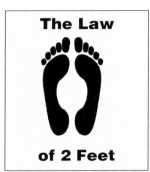

## The Law of 2 Feet

*The 'Law of 2 feet'*
*If at any time you feel you are neither learning nor contributing, move elsewhere (to another workshop or to have a coffee).*

## The four principles

- Whoever comes are the right people.
- Whenever it starts is the right time.
- When it's over, it's over.
- Whatever happens is the only thing that could happen.

*Four principles*
*In other words: participation is voluntary; be relaxed about timetabling; move on when there's no more to say; let go of expectations.*

*"It was fantastic. I felt really heard. I learnt lots I didn't know about my local area, and we created some brilliant ideas of what to do. I wish I had brought more of my friends."*
**Workshop participant**
Hammersmith & Fulham.

Open space workshops provide a highly democratic framework for enabling any group of people to create their own programme of discussions on almost any theme without much preparation. They are particularly useful for dealing with general policy issues, for generating enthusiasm and for dealing with urgent issues needing quick action.

- A theme, venue and time are determined and publicised by the organisers.

- Participants start by sitting in a circle and decide themselves on the issues to discuss, using a simple procedure (see format, right) usually guided by a facilitator.

- Workshop sessions are self managed by the participants within a framework of simple principles and 'laws' (see margin, left). Each workshop session develops a list of actions required and who should take them.

- A report of the event is circulated to all participants.

✎ The framework is flexible and can easily be adapted by the facilitators or participants. The 'principles', 'laws' and timetable can be adjusted to take account of local conditions and experience.

✎ Good facilitation is important for setting up the workshop and getting people started. Once up and running, the facilitator can fade into the background.

$ Main costs: venue, refreshments, stationery (A4 paper, large marker pens, Post-it notes, flipchart paper and masking tape) and facilitator's fee (if any).

# Open space workshop format

For minimum length session. For longer events, workshops sessions and open sessions (steps 5 & 6) are repeated.

### 1 Preparation
Set up the space as shown in sketch, right.

### 2 Introduction
Participants sit in a circle. Facilitator explains purpose and procedure. (10 mins)

### 3 Opening circle – declaring issues
Participants are invited to identify issues they want to convene workshops on. People write their issue on a sheet of paper with their name, read it out ("My name is.... My issue is ......") and place the sheet on the bulletin board in a suitable workshop slot. Several issues can be dealt with in one workshop if there are more issues than slots. (15 mins)

### 4 Signing up
Everyone gathers round the bulletin board and signs up for the workshops they wish to take part in. (15 mins)

### 5 Workshop sessions
Sessions take place. Results are recorded, usually as a simple list of actions required and by whom for each issue. These are posted on the bulletin board. (60 mins)

### 6 Open session
General debate in a circle after refreshment break. (30 mins)

### 5 Final plenary circle
Participants make any final statements they wish. (15 mins)

### 6 Report circulated
Preferably at the end of the event or the next day. Needs only contain the action points and responsibility for them.

**Running time: 2.5 hours – 3 days**
**Ideal numbers: 20 to 500.**

**Bulletin Board**

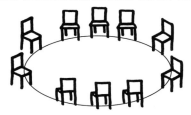

| The Law | Theme | Improving Anytown | | | | | | | Principles | Timetable |
|---------|-------|----|----|----|----|----|----|----|------------|-----------|
|  of 2 Feet | Space | A | B | C | D | E | F | G | | 10.00 ___ 11.00 ___ 12.00 ___ 14.00 ___ 15.00 ___ 16.00 ___ |
| | Topic am | | | | | | | | | |
| | Topic pm | | | | | | | | | |

*Starting point*
*Circle of chairs; bulletin board with workshop locations identified; timetable; posters of 'principles' and 'laws'.*

*Creating an agenda*
*Participants sign up for which issues they want to discuss in workshop groups, selecting from the menu created by the participants themselves. Reports from the workshops can later be posted on the same bulletin board.*

---

## FURTHER INFORMATION

☞ Scenario: *Local neighbourhood initiative.*

ᗧ *Open Space Technology*

✉ Wikima.

☆ Romy Shovelton, Adele Wilter.

# Participatory editing

**Participatory editing allows people to help shape reports and news-sheets without necessarily leaving their own homes. Reports have a crucial role to play in crystallising the results of community planning initiatives and communicating to others.**

- The nature and structure of the product are determined by the organisers. A draft is drawn up by writers, editors, designers and illustrators.

- Drafts are circulated, or displayed, for comment. Participants make comments on the draft with coloured pens or Post-its.

- Editors go through the comments and produce a revised draft which is approved by the organisers. The process is repeated as necessary.

---

Dear.............

FOREST ACTION REPORT
COMMENTS PLEASE

A draft mock up of the report arising from the recent design workshop is enclosed.

Please let me have your comments by midday Friday 4 May by tel., fax, post or email.

Any reactions would be useful. But the best help would be if you could mark up all comments as proposed alterations in red pen on the draft and return it. And, if possible, let me have any long sections of new copy by email so I can cut and paste it to reduce the chance of typing errors.

The editing team will produce a revised draft and there will be a final opportunity to see and discuss this on Saturday 5 May from 2 to 6 at the warden's office on Hill Street.

Your help will of course be acknowledged unless you let me know to the contrary.

sincerely

Report Editor

**Participation by post and email**
*Sample letter inviting comments on a report.*

---

✎ Explain the process clearly at the outset. Stress that comments are not automatically included but help the editors make improvements. Appoint one person as editor-in-chief to avoid lengthy wrangling in the event of disagreements. Collective editing sounds good in principle but rarely works well in practice.

✎ Secure a good cross-section of participants. It is quite extraordinary how few comments will normally be duplicated, even with many people responding.

✎ Holding an 'editing workshop' can generate ideas that would not emerge from individuals. Use pages pinned up on the walls as a basis for discussion (☞ p222).

✎ Always circulate material as close as possible to its final form. Sending out text without pictures for instance has limited use.

$ Main costs: photocopying; binding; postage; time.

**Respect cultural context**
Make sure that your approach is suitable for the cultural context in which you are working. Consider local attitudes to gender, informal livelihoods, social groupings, public engagement and so on.

*(handwritten: * Citizen control can amount to zilch in the end if the authorities have not been properly engaged.)*

*(EH?)*

**Shared control**
The extent of public participation in any activity can vary from very little (manipulation by authorities) to a great deal (citizen control). Different levels are appropriate at different stages of the planning process but most effective community planning operates at the shared control level (see diagram). *The most important thing is to engage all of the stakeholders*

*(handwritten: MAYBE ALIENATE? HEALTHFUL AUTHORITIES DELETE?)*

**Spend money** *opposite/on this page.*
Effective participation processes take time and cost money. Over-tight budgets invariably lead to cutting corners and poor results. Remember that community planning is an important activity, the success or failure of which may have dramatic implications for future generations as well as your own resources. The costs of building the wrong thing in the wrong place can be astronomical and make the cost of proper community planning pale into insignificance. Budget for it generously. *+ INVOLVE/TAP e.g.*

**Think on your feet** *PARISH COUNCILS + OTHER*
Once the basic principles and language of participatory *LOCAL AUTHORITIES*

*Shared control.*
*Ladder of participation showing areas where community planning works best.*

***Making comments***
*Specific suggestions for alterations marked on a draft are more useful than general comments (example shown is from a draft of this book).*

## Tips on producing reports

- Keep the structure simple.
- Be concise. People don't read much. Lengthy reports are only useful for massaging egos. Concentrate on getting the argument right. Using bullet points and headings will help this.
- Be visual. Good images are worth thousands of words. 'Before and After' images are particularly good for conveying proposed changes.
- Using short quotes or 'soundbites' from people can be very powerful.
- Make sure you credit everyone accurately.

## Workshop report structure
Simple format to avoid tedious blow-by-blow accounts and assist with compiling reports.

1 Workshop title.
2 People present – name and organisation.
3 Issues raised – heading and bullet points.
4 Proposals – heading and bullet points.

## Sample report structure
Simple format which works in most situations.

1 **Recommendations** (1,2,3 etc. The only thing many people will read)
2 **The Way Forward** (issue 1, issue 2 etc. summary paragraphs)
3 **Background** (why the report is necessary and how it was produced)
4 **Issues** (Main issues in depth – optional)
5 **Ideas** (Everything suggested even if not agreed by everyone – optional)
6 **Proposals** (what should happen – in detail)

**Appendices** (may be separate document)
A Workshop notes
B Credits
C Other relevant info

### FURTHER INFORMATION

☞ Methods: *Design assistance team. Local design statement.* Scenario: *Planning study.* See also editing workshop format on page 222.

# Photo survey

**Photo surveys help groups develop design ideas by taking and discussing photos of their existing environment. They can be used as part of a wider community profiling or action planning event or as an independent exercise.**

**Taking photos**
*Making images of what is important for you in the local environment for sharing with others.*

- Participants go around their neighbourhood individually or in teams, taking photos of places and images according to a general or specific theme.

- After processing, the photos are sorted, selected and placed on large sheets of blank paper or maps. Photos can be grouped or cut up and comments may be added using Post-its or felt tips.

- The completed sheets or maps are used as a basis for discussion, analysis and design.

✎ Undertaking the whole exercise in one stretch builds a useful momentum but requires polaroid cameras, a fast development service (over lunch perhaps) or digital cameras and computers. Letting people take photos individually over a week can allow more thought but requires more self discipline.

✎ If not done automatically, record negative numbers on the back of prints before they are used. Get two sets of prints and keep negatives safe.

✎ Before and after photos can be highly effective. Dig out historical photos and take new ones from the same spot.

✎ After the photo survey is completed it can be useful to introduce photos from other places and make comparisons.

*"I was surprised how the photographs added a new dimension to everyone's perception."*
**Ning Tan, facilitator**
Philippine workshop, 1995.

$ Film and processing are expensive. If budgets are tight, give one film to each team and ensure the camera gets handed around. Using digital cameras is cheaper but requires more initial investment in equipment.

# Photo survey process

Assuming a rapid 1-hour film processing facility is available nearby. If not, use polaroid cameras or split into 2 sessions.

**1 Briefing. Agree priorities**
Briefing by facilitator. Agreement of objectives, timescales and themes.
Theme examples:
- memorable places and images;
- beautiful places, ugly places;
- places to be alone, to socialise, to play;
- private places, public places;
- ugly buildings, beautiful buildings;
- threats.
Divide into teams and hand out cameras and film. (30 mins).

**2 Take photographs**
Teams go round taking photos. (Teams can have the same or different themes.)
(1 – 3 hours, depending on size of area)

**3 Process films during lunch break**
Prints produced – standard size are fine. (1.5 hours)

**4 Prepare presentation**
Teams arrange photos on boards or paper sheets. Symbols and words added on Post-its to record comments, feelings and evaluations. Relevant photos grouped together. When completed (or time up) photos pinned or glued down. Sheets named and put up on wall. (1 hour)

**4 Exhibit**
Viewing of exhibits. Tea break. (30 mins)

**5 Presentation**
Each team presents their images and conclusions to a plenary session. Debate and discussion. Areas of agreement and disagreement recorded. (1 hour)

Ideal numbers: **6 teams of 6–8 max**

Running time: **5.5 hours minimum.**

***Sorting photos***
*Villagers place photos of their own houses on a large map as an early step in a week-long planning workshop.*

***Cutting up photos***
*Photos being cut up and pasted on a large map to create a jigsaw display. Using this technique, people contribute photos which they think characterise their particular area. These are cut up to fit the given area of the map (perhaps a parish or plot). The end result is a vivid pictorial comparison of how people see their locality.*

### FURTHER INFORMATION

☞ Methods: *Elevation montage. Local design statement. Mapping.*
Scenario: *Village revival.*

✉ Countryside Commission.

✭ Peter Richards, Deike Richards, Debbie Bartlett.

# Planning aid scheme

**Planning aid schemes provide free and independent planning advice to groups or individuals who cannot afford to employ a consultant. They aim to give people the knowledge, skills and confidence to deal with the planning system and to become involved in wider planning issues.**

- Planning aid schemes are normally set up and run by national or regional professional institutions.

- A register of qualified professional planners prepared to volunteer their time is established.

- People needing help are put in touch with the nearest suitable volunteer on the register.

- The volunteer assists as much as possible, referring queries to the authorities or consultants if appropriate.

- As schemes become well established they may employ paid workers, establish telephone helplines, produce publications and become more pro-active in encouraging community participation.

✎ Government grant assistance is useful for setting up and administering planning aid systems.

✎ Producing information sheets on the planning system and common problems and issues can make the volunteer's job much easier.

✎ Need not be restricted to planners. 'Architectural aid', 'Surveying aid' and so on can also be very valuable.

**$** Setting-up costs: administration in compiling register; distributing publicity material. Ongoing costs: dealing with enquiries.

**Promotion leaflets**
*Ingredients: Title; Area covered; What planning aid is; What kind of help can be given; How much it will cost; Examples of help given; Who to contact.*

## Planning aid advice services checklist

- ☐ Appealing against a refusal of planning permission.
- ☐ Appearing at a public inquiry.
- ☐ Applying for planning permission.
- ☐ Drawing up community plans and local design statements.
- ☐ Guidance on development proposals and specific site problems.
- ☐ How the planning system works.
- ☐ How to find information and contact the right people.
- ☐ Objecting to or supporting a planning application or planning appeal.
- ☐ Putting forward your own views when local plans are being prepared.
- ☐ The rights of an individual or group on planning matters.
- ☐ The need for planning permission.
- ☐ Understanding enforcement procedures.
- ☐ Understanding the many types of development plans.
- ☐ Using the most effective public participation methods.
- ☐ .....................................................
  .....................................................

**Government funding**

**National office**
Overall scheme publicity and funding.

**Regional offices**
Register of local professional volunteers.
Local publicity.

**Professional volunteers**

### Planning aid network
*The scheme is coordinated by the national office of a professional institution. Regional branches publicise the scheme locally and maintain registers of professional planners willing to work in a voluntary capacity.*

## Benefits for professionals

- Opportunity to take part in a wide range of activities including environmental education.
- Satisfaction in helping people participate in the development of their communities.
- Useful source of continuing professional development.
- Valuable insight into the planning system from a user's point of view.

### FURTHER INFORMATION

☞ Scenario: *Regeneration infrastructure.*

✉ Royal Town Planning Institute  (National Planning Aid Co-ordinator).

# Planning day

**Planning days are a good way for getting the key parties to work creatively together to devise and explore options for a site, neighbourhood or city.**

- Participants will normally be personally invited by the event instigators. The aim is to have a cross-section of main stakeholders.

- A briefing pack is sent to all those attending. As well as setting out the aims of the day, the pack will contain background information about the area and the development process so that everyone starts the day with the maximum up-to-date knowledge.

- Workshop formats are designed to encourage the development of creative ideas (☞ *Design workshop*).

- Facilitators will often be from outside the area to provide a measure of independence.

- A printed summary is produced as soon as possible afterwards and the proposals may be exhibited to a wider public (☞ *Open house event*).

✎ Personal invitations can ensure a balanced attendance. But avoid criticism of exclusivity by having spare places for others.

✎ One-day events can generate a wealth of information and ideas which can easily be lost. Make sure there are resources available for recording, presenting and following up the results.

✎ Holding an 'awareness raising' day (☞ glossary) a couple of weeks beforehand can be helpful to generate momentum.

$ Main costs: venue, catering, organiser's time (10 person days minimum), facilitator's fees.

---

Dear_____,

I have pleasure in inviting you to participate in a special planning day on Tuesday 25th April at 25 High Street. A timetable, guest list and briefing pack will be sent out prior to the event.

The aim is to help develop practical but exciting development options for the area and encourage further collaboration between those concerned. The outcome will form the basis for wider public consultation shortly afterwards.

The format of the day has been carefully designed to achieve results. As well as all major local stakeholders we are also inviting a few specialist advisors to provide the breadth of input required. If there are others you think should be present, please let me know, though space is limited.

To help us in making arrangements, please confirm that you can attend.

Yours sincerely

*Sample invitation letter*

*"We need more events like this."*
**Participant, Planning day**
Oxpens Quarter Initiative, Oxford, 1997.

**Workshop sessions**
*Participants divided into groups working round tables with flipchart to one side.*

**Plenary sessions**
*Reporting back from the workshops with drawings and flipchart sheets pinned on the wall.*

## Sample planning day timetable

### Ideal numbers: 40–80
Larger numbers comfortable if enough space and facilitators; 10 max per workshop.

**10.00 Arrivals and coffee**
Viewing of display material.

**10.30 Introductions and briefings**

**11.00 Briefing workshops: issues and opportunities**
Participants allocated to one of four workshop groups, eg:
**1** Transport (access and movement)
**2** Activities (land uses)
**3** Strategic issues (regional context)
**4** Quality of life (environment)

**12.15 Plenary session**
Report back from workshops

**12.45 Lunch and site walkabouts**

**14.00 Design workshops: options and proposals**
Participants work in one of several design workshop groups focusing on different aspects of the site, eg:
**1** Regional context **2** Town context
**3** The site **4** River edge **5** New square?

**15.15 Plenary session**
Report back from workshops.

**15.45 Tea**

**16.15 Next steps**
Planning future activity.

**17.30 Presentation**
To councillors, press.

**18.00 Reception**

### FURTHER INFORMATION

☞ Methods: *Briefing workshop. Design workshop. Newspaper.* Scenarios: *Inner city. Planning study. Town centre.*

***Suggestion cards***
*These can be pre-prepared
with blanks for people to add
any ideas of their own. The use
of colour and visual symbols
makes the process accessible to
those with low literacy levels.*

***Priority cards***
*These are used to record all
suggestions and their locations.*

*"Compromise and consensus
become easier because
everyone's line of vision
converges on the subject
matter – the model itself –
allowing for practical ways of
non-threatening communication
and participation."*
**Neighbourhood Initiatives
Foundation**
leaflet, 1997.

# Planning for Real

**Planning for Real uses simple models as a focus
for people to put forward and prioritise ideas
on how their area can be improved. It is a
highly visible, hands-on community development
and empowerment tool, which people of all
abilities and backgrounds find easy and
enjoyable to engage in.**

■ A large 3-dimensional model of a neighbourhood is
constructed, preferably by local people, using
cardboard cut-outs for buildings pasted onto a base
plan fixed to polystyrene or cardboard.

■ The model is used at pre-advertised sessions held in
various locations in the community.

■ Participants place suggestion cards on the model
indicating what they want to see happen and where
(eg playground, parking, standpipe, tree, shopping).

■ The cards are sorted and prioritised to establish an
action plan which is followed up by working groups.

✎ Kits with building cut-outs and cards can be purchased (☞ further
info), or you can make up your own using available materials.

✎ Events work best if facilitated by someone who has done it
before but the basic idea is easy to pick up from the kits. The
kits' manufacturers – the Neighbourhood Initiatives Foundation –
recommends that users should be fully trained by them.

✎ The model kits are good for generating interest and creating an
initial vision. After that they need some creative adaptation if
they are to be used for detailed design.

$ From US$800 (venue and materials) to $24,000 (trained
facilitator to prepare for several months).

# Typical Planning for Real process

1  **Initiation.** Define area. Set up Steering Group. Get support. Purchase model pack (optional) or gather materials. (3 months)

2  **Make model.** A collective exercise by Steering Group, often with school children or students. Usually to a scale of 1:200 or 1:300 – which allows people to identify their own homes – and in sections so that it is easily transportable. (2 days)

3  **Publicise activity.** Take model around the area to generate interest. (2 weeks)

4  **Training session.** Run through process with Steering Group. (2 hours)

5  **Open sessions.**
   One or more times in different locations.
   • People gather around model.
     **Introduction** by facilitator explaining objectives and process. (10 mins)
   • Participants individually place **suggestion cards** on the model. Professionals watch and answer questions but do not take part. (30 mins)
   • Participants **discuss results** and rearrange cards until collectively happy with the result. (30 mins)
   • Participants **record results**, usually on priority cards setting out the suggestion and its location. (30 mins)
   • Participants **prioritise suggestions** by placing priority cards on Now, Soon or Later boards and identifying who should take action. (30 mins)
   • **Discussion on next steps** and establishing working parties on the main issues. (20 mins)
   .(Total: 2.5 hours – possibly broken up into a series of separate drop-in 'suggestions' sessions, and then a prioritising session.)

6  **Working parties.**
   Follow up suggestions. (2 months)

7  **Feedback.**
   Circulation of newsletter. (1 month)

**Making suggestions**
*Participants mill around the model, and make their views known by placing pre-written or self-completed suggestion cards onto it.*

**Prioritising**
*Working in small groups, participants order the suggestions by placing cards onto a chart which is divided into three bands –'Now', 'Soon', 'Later' – on one axis and those who should be responsible for taking action on the other.*

---

**FURTHER INFORMATION**

☞  Method: *Models.* Scenario: *Inner city.*

↪  *Building Design Pack. Do-ers Guide to Planning for Real. Planning for Real Community Pack. Planning for Real – the Video. Power in our Hands.*

✉  Neighbourhood Initiatives Foundation supplies kits with instructions.

★  Margaret Wilkinson. 'Planning for Real'® is a registered trademark of the Neighbourhood Initiatives Foundation.

# Planning weekend

**Planning weekends are an elaborate but highly effective way of generating momentum for change and getting all parties involved in producing a plan of action for a site, neighbourhood or city.**

**Briefing**
*Team members are briefed by community leaders and officials at the start of a planning weekend.*

**Public presentation**
*Team members present their proposals for the area to a public meeting after four intensive days of workshops, brainstorming and team working.*

*"In many ways, the process has transformed the way that Americans shape community development policies and take those actions that most directly affect their community's growth or change."*
**American Institute of Architects**
*R/UDAT Handbook*, 1992.

■ Planning weekends comprise an intensive and carefully structured programme of activities spanning a weekend. They usually last for 4 full days – Friday to Monday – but may be longer or shorter. The main workshop sessions are open to the general public.

■ The weekends are facilitated by a multidisciplinary team. This may be comprised of outsiders or locals or a combination of the two.

■ The end result is a set of proposals for action which is presented to the community on the last evening and produced in exhibition and print form.

✎ Planning weekends – often called *community* planning weekends – work best when there is at least 6 months preparation time and a commitment by all parties to follow up afterwards.

✎ The most effective long-term results are likely to be when events are organised locally with back-up and support from people who have done it before.

✎ Employing a local resident as event co-ordinator can help ensure local support and follow-up.

✎ Get journalists involved, ideally as Team members.

**$** Average costs: US$30,000 excluding organisers' time and assuming team members come free. Professionally organised events can cost over $100,000.  Locally organised events can be done for under $15,000.

# Planning weekend timetable
Sample for a 4-day event. Customise.

**THURSDAY**

| | |
|---|---|
| 14.00 - 18.00 | **Setting up**<br>Room layout. Equipment delivery. Sign making. |
| 18.00 - 20.00 | **Organisers' final meeting** |
| 20.00 - 22.00 | **Team arrivals** |

**DAY 1    FRIDAY**

| | |
|---|---|
| 10.00 - 10.30 | **Event launch/introduction**<br>Welcome by hosts. |
| 10.30 - 12.30 | **Reconnaissance**<br>Tour of area by bus, train, plane or foot with visits to interest groups. |
| 12.30 - 13.30 | **Buffet lunch** |
| 14.00 - 17.00 | **Briefings**<br>Short presentations by key interested parties outlining opportunities and constraints. |
| 18.00 - 19.00 | **Team review meeting** |
| 19.00 - 20.00 | **Dinner and social** |

**DAY 2    SATURDAY**

| | |
|---|---|
| 9.00 - 10.00 | **Team briefing & preparation** |
| 10.00 - 11.30 | **Briefing workshops 1**<br>Open to all. Several parallel groups, ending with a plenary report back. |
| 11.30 - 13.00 | **Briefing workshops 2** |
| 13.00 - 14.00 | **Lunch & walkabouts** |
| 14.00 - 15.30 | **Design workshops 1**<br>Open to all. Ending with plenary report back. In parallel groups of 10-15. |

| | |
|---|---|
| 15.30 - 17.00 | **Design workshops 2** |
| 17.00 - 19.00 | **Breather**<br>Minute writing, exercise. |
| 19.00 - 23.00 | **Team brainstorm dinner** |

**DAY 3    SUNDAY**

| | |
|---|---|
| 11.00 - 12.00 | **Team editorial meeting**<br>Presentation structure. Production strategy. |
| 12.00 onwards | **Report, exhibition and slide show production**<br>Writing, editing, drawing, slide making. Review sessions as necessary. Team only. Sleep and eat as and when possible. |

**DAY 4    MONDAY**

| | |
|---|---|
| All day | **Report, exhibition and slide show production** |
| Late as possible | **Report to printers** |
| Late as possible | **Colour slides processing** |
| All day | **Clearing up**<br>Tidying and packing up. |
| 19.00 - 21.00 | **Public presentation**<br>Slide show. Discussion. Formal thanks. Distribution of report. |
| 21.00 - 23.00 | **Farewell social event** |

**Ideal numbers: 100 – 250. Team: 10 – 30**
Larger numbers can be catered for if enough space and workshop facilitators.

---

### FURTHER INFORMATION

☞ Methods: *Briefing workshop. Design workshop.* Scenarios: *Inner city regeneration. Local neighbourhood initiative. Newspaper supplement.*

๑ *Action Planning. Creating a Design Assistance Team for Your Community.*

# Prioritising

| | NOW | SOON | LATER |
|---|---|---|---|
| We can do it on our own | | | |
| We can do it with a little help | | | |
| We can do it with help plus some money | | | |
| We can do it jointly with the local authority | | | |
| We cannot do it but can tell the local authority or other agency what needs doing | | | |
| Who else could help? | | | |

**Prioritising projects**

*Matrix for placing cards identifying possible projects or actions needed.*

**Prioritising is a way of placing in order of priority what needs doing and when. This is an important aspect of all decision-making and often needs to be done as a group activity if the results are to be generally agreed on.**

- The various options are worked out using brainstorming, surveys or other methods.

- A graphic format is selected to allow the prioritising of options to be simply and visually displayed. There are many ways of doing this, including the three examples shown on these pages (and on pages 36-37, 71 and 78-79).

- After discussion of the issues, and perhaps presentations, participants make individual choices using stickers or cards.

- The results are analysed and provide the basis for decision-making or further discussion.

✎ Often worth allowing people an opportunity to change their votes after seeing how others vote and discussing the results. This allows people to think through situations which are often quite complex.

✎ Facilitator's skill is finding the appropriate graphic format for the issues being considered.

✎ Great scope for using computers to process results, especially where large number of people and choices are involved.

$ No significant costs involved apart from facilitator's fees if any.

# Wheel of fortune group prioritising method

Way for a group of people to collectively rank up to 20 competing priorities. Suitable for a workshop or public meeting.

**1 Preparation**

Large sheets of paper are taped together to create a big square on the floor or a table. The bigger the group, the larger it needs to be. A large circle is drawn on the paper, divided into as many slices as there are options. Each slice is labelled.

**2 Coloured sticky notes**

Participants are each given 3 cards or Post-it notes. Different colours can be given to people representing different interest groups.

**3 Voting**

Participants vote for their top three priorities by placing their cards or Post-its in the relevant slice.

**4 Discussion and recording**

Votes are counted and recorded for further discussion.

The process is repeated with different groups.

**Ideal numbers: 10 – 15**
**Running time: 20 minutes**

# Fence prioritising method

Way for a group to arrive at a majority view on issues where there are conflicting options. Likely to be done after presentations, and discussion of the issues involved.

1 A list of issues is prepared, perhaps by a consultant.
2 The issues are illustrated graphically on lines with a 'fence' in the middle (see below).
3 Participants discuss each issue in turn. After discussion, each participant places a dot somewhere along the line. A dot placed towards the end of a line indicates strong agreement for the given option. A dot in the middle indicates no strong views either way (ie 'sitting on the fence').
4 The strongest concentration of dots (or the mean position of the sum of all the dots) is taken as the collective view.

Example below: planning a new settlement.

| | FENCE | |
|---|:---:|---|
| **Neighbourhoods.** Based on 5-minute walk (400m) ●●●●● | ● | No identifiable neighbourhood structure ●●● |
| **Shopping.** Small retail centres you can walk to ●●●●●● | ● | Larger retail centres you can drive to ●● |
| **Roads.** New road with 50km/hr speed limit ●●● | ● | New road as by-pass with 80km/hr speed limit ●●● |
| **Streets.** Interconnected streets with calmed through-traffic ●●● ● | ● | Curvilinear street system with cul-de-sac streets ●●●● |
| **Working/Living.** Mixing working and living places ●● | ●● | Separate working and living places ●●●●● |
| **Integration.** Development linking with surrounding area ●● | ● ● | New self-contained communities ●●● |

## FURTHER INFORMATION

☞ Methods: *Design workshop. Ideas comp. Microplanning. Planning for Real.*

☆ Matrix: Neighbourhood Initiatives Foundation. Wheel of fortune: Robin Deane, 1066 Housing Association. Peter Richards, Deicke Richards Architects.

# Process planning session

Process planning sessions allow people to work together to determine the most suitable public participation process for their particular situation. It is particularly useful to hold them at an early stage in a community planning initiative and then at periodic intervals.

- As many as possible of the key interested parties or 'stakeholders' are invited to ensure that the outcome is supported by all parties.

- Participants are introduced to the various options available and helped to design a process of their own, usually by an external facilitator.

- A formal workshop format is normally followed (example in box, right) to make the procedure equitable and transparent.

- Sessions are held periodically whenever there is a need to review the overall process.

**Evening session**
*Police, residents and other stakeholders taking part in an evening process planning session in a community centre. It led to an action planning weekend seven months later.*

✎ Make people feel comfortable and relaxed. Spanning lunch can work well for officials and business people with participants seated around circular tables. Evening sessions spanning a buffet supper will normally work better for residents.

✎ Be on guard for sabotage by those who don't want any kind of process to take place.

✎ Showing slides or videos of methods in use is usually a good way to generate enthusiasm.

✎ Invite external facilitators to present options, but keep ownership local from the start.

$ Main costs: Venue; catering; fee for presenter.

# Process planning session sample format

**1 Introductions**
Facilitator explains event objectives and structure. Everyone says briefly who they are and what their hopes are for the session. (15 mins)

**2 Presentation**
Slide show or video of possible processes to provide inspiration. (45 mins max)

**3 Aims**
Short debate on overall objectives and specific constraints. (15 mins)

**4 Refreshment break**

**5 Individual ideas**
People fill in a process planner (☞ box, right, or p166-71) OR develop their ideas on a blank sheet of paper. (10 mins minimum)

**6 Group ideas**
People are divided into groups (4 – 8 ideal). Individuals present their idea to group. Group votes to pursue one idea only and develop it further. (20 mins min)

**7 Report back**
Each group makes semi-formal presentation of their idea to plenary of all participants. (5 mins each group)

**8 Selection**
Vote on which idea to pursue and then discuss improvements and next steps. (10 mins minimum).

**Ideal numbers: 16 – 20**.
Larger numbers no problem.

**Running time: 2 – 4 hours.**
3 hours comfortable.

**Note:** This format can also be used for general training purposes with no specific location or issue in mind.

*Lunchtime session*
*One of four tables at a working lunch for key players (property owners, authorities, amenity groups) to determine a development process for a major town centre regeneration initiative. It led to a design workshop and open house event one year later.*

---

## Sample process planner
Customise and leave space for responses.

**Aims**
1 What do you want to **achieve**? _____
2 What are the main **issues**? _____
3 What geographical **area** are you concerned with? _____

**Process**
4 What **methods** do you favour? _____
5 **When** should activities take place? _____
6 **Who** are the key people to involve? _____
7 What **expertise** do you need? _____

**Organisation**
8 Which **organisation/s** should lead? ____
9 Who else should **help**? _____
10 How much will it **cost** and **who pays**? __
11 Who does **what next**? _____

12 **Other** thoughts and ideas _____

---

**FURTHER INFORMATION**

☞ Getting started p6. Useful formats pp166-171.
Scenarios: *Local neighbourhood initiative. Planning study. Town centre upgrade.*

# Reconnaissance trip

Reconnaissance trips involve direct inspection of the area being considered by mixed teams of local people and technical experts. They are used to familiarise everyone with the physical environment and key issues at the start of many community planning processes and to review progress at intervals.

- A route is carefully planned to include key local features and issues. The route may be walked or toured by bus, boat or other forms of transport. It may include visits to buildings or facilities.

- The trip is undertaken by a mixed group of local people and technical experts. Usually a team leader will direct the group and determine the pace.

- The group make notes, sketches, take photos and talk informally to people in their own setting. They may check existing plans for accuracy.

- At the end of the trip a debriefing is held, and the notes and other materials compiled into a form useful to the next stage of the planning process.

✎ Where little information exists, the route can be planned with a view to producing a specific 'transect' diagram or map *(see right)*.

✎ Groups of more than 15 can be unwieldy. Split into smaller groups, perhaps taking different routes and comparing notes afterwards.

✎ Viewing from a hill or high tower is particularly useful. If funds allow, a trip in a helicopter or light aircraft can be worthwhile.

✎ Good opportunity for engaging with media, especially TV.

$ Main costs: Transport; organiser's time.

**Tour of neighbourhood**
*Well planned route map with important features marked (above). Viewing from the air, with the media and on the ground (below).*

## Reconnaissance trip timetable

Sample for a complex trip lasting most of a day with advance planning.

1 **Briefings.** By a number of key parties (in a hall or meeting room).

2 **Bus.** Tour of wider area. Commentary by local residents and planners. Stops at high viewing point and key buildings and sites.

3 **Lunch.** In a local bar with business people.

4 **Walk.** Around central area. Semi-structured interviews with traders. Detailed checking of land use plan.

5 **Tea.** At a community centre with local residents. Discussion.

6 **Visit.** To arts centre. Viewing of local crafts exhibition. Discussion with artists.

7 **Team meeting.** Debriefing and review.

## Transect walk format

For a simple walk where little information exists and with little advance planning.

1 **Select people.** Decide who will do the walk. Ensure a cross-section of interests.

2 **Decide route and issues.** Plan a route which covers the issues under consideration (eg land use changes, development pressures, hazards).

3 **Walk.** Walk the route making sketches, taking notes, holding informal interviews, taking photos.

4 **Construct profile.** Compile all notes and sketches. Prepare a profile in map or diagram form.

5 **Display.** Use profile as a basis for consultation and planning.

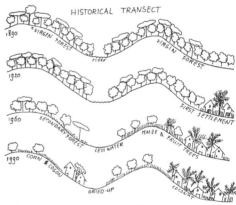

***Historical community profile***
*Diagram resulting from a transect walk showing the evolution of the landscape over the last century.*

***Looking round***
*Exploring and discussing a site proposed for development and a factory in a proposed conservation area.*

---

### FURTHER INFORMATION

☞ Methods: *Diagrams. Design assistance team. Mapping. Planning weekend. Review session.*
Scenario: *New neighbourhood.*

# Review session

Review sessions are a useful way of monitoring progress and maintaining momentum. They can be held weeks, months, or even years after an action planning event or other community planning initiative.

**Reunion**
*Cakes made by a local resident set the tone for team members returning to the scene of an action planning event for a review session.*

Was it a useful thing to do?

What did it achieve?

How could we have done it better?

What happens next?

**Sample brief**
*For a review session on an action planning event.*

- Background material is produced evaluating the outcome of initiatives and reviewing progress.

- All those involved in previous activity are invited back to a session, normally lasting for one day. Invitations can also be sent to those who may wish to become involved in the future.

- A programme is designed to review progress, evaluate earlier initiatives and determine the next steps (see sample timetable, right).

- A report of the session is written up and circulated.

✎ Timing is important. Holding a review session too soon will be pointless. Left too long and you may lose momentum.

✎ Make it an enjoyable event by including opportunities for socialising and networking.

✎ Evaluating precisely what outcomes have resulted from any particular initiative is always difficult because there are so many variables. No one is likely to have the whole picture. Produce a draft of the Progress Monitor (p170) and circulate it for comment.

✎ Good opportunity to get new people and groups on board, particularly those feeling excluded by not being involved previously.

$ Main costs: venue, preparation, travel costs, refreshments.

## Review Session Timetable

**10.00** **Arrivals and refreshments**
Viewing of display material.

**10.30** **Walkabout**
To observe progress on the ground.

**11.15** **Report back**
By those undertaking initiatives.

**12.15** **Evaluation sessions**
General review as a group.

**12.45** **Lunch**
(plus evaluation sessions for special
groups, eg external team members).

**14.00** **Next steps**
List actions needed now and by who.

**15.15** **Refreshments and networking**

**Ideal numbers: 30 – 40**

*Reviewing progress*
*Team members and participants of an action*
*planning week meet 16 months later to review*
*progress and plan further initiatives.*

| **FURTHER INFORMATION** |
| --- |

Scenarios: *Inner city regeneration. Local
neighbourhood initiative. Village revival.*
Useful formats: *Progress monitor.
Evaluation form.*

✉ Mount Wise Action Planning.

☆ Dick Watson

# Risk assessment

## Is your community ever threatened by:

- ☐ Accidents (car, rail, air)
- ☐ Armed conflict
- ☐ Civil unrest
- ☐ Cyclone
- ☐ Deforestation
- ☐ Drought
- ☐ Earthquakes
- ☐ Environmental degradation
- ☐ Epidemics
- ☐ Fire
- ☐ Flooding
- ☐ Migrations (forced)
- ☐ Over-development
- ☐ Pests
- ☐ Pollution
- ☐ Tidal waves
- ☐ Tornadoes
- ☐ Tourism (excessive)
- ☐ Traffic congestion
- ☐ Tribal wars
- ☐ Typhoon
- ☐ Volcanic eruption

**Hazards checklist**
*Typical hazards that may face a community but are often ignored until it is too late. They range in seriousness but the same principles for assessing and reducing risks apply to all.*

**Risk assessment involves analysing threats (or 'hazards') facing a community. It should ideally be used in all planning – since most communities face some kind of threat. But it is most necessary for vulnerable communities prone to natural or human-made disasters.**

- Risk assessment comprises three elements:
  - **hazard analysis** – understanding what hazards exist, the likelihood of them occurring, their likely intensity, and their effect.
  - **vulnerability assessment** – understanding who or what is vulnerable to the hazards.
  - **capacity assessment** – understanding what capacities exist within the community to reduce vulnerability.

- A range of methods can be used to make it easy for communities to make their own risk assessments as a basis for taking action to reduce risks (see box right). Most involve group work, preferably with trained facilitators.

- The end result is a clear understanding by the community of the nature and scale of the risks it faces. It is then possible to determine what is needed to reduce the risk; for instance new local initiatives, outside resources, technical expertise.

✎ Big benefit is in obliging planning to consider natural and human-made hazards and infrequent threats all too often ignored.

✎ Involve local emergency services; an invaluable source of knowledge.

$ Varies depending on approaches adopted and numbers involved.

## Vulnerability and capacity matrix

| POTENTIAL HAZARD  Flooding | VULNERABILITIES | CAPACITIES |
|---|---|---|
| **PHYSICAL and MATERIAL**<br>What is vulnerable?<br>What resources exist to address vulnerability? | · Houses & farmland in low lying areas.<br>· Water supplies easily contaminated by floods.<br>· Food supplies get cut. | · People have boats to save belongings.<br>· Identifiable evacuation centre exists. |
| **SOCIAL and ORGANISATION**<br>Who is vulnerable?<br>What resources exist to make them less so? | · People in outlying areas (15 families).<br>· Migrant workers.<br>· People unable to swim (particularly women). | · People's organisation at community level.<br>· Warning system exists. Disaster response committee functions. |
| **MOTIVATION and ATTITUDE**<br>What attitudes lead to vulnerability?<br>What capacities exist to improve the situation? | · Individualism.<br>· Lack of community spirit/cooperation. | · New positive attitude by young people.<br>· Voluntary organisations. |

# Some participatory risk assessment methods

### Hazard and risk mapping
Locating hazards on maps along with people, buildings and infrastructure at risk from those hazards (☞ Mapping).

### Simulation exercises
Acting out the effect of possible hazards. Either to assess the impact of new initiatives on existing risk levels or to understand the impact of past hazards (☞ Simulation).

### Hazard or threat ranking
Prioritising the importance of various hazards according to community perceptions and needs (☞ Community profiling).

### Vulnerability and capacity analysis
Compiling a matrix of a community's vulnerabilities to, and capacities to cope with, each hazard identified (see example, above).

### Completing a vulnerability and capacity matrix
General and risk-specific information from secondary sources and community profiling sessions is ordered into categories and placed in a matrix as shown above. This is usually done in group sessions using a large wallchart. A separate matrix is completed for each hazard. Separate charts can be completed for men and women and for different ethnic groups. Completed matrices can be used to test a proposed initiative's impact on a community's vulnerability and capacity, and to monitor it during implementation.

### FURTHER INFORMATION

☞ Method: *Community profiling. Mapping. Simulation.*
Scenarios: *Disaster management. Shanty settlement upgrading.*

⊘ *Rising from the Ashes*

☆ Roger Bellers. Nick Hall.

# Roadshow

**Roadshows combine a series of workshops, exhibitions and a symposium to generate professionally produced urban design proposals based on local people's wishes. They are a good way of generating a critical mass of energy for securing wide debate and an impetus for implementation.**

*Sample advertising leaflet*
*Key components: Map showing sites; times and locations of workshops, exhibitions and symposium; details of organisers, sponsors etc; aims and objectives.*

- An overall theme is agreed by the organisers (such as vacant sites or rundown estates) and a number of sites in a neighbourhood selected for attention.

- Teams of professionals are selected by open competition to prepare improvement schemes for each of the selected sites.

- The chosen teams facilitate design workshops with local residents, prepare proposals and present them in an interactive exhibition.

- A final, highly publicised symposium is held to debate the results and generate momentum for the scheme's implementation.

*"It's a wonderful format; this teach-in on matters that we all have opinions about with people who are knowledgeable. It's started a discussion that's desperately needed about taking control of our own environment. May the debate roll on."*
**Roger de Freitas, Hammersmith Society**
Summary Symposium, Architecture Foundation Roadshow, 28 May 1998.

✎ Roadshows are most likely to succeed if organised by an independent body with the active support of the local authorities and community groups.

✎ Other publicity and involvement activity undertaken at the same time (eg school workshops, video soapboxes, radio phone-ins) can help generate momentum.

$ Main costs: organisers' time (3 person months at least); publicity material, fees for design teams (optional); venue for symposium.

# Sample roadshow timetable

Jan-Mar   **Preparation.** Decide on area, theme and sites. Secure support from key groups, and funding. Prepare format and logistics.

Apr   **Announce competition for design teams.** Open competition to select professional teams.

June   **Select teams.** Based on ability to work with local communities as well as on technical ability.

July   **Official public launch.** To secure media publicity.

Aug-Sep   **Public workshops.** To brief design teams (one workshop for each site). **Schools programme.** Workshops generating proposals from children. **Video soapbox.** Prominently located to gain views of wider public.

Oct   **Design time.** All-day crit for all design teams and key local stakeholders to share approaches prior to finalising proposals.

Oct   **Exhibition of proposals.** With provision for people to comment. Preferably held at on-site locations as well as at a locally prominent venue where the symposium is to be held.

Oct   **Symposium.** With high profile speakers and media.

Nov   **Scheme revision.** In the light of comments.

Dec   **Report published.**

        **Ideal numbers: 10 sites and design teams**
        **Total time period: 1 year**

***Exhibition of proposals***
*Proposals from the design teams are publicly exhibited to encourage discussion and dialogue which is continued at a public symposium.*

| **FURTHER INFORMATION** |
| --- |
| ☞   Methods: *Design workshop. Ideas competition. Interactive display. Design fest. Video soapbox.* |
| ✉   Architecture Foundation. |

# Simulation

**Simulation can be used to act out a real event or activity, helping both participants and observers gain information and insights prior to formulating plans. It can also be used to test draft plans.**

*Look at the sky, the clouds are dark. It may be a storm coming. Let's turn on the radio.*

*Local radio channel: "Flood warning No 3."*

*Quick, let's go home and sandbag our house.*

*I'll go and move the animals to higher ground.*

*Tell grandpa to come and stay at our house - just in case the stream banks burst.*

*Do you think we could move our belongings into the school hall if things get too bad?*

*Not sure. Drop in at the store on the way back and ask.*

- An event or activity to be simulated is chosen. This could be a natural or human-made hazard – such as an earthquake – or daily life in a street or building.

- People who have experienced the event or activity from a variety of perspectives are brought together for a workshop session.

- People act out the event or activity as a drama, individually or in groups. Usually, a carefully structured exercise is prepared in advance by a facilitator (see example in box, right).

- Key information and issues arising are recorded for future use.

- Recommendations are identified for future actions.

✎ Enjoyable way of getting information that would be hard to obtain any other way.

✎ Good process for team building and clarification of roles.

✎ People may need time to prepare, so the method should be explained in advance.

✎ Allocate time for discussion after each simulation exercise to allow people to reflect on their own performance.

$ Minimal costs involved for materials, plus facilitator's fees if any.

## Sample simulation exercise

**1 Determine event or activity to simulate**
Eg: A recent flood.

**2 Design the exercise**
Objectives. Process. Materials required.

**3 Assemble participants/cast of characters**
Eg: A cross-section of the local community
affected in different ways by the flood,
plus officials and technical experts dealing
with flood relief and avoidance measures.

**4 Explain purpose**
Eg: To understand how people reacted to
the recent flood in order to decide on
measures to reduce the impact of future
ones. (10 mins)

**5 Divide into groups**
Ask each group to prepare to act out a
different aspect of the event or activity in
the form of a drama. Eg: Before the flood;
during the flood; after the flood. Each
group also to appoint a reporter. (10 mins)

**6 Group working**
Each group prepares its drama through
discussion prompted by responding to key
questions. Eg: "When and how did you
know a flood was coming?" "What did
people do and when?" Reporter notes
main issues arising. (60 mins)

**7 Plenary: dramas and presentation**
Each group acts out its drama followed by
a presentation by the reporter summing up
the main issues. General discussion. (60-90
mins)

**8 Review** (perhaps later or after a break)
Review of issues and concerns raised.
Discussion on next steps. (30 mins)

**Ideal numbers: 18–24** (3 groups of 6-8)
**Running time: 140–170 mins** (plus 30
mins for review)
**Note:** The same exercise could be used to
simulate an event that has not yet
happened but might do in the future.

***Acting out an event***
*Local residents dramatising how they were
affected by a recent typhoon during a field
workshop to improve disaster management.*

| FURTHER INFORMATION |
| --- |
| ☞ Methods: *Community profiling. Field workshop. Gaming. Risk assessment.* |
| ☆ Roger Bellers. Nick Hall. |

# Street stall

**Street stalls are interactive displays held out of doors. They make it possible to secure the views of larger numbers of people than is normally possible indoors. They are particularly useful where the views of people using a particular street or public space are required.**

■ A highly public location is selected and exhibition and interactive display material mounted for a selected period.

■ Facilitators are on hand to encourage people to make comments and engage in debate.

■ The event may be advertised in advance but this is not essential.

✎ Arcades and colonnades are good venues as they provide shelter from the rain. Ideal if you can also have the use of a shop.

✎ Can benefit from, and be attractive for, radio and television coverage. Leaflets can also be handed out to passers-by and placed in shop windows.

✎ Be careful when using Post-it notes and leaflets if windy conditions are likely – they may blow away!

✎ Getting formal permission to set up a stall in a public area can take forever. Plan well ahead or just do it and be prepared to move if necessary.

✎ Likely to attract a broader range of people than an indoor event, but marginalised groups or reticent individuals may still need special inducement to participate. Have a 'postbox' so that people can make contributions anonymously.

**$** Main costs: display material; staff time.

*"The street stall proved to be an invaluable and invigorating experience for us all. We were overwhelmed by the interest taken... and all subsequent developments of our scheme were made against the backdrop of what the people of Bath wanted to see."*
**Student report, Prince of Wales's Institute of Architecture**
Bath Project, 1996.

*"The day had a certain verve which boosted – and was reinforced by – the strong level of interest of passers-by. It was good for the Trust to be involved in something as popular and constructive – we are often portrayed as being elitist and negative."*
**Timothy Cantell, Chairman, Planning Committee, Bath Preservation Trust**
letter, March 1997.

**Taking to the streets**
*Shoppers join in a debate on the future of the town centre by writing on Post-it notes, sketching their own ideas and holding discussions with the organisers. Over 2,000 Post-it notes were posted up over 5 hours on a cold winter day and two books filled with comments. The results were used to prepare a scheme for one of the most important development sites in the town.*

### FURTHER INFORMATION

☞ Methods: *Interactive display. Open house event. Table scheme display.* Scenario: *Community centre.*

# Table scheme display

**Table scheme displays allow large numbers of people to understand and make an input into development proposals, with or without engaging with others. They can be used as part of an exhibition or open house event.**

- Drawings or models of a proposed scheme are placed on a table with the main elements identified on separate voting sheets around the edge.

- Separate tables can be used for different scheme options.

- People vote on what they like or dislike by placing sticky dots on the voting sheets.

- More detailed comments can be made using Post-it notes, either on the same tables or on separate displays.

- The results are analysed afterwards to inform the next stages of the planning process.

**THE MAIN ELEMENTS OF THE SKETCH SCHEMES ARE HIGHLIGHTED.**

Please indicate whether you agree or disagree with the ideas by using the stickers provided.

● Green = Agree

● Red = Disagree

○ Yellow = No opinion

**YOU MAY HAVE YOUR OWN IDEAS OR SUGGESTIONS.**

Please write these on the comment sheet or sketch them on the blank plan provided. It will help if you add your name and address.

*Sample instructions*

✎ Good way of introducing people to the design process. Works particularly well for getting comments on rough sketch schemes developed at design workshops. Redrawing is not usually necessary though it can help if time allows.

✎ Useful debate will invariably take place around the tables. It can be helpful to have organisers present at each table to respond to questions and to take notes.

✎ Have a spare table with a blank plan for those wanting to draw up their own ideas in more detail.

$ Few costs involved unless proposals are professionally redrawn.

**Table scheme display**
*Voting with sticky dots on town centre
improvement ideas proposed by a design
workshop focusing on transport. Part of a one-day
open house event.*

---

**FURTHER INFORMATION**

☞ Methods: *Interactive display. Open house
event.* Scenario: *Community centre.*

---

# Task force

***Recruiting team members***
*Sample poster for a task force.*

*"The task force is valuable because when people come from outside they have a special vision, with a certain objectivity, and they see things we don't see. That vision is very very good for developing new approaches."*
**Yves Dauge, Mayor of Chinon**
France, 12 August 1994.

*"Before the Task Force, all discussion about the future of the city – what should happen, when and where – took place in small rooms with one or two people. Now everyone is discussing it."*
**Lorenzo Piacentini, engineer**
Viterbo, Italy, 1994.

*"It was an absolutely exceptional experience. We were exposed to so many inspiring people and it was very intensive. It had a great influence on my life."*
**Joanna Wachowiak,
architecture student**, 1994.

**Urban design task forces are multidisciplinary teams of students and professionals which produce proposals for a site or neighbourhood based on an intensive programme of site studies, lectures, participatory exercises and studio working, normally lasting several weeks. They are an efficient way of securing high quality design proposals at the same time as providing a first-rate educational opportunity.**

- Task forces combine an academic and practical training in urban design with the development of realistic proposals for improving a site, neighbourhood or city.

- Staff and student team members will come from a range of backgrounds, ages and, normally, countries.

- The programme begins with academic input and skills training and then moves into engaging with the community and producing urban design proposals (see sample format, right).

- Task forces are likely to be organised by academic institutions in partnership with local agencies.

✎ Plan at least one year in advance in order to have time to secure support from all relevant local organisations and make the necessary logistical arrangements.

**$** Cost dependent on numbers involved. Main costs: travel; accommodation; staff time; presentation materials. Cost for a 4-week event likely to be around US$130,000. Contributors: host city, student members, academic institutions. Scope also for sponsorship and international exchange funding.

# Task force sample format

**1 Building a skill base**
Seminars, practical experience and visits for the team designed to develop skills in:
- observational drawing and painting
- urban analysis
- local building crafts
- measuring buildings
- modelmaking
- team working
- participatory design
(1 week)

**2 Small live projects**
Developing urban design proposals for small sites. These may be of real practical value but are primarily designed to develop skills in urban design, presentation and team working. (1 week)

**3 Public engagement on large live project**
Public lectures, meetings or workshops with various interest groups, action planning event (eg *Community planning forum*). (3 days)

**4 Studio working**
Developing urban design proposals. (2 weeks)

**5 Presentation**
Exhibition and public presentation of proposals with newsletter. (1 day)

**6 Publication**
Publication of book or report of proposals. (6 months)

**Ideal numbers: 20–30 students**
**10 tutors**

**Running time: 3–6 weeks**

***Public engagement***
*Finding out local views on the city.*

***Studio working***
*Task force members prepare proposals in a temporary locally-based studio.*

***Presentation***
*Task force members explain their proposals to local politicians at the final presentation.*

## FURTHER INFORMATION

☞ Methods: *Community planning forum. Urban design studio.* Scenario: *New neighbourhood.*

⊘ *Viterbo; Santa Maria in Gradi.*

✉ Prince's Foundation.

☆ Brian Hanson and Richard John.

# Urban design studio

**Urban design studios are special units attached to a university or other educational establishment which undertake environmental project work, usually in the immediate locality. They can provide both a valuable educational experience for students and an important resource for local communities.**

***Academic rigour***
*Combining theory and practice.*

"It allowed me to apply things I learned in school in a no-longer fictitious environment. It's not the community being treated as a laboratory for students to exercise their creative will. Both sides are getting something out of it."
**J B Clancy, student**
**Yale Urban Design Workshop**
*New York Times*, 19.11.95.

"Students are increasingly interested in what it means to be a participant in the public realm. The idea of a citizen architect is back."
**Alan Plattus, Director**
**Yale Urban Design Workshop**
*New York Times*, 19.11.95.

- Urban design studios are set up by an educational establishment, usually at a school of architecture or planning. They will normally be independent units.

- The studios have access to all the resources of the establishment; staff, students, researchers, facilities and equipment.

- Relationships will be built up with local agencies and community organisations and a variety of project work will be undertaken.

- Once established, the studios will start advertising their services and take on consultancy work.

✎ Independence is essential to overcome the incompatibility of curriculum and real project timetables. Academics and administrators sometimes find such units threatening because students often enjoy the work more than academic studies. Also, live projects generate their own momentum and are hard to dovetail into predetermined time slots. Studios rarely survive unless given enough time to build up a reputation, so making it possible to attract funding for projects and become self-sufficient.

✎ Core staff are needed to maintain momentum of projects during school vacations and other times when students are unavailable.

✎ Studios may work best if student involvement is voluntary.

$ Main costs are staff, travel and equipment. Initially funded as part of architecture school. Later, can secure consultancy fees.

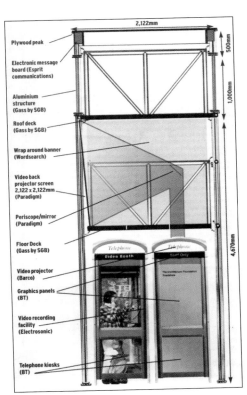

Plywood peak

Electronic message board (Esprit communications)

Aluminium structure (Gass by SGB)

Roof deck (Gass by SGB)

Wrap around banner (Wordsearch)

Video back projector screen 2,122 x 2,122mm (Paradigm)

Periscope/mirror (Paradigm)

Floor Deck (Gass by SGB)

Video projector (Barco)

Graphics panels (BT)

Video recording facility (Electrosonic)

Telephone kiosks (BT)

2,122mm

500mm

1,000mm

4,670mm

### Public viewpoint

*A resident's comments on the state of the local area are screened prominently in a shopping street. Passers-by can add their views to the debate by stepping into one the converted telephone booths, picking up the handset and pressing 'record'.*

### Design details

*Four telephone boxes are modified for people to record their views. Each booth contains a telephone handset which triggers the automatic video recording programme. Simple written and spoken operating instructions are provided. The scaffold tower above has a message board using moving text to invite the public to participate, a light cube with images relevant to the issue being considered and a back projection video screen on which the recorded messages are projected.*

---

### FURTHER INFORMATION

Method: *Roadshow.*

Architecture Foundation.

Example shown designed by Alex de Rijke as part of an Architecture Foundation Roadshow. Illustration and screen shots courtesy of *Building Design*.

# Scenarios A–Z

**A range of scenarios covering some common development situations. Each illustrates one way in which methods can be combined in an overall strategy.**

Use for inspiration, not as blueprints. It is important to stress that in each case, there are many other ways of achieving the same objective. Note also that the timescales shown may be over-optimistic in some contexts as they assume that securing permissions, raising finance and setting up organisational frameworks takes place fairly smoothly.

*Community mapping,*
*Yunan, China, 1997*

# Community centre

This scenario applies to the design and construction of any building for community use.

The conventional approach would be for a local authority to commission architects to plan and design a building which is then managed by that authority. All too often such facilities are inappropriate and uneconomic. Sometimes they are rejected by the local communities they are intended for. Occasionally they are even vandalised and destroyed.

In the scenario shown here, the need for the building is established by the community. Planning and design are then coordinated by a special project group which involves everyone interested at key stages.

The end result is a facility which has been shaped by members of the community to suit their needs and is then looked after by the people who use it.

## FURTHER INFORMATION

☞ Methods:
*Community planning forum.*
*Community profiling.*
*Feasibility fund.*
*Interactive display.*
*Open house event.*
*User group.*

⊘ *Plan, Design and Build.*
*Brick by Brick.*
*User Participation in Building Design and Management.*

# Community centre

A community needs a new social centre, sports facility, school, health centre or village hall.

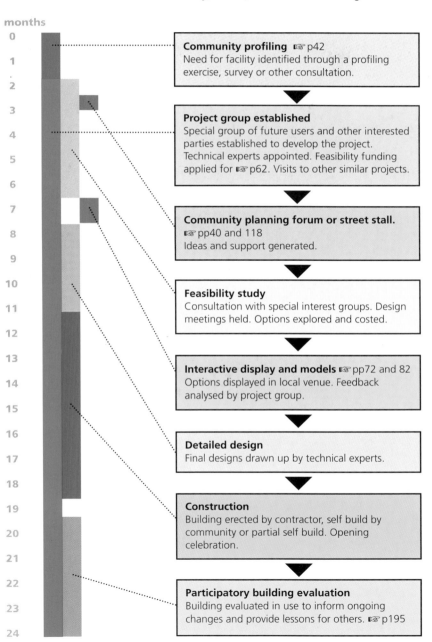

months

0
1
2
3
4
5
6
7
8
9
10
11
12
13
14
15
16
17
18
19
20
21
22
23
24

**Community profiling** ☞ p42
Need for facility identified through a profiling exercise, survey or other consultation.

▼

**Project group established**
Special group of future users and other interested parties established to develop the project. Technical experts appointed. Feasibility funding applied for ☞ p62. Visits to other similar projects.

▼

**Community planning forum or street stall.**
☞ pp40 and 118
Ideas and support generated.

▼

**Feasibility study**
Consultation with special interest groups. Design meetings held. Options explored and costed.

▼

**Interactive display and models** ☞ pp72 and 82
Options displayed in local venue. Feedback analysed by project group.

▼

**Detailed design**
Final designs drawn up by technical experts.

▼

**Construction**
Building erected by contractor, self build by community or partial self build. Opening celebration.

▼

**Participatory building evaluation**
Building evaluated in use to inform ongoing changes and provide lessons for others. ☞ p195

# Derelict site re-use

This scenario shows an initiative to make use of a derelict area of land in public ownership. Such land exists everywhere, usually attracting rubbish and having a depressing effect on the local neighbourhood.

Often, sites are left vacant for many years. Alternatively, local authorities may carry out some landscaping or sell the land to the private sector for development.

The scenario here shows how a popular use for the site can be generated and implemented, starting off with an ideas competition.

The initiative can be taken by anyone; a local authority, regeneration agency, community group individual or urban design studio at a school of architecture or planning.

## FURTHER INFORMATION

☞ Methods:
*Art workshop.*
*Ideas competition.*
*Open house event.*
*Street stall.*
*Urban design studio.*

# Derelict site re-use

**An initiative to make use of a derelict urban site in public ownership.** Timescale assumes relatively simple option adopted such as a pocket park. A building would take longer to construct.

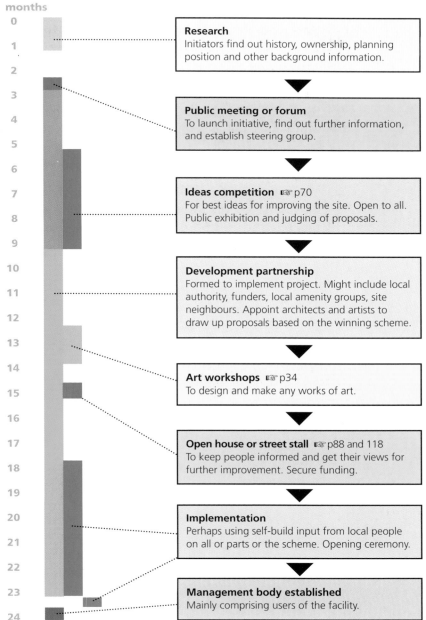

months

0
1
2
3
4
5
6
7
8
9
10
11
12
13
14
15
16
17
18
19
20
21
22
23
24

**Research**
Initiators find out history, ownership, planning position and other background information.

▼

**Public meeting or forum**
To launch initiative, find out further information, and establish steering group.

▼

**Ideas competition** ☞ p70
For best ideas for improving the site. Open to all. Public exhibition and judging of proposals.

▼

**Development partnership**
Formed to implement project. Might include local authority, funders, local amenity groups, site neighbours. Appoint architects and artists to draw up proposals based on the winning scheme.

▼

**Art workshops** ☞ p34
To design and make any works of art.

▼

**Open house or street stall** ☞ p88 and 118
To keep people informed and get their views for further improvement. Secure funding.

▼

**Implementation**
Perhaps using self-build input from local people on all or parts or the scheme. Opening ceremony.

▼

**Management body established**
Mainly comprising users of the facility.

# Disaster management

This scenario applies particularly to communities facing the threat of natural or human-made disasters such as floods, earthquakes, wind storms and industrial accidents.

Disasters tend to happen to people at risk. They are at risk because they are vulnerable to hazards. This vulnerability can best be reduced by increasing people's capacity to deal with a range of social, cultural, economic and physical factors.

The key to successful disaster management is ensuring that victims and potential victims are involved. Much formal disaster management does not do this and is often unsustainable, costly and ineffective.

Participatory community-level disaster management involves a cross-section of people and interests in researching, planning and implementing projects. Because the projects are developed for and by local people, there is more interest, understanding and success in reducing suffering and losses.

The key principles of this approach are:
- **Communities themselves are best placed to prioritise threats and take effective risk reducing actions.**
- **The best time to reduce the impact of disasters is before the next disaster occurs.**
- **The identification of hazards and who and what may be affected by them is necessary before risk reduction plans can be made.**
- **Progress has to be well publicised to maintain interest and strengthen the culture of disaster reduction.**

**FURTHER INFORMATION**

☞ Methods:
*Prioritising.*
*Risk assessment.*

ⓐ *Development at Risk.*
*Disaster Mitigation.*

✉ Federal Emergency Management Agency (FEMA).
South Bank University.

☆ Roger Bellers, Nick Hall. Based in part on Project Impact programme run by FEMA.

# Housing development

**A large new housing development is built with the future occupants involved from the outset.**

Timescale assumes rapid approvals and efficient main contractor.

**months**

0
1
2
3
4
5
6
7
8
9
10
11
12
13
14
15
16
17
18
19
20
21
22
23
24
25
26
27
28
29
30
31
32
33
34
35
36

### Occupants form group
Families come together and form an association or cooperative with help from advisors. Funding mechanism agreed. Committees formed. Architects appointed.

### Briefing
Visits to other projects, illustrated questionnaires, slide shows, skills survey, briefing workshops ☞p34.

### Site office
Design base established in local hall or shop ☞p84.

### Design meetings
Regular sessions between architects and occupants' committees using models ☞p82, choice catalogues ☞p36 and drawings to determine scheme concept and layout.

### Design surgeries
Between architects and individual occupants to agree room layouts, fixtures and fittings using models ☞p82, mock-ups and choice catalogues ☞p36.

### Construction
Regular site visits. Possibly self build of all or part of the scheme.

### Other projects started
Such as child care facilities, social facilities, employment projects.

# Industrial heritage re-use

This scenario applies where industrial buildings become redundant, particularly if they have heritage value or could be used for other purposes.

Typically, as industrial buildings cease to be used, they will be left empty and become derelict. The area where they are situated becomes increasingly run down, and other businesses and landowners suffer. Unless an initiative is taken the buildings will eventually fall down or there will be little option but to demolish them and start again from scratch.

Industrial areas often contain fine, sturdy structures which contribute to local character. Often they are ideally suited for conversion for other purposes. The difficulty is in making a sufficiently bold transformation of an area to change its image, attract new uses and persuade landowners and others to invest.

In this scenario, a partnership is established between the main parties, and an academic institution plays a key role in raising the profile of the area, assembling expertise and helping organise an action planning event to firm up a strategy agreed by all.

---

**FURTHER INFORMATION**

☞ Methods:
*Action planning event.*
*Design assistance*
*team.*

☆ John Worthington.

---

**142**

# Industrial heritage re-use

An academic institution helps a local authority regenerate a run-down industrial area in a variety of ownerships.

months

0

1

2

3

4

5

6

7

8

9

10

11

12

13

14

15

16

17

18

19

20

21

22

23

24

**Local partnership established**
Between local authority, local businesses and civic societies. Local authority provides administration.

**Draft regeneration brief**
Drawn up by Partnership.

**National and academic support**
Links made with academic institutions and national charitable bodies.

**Consultant advice on participation options**
Help to the Partnership in developing and organising the most suitable participation process.

**Conference**
National conference held at academic institution on the generic issues faced, eg reviving our industrial heritage. Local issue introduced. Key local players invited.

**Action planning event** ☞ p24
**(following immediately from conference)**
Two days of action planning workshops for local interests facilitated by a design assistance team made up from seminar members. Report of recommendations circulated widely.

**Implementation**
Partnership considers report and sets up implementation mechanisms.

# Inner city regeneration

This scenario shows how a deprived inner city area can transform itself over a period of almost a decade.

Starting by tenants gaining control of the management of their housing, a series of initiatives are taken as local people and their advisors become increasingly confident and competent in managing the regeneration process and forming partnerships. These include an improvement programme for existing housing estates, new housing development on infill sites, landscaping of open spaces, community arts and youth projects and, finally, the development of a community masterplan for attracting the private sector to invest in new housing, leisure and commercial projects, so leading to the creation of a balanced and sustainable community or 'urban village'.

## FURTHER INFORMATION

☞    Methods:
     *Action planning event.*
     *Art workshop.*
     *Choice catalogue.*
     *Design game.*
     *Development trust.*
     *Neighbourhood*
     *planning office.*
     *Planning day.*
     *Planning for Real.*
     *Review session.*

☆    Dick Watson.

**144**

# Inner city regeneration

Rejuvenation of a deprived inner city area dominated by blocks of local authority flats and lacking amenities.

months

0
3
6
9
12
15
18
21
24
27
30
33
36
39
42
45
48
51
54
57
60
63
66
69
72
75
78
81
84
87
90
93
96
99

**Tenant management organisation formed**
Authority hands over management of flats to tenants. Tenants appoint community architect.

**Neighbourhood planning office opened** ☞ p84
For tenant committees and consultants.

**Housing estate improvement programme**
Scheme developed using Planning for Real ☞ p100 and choice catalogues ☞ p36.

**New housing**
Designed and built by a local housing association after a planning day ☞ p98.

**Open space projects**
Devised by special projects committee using design games ☞ p48.

**Community arts and young people's projects**
Using arts workshops ☞ p30 and projects in schools.

**Action planning event** ☞ p24
To take stock and produce a strategy for future action. With outsider and local design assistance team members. Lasting several days.

**Review session** ☞ p110.

**Masterplan**
Drawn up by development partnership and local development trust ☞ p52.

# Local neighbourhood initiative

This scenario applies to any area where there are a number of institutional landowners and agencies operating and where local people want to break through inertia and improve the environment and quality of life.

So often the difficulty is getting all the various landowners and agencies to agree on a development strategy that is both visionary and based on what local people want. Without such agreement, development takes place in a mundane and piecemeal fashion, if at all, the most important local needs may not be addressed and opportunities offered by the natural environment are missed. At worst, new initiatives may be destroyed by vandalism and crime.

The scenario shown here ensures that local people start off and remain at the centre of the regeneration process but that all the agencies and land owners are also involved and can play their part.

**FURTHER INFORMATION**

☞ Methods:
*Planning weekend.*
*Process planning session.*
*Neighbourhood planning office.*
*Open space workshop.*
*User group.*

    THE **COMMUNITY PLANNING** HANDBOOK

# Local neighbourhood initiative

Local people in a rundown neighbourhood and agencies working with them take the initiative to speed up the regeneration process.

months

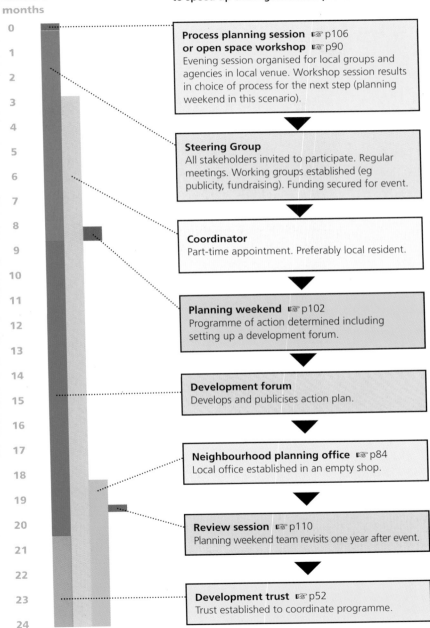

**Process planning session** ☞p106
**or open space workshop** ☞p90
Evening session organised for local groups and agencies in local venue. Workshop session results in choice of process for the next step (planning weekend in this scenario).

**Steering Group**
All stakeholders invited to participate. Regular meetings. Working groups established (eg publicity, fundraising). Funding secured for event.

**Coordinator**
Part-time appointment. Preferably local resident.

**Planning weekend** ☞p102
Programme of action determined including setting up a development forum.

**Development forum**
Develops and publicises action plan.

**Neighbourhood planning office** ☞p84
Local office established in an empty shop.

**Review session** ☞p110
Planning weekend team revisits one year after event.

**Development trust** ☞p52
Trust established to coordinate programme.

# New neighbourhood

This scenario shows how creative proposals can be developed for a new neighbourhood, extension to a neighbourhood or completely new settlement.

Mostly with such developments, it is left to the private sector to come up with proposals, or else consultants might be invited to prepare a masterplan for consideration by the authorities. In both cases, the crucial design conception stage tends to take place without engaging local people or a sufficiently broad range of expertise. When consultation does finally take place, it is too late for all but minor changes to be incorporated.

In the scenario shown, initial proposals are developed, at relatively little cost, by a task force of experts and students from a wide range of disciplines and backgrounds, in close consultation with local interested parties. These are then refined through further local input and drawn up in detail by a professional team.

The organisers are likely to be an urban design consultancy, architecture centre or urban design studio at a school of architecture or planning.

---

**FURTHER INFORMATION**

☞ Methods:
*Architecture centre.*
*Newspaper supplement.*
*Mobile unit.*
*Open house event.*
*Reconnaissance trip.*
*Task force.*
*Urban design studio.*

---

**148**

# New neighbourhood

Devising proposals for a new neighbourhood by involving a task force of experts and students working closely with local interested parties. Timescale assumes co-operative landowner.

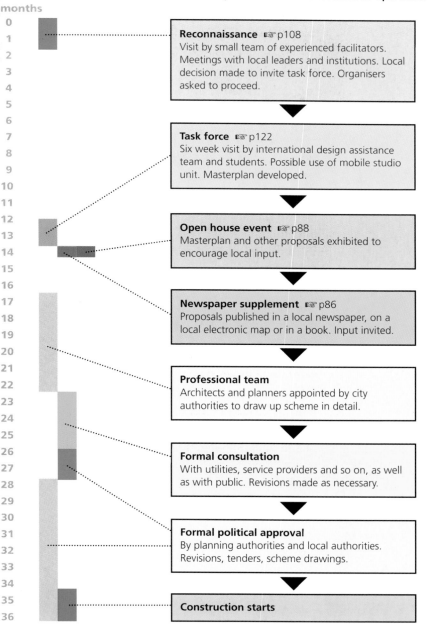

months
0
1
2
3
4
5
6
7
8
9
10
11
12
13
14
15
16
17
18
19
20
21
22
23
24
25
26
27
28
29
30
31
32
33
34
35
36

**Reconnaissance** ☞ p108
Visit by small team of experienced facilitators. Meetings with local leaders and institutions. Local decision made to invite task force. Organisers asked to proceed.

**Task force** ☞ p122
Six week visit by international design assistance team and students. Possible use of mobile studio unit. Masterplan developed.

**Open house event** ☞ p88
Masterplan and other proposals exhibited to encourage local input.

**Newspaper supplement** ☞ p86
Proposals published in a local newspaper, on a local electronic map or in a book. Input invited.

**Professional team**
Architects and planners appointed by city authorities to draw up scheme in detail.

**Formal consultation**
With utilities, service providers and so on, as well as with public. Revisions made as necessary.

**Formal political approval**
By planning authorities and local authorities. Revisions, tenders, scheme drawings.

**Construction starts**

# Planning study

This scenario applies where professional planning consultants are commissioned by a local authority or landowner to produce recommendations on future development options in a relatively short period of time.

The conventional approach would be for the consultants to prepare a report based entirely on their past experience and researching available literature.

In the scenario shown here, the consultants also include a consultation process which has to be tightly time-tabled to suit their client's timescale. This ensures that the consultants' proposals are based on up-to-date knowledge of local people's views and that local people begin to become involved in the development process.

**FURTHER INFORMATION**

☞   Methods:
     *Participatory editing.*
     *Planning day.*
     *Process planning*
     *session.*

# Planning study

Planning consultants are asked by a local authority to prepare a study of the potential of a large sector of a city. The timescale is short.

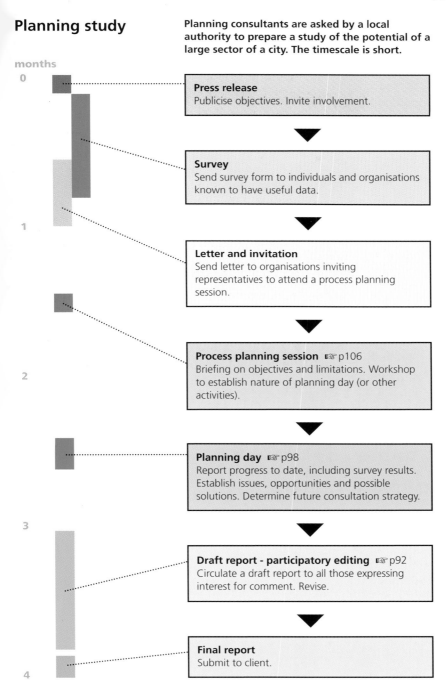

months

0

**Press release**
Publicise objectives. Invite involvement.

**Survey**
Send survey form to individuals and organisations known to have useful data.

1

**Letter and invitation**
Send letter to organisations inviting representatives to attend a process planning session.

**Process planning session** ☞p106
Briefing on objectives and limitations. Workshop to establish nature of planning day (or other activities).

2

**Planning day** ☞p98
Report progress to date, including survey results. Establish issues, opportunities and possible solutions. Determine future consultation strategy.

3

**Draft report - participatory editing** ☞p92
Circulate a draft report to all those expressing interest for comment. Revise.

**Final report**
Submit to client.

4

# Regeneration infrastructure

**This scenario shows how the framework for encouraging community planning can be improved by government and private and voluntary agencies. It can be applied at national, regional or even international level.**

**The focus is on supporting and promoting the setting up of enabling mechanisms, some of which will become self-financing after a period of time.**

**The costs involved are a fraction of the support normally given to regeneration programmes and the long-term benefits are likely to be far greater.**

**FURTHER INFORMATION**

☞ Methods:
*Architecture centre.*
*Award scheme.*
*Community design centre.*
*Feasibility fund.*
*Ideas competition.*
*Neighbourhood planning office.*
*Planning aid.*
Useful checklists:
*Initiatives needed.*

# Regeneration infrastructure

**Leading institutions and government collaborate to set up a framework to support community planning initiatives at local level.**

months

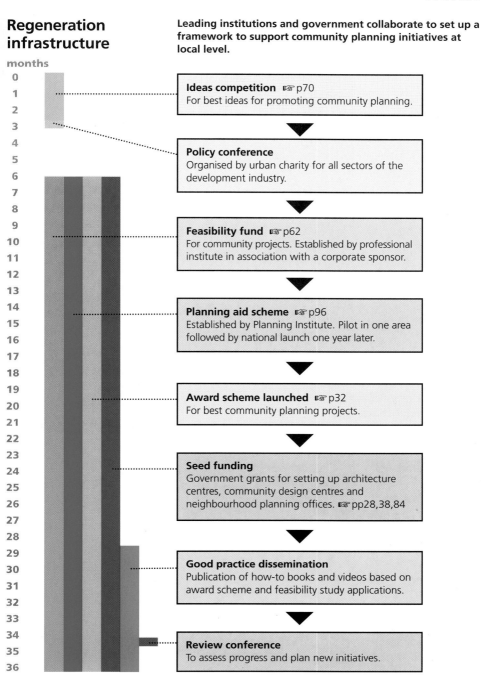

**Ideas competition** ☞ p70
For best ideas for promoting community planning.

**Policy conference**
Organised by urban charity for all sectors of the development industry.

**Feasibility fund** ☞ p62
For community projects. Established by professional institute in association with a corporate sponsor.

**Planning aid scheme** ☞ p96
Established by Planning Institute. Pilot in one area followed by national launch one year later.

**Award scheme launched** ☞ p32
For best community planning projects.

**Seed funding**
Government grants for setting up architecture centres, community design centres and neighbourhood planning offices. ☞ pp28,38,84

**Good practice dissemination**
Publication of how-to books and videos based on award scheme and feasibility study applications.

**Review conference**
To assess progress and plan new initiatives.

# Shanty settlement upgrading

This scenario applies to the informal settlements which proliferate around many cities in developing countries. The residents may be squatters, tenants or owner-occupiers.

Often, authorities ignore such places, leaving them to their own devices. Alternatively they may attempt to have them demolished on the grounds that they are unsightly, unhealthy or unlawful.

In this scenario the authorities support the residents to upgrade their settlement by providing technical assistance. Over the years, services are installed, roads are improved and building construction standards raised.

Eventually such settlements can become almost indistinguishable from other parts of the city.

## FURTHER INFORMATION

☞ Methods:
*Community design centre.*
*Community profiling.*
*Field workshop.*
*Microplanning workshop.*
*Risk assessment.*

∂ *Action Planning for Cities.*

✉ Centre for Development and Emergency Practice. International Institute for Environment and Development.

☆ Nick Hall.

# Shanty settlement upgrading

**Residents gradually upgrade their homes and neighbourhood with assistance from the authorities, technical experts and support agencies.**

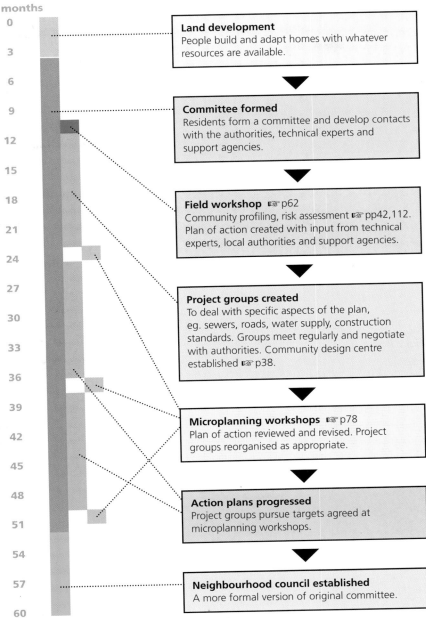

months

0

3

6

9

12

15

18

21

24

27

30

33

36

39

42

45

48

51

54

57

60

**Land development**
People build and adapt homes with whatever resources are available.

**Committee formed**
Residents form a committee and develop contacts with the authorities, technical experts and support agencies.

**Field workshop** ☞ p62
Community profiling, risk assessment ☞ pp42,112.
Plan of action created with input from technical experts, local authorities and support agencies.

**Project groups created**
To deal with specific aspects of the plan, eg. sewers, roads, water supply, construction standards. Groups meet regularly and negotiate with authorities. Community design centre established ☞ p38.

**Microplanning workshops** ☞ p78
Plan of action reviewed and revised. Project groups reorganised as appropriate.

**Action plans progressed**
Project groups pursue targets agreed at microplanning workshops.

**Neighbourhood council established**
A more formal version of original committee.

# Town centre upgrade

This scenario applies when a planning authority wants to initiate improvement of a town centre area.

Many town centre areas have developed in a piecemeal fashion over a number of years. Land will be in a variety of ownerships. Buildings are likely to have been designed with little respect for overall urban design.

If the planning department does nothing, the piecemeal approach will continue and fundamental issues will never be solved.

The approach shown here allows a planning authority to involve all the many different interests in developing an overall strategy which can be incorporated into the planning framework.

**FURTHER INFORMATION**

☞ Methods:
*Open house event.*
*Planning day.*
*Process planning session.*
*User group.*

# Town centre upgrade

A planning department initiates development of part of the town centre without the conflict between developers and citizens so common in much town centre development.

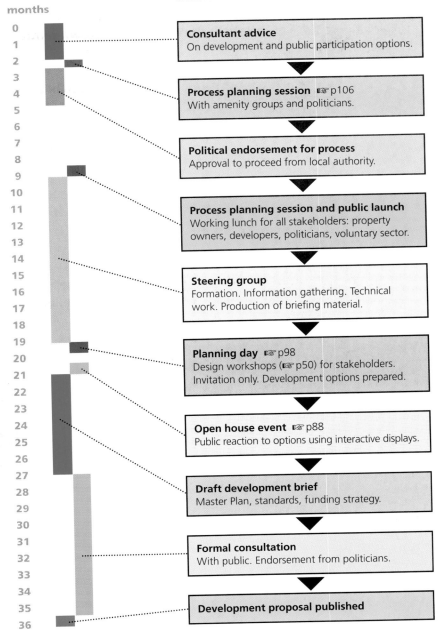

**months**

| | |
|---|---|
| 0 | |
| 1 | **Consultant advice** |
| 2 | On development and public participation options. |
| 3 | |
| 4 | **Process planning session** ☞ p106 |
| 5 | With amenity groups and politicians. |
| 6 | |
| 7 | |
| 8 | **Political endorsement for process** |
| 9 | Approval to proceed from local authority. |
| 10 | |
| 11 | **Process planning session and public launch** |
| 12 | Working lunch for all stakeholders: property |
| 13 | owners, developers, politicians, voluntary sector. |
| 14 | |
| 15 | **Steering group** |
| 16 | Formation. Information gathering. Technical |
| 17 | work. Production of briefing material. |
| 18 | |
| 19 | |
| 20 | **Planning day** ☞ p98 |
| 21 | Design workshops (☞ p50) for stakeholders. |
| 22 | Invitation only. Development options prepared. |
| 23 | |
| 24 | **Open house event** ☞ p88 |
| 25 | Public reaction to options using interactive displays. |
| 26 | |
| 27 | |
| 28 | **Draft development brief** |
| 29 | Master Plan, standards, funding strategy. |
| 30 | |
| 31 | |
| 32 | **Formal consultation** |
| 33 | With public. Endorsement from politicians. |
| 34 | |
| 35 | **Development proposal published** |
| 36 | |

# Urban conservation

This scenario covers an initiative to improve the state of historic buildings in a town.

Restoring buildings is very costly and sufficient public funds are rarely available to meet the demand. In this scenario the local authorities allocate funding for three years to start up an independent project providing technical assistance and taking initiatives. As well as administering grants to pump-prime quality repairs by private owners, the project undertakes a wide range of education programmes aimed at raising awareness and stimulating initiatives by both private individuals and community groups.

When the funding period expires, the project is converted into a development trust controlled by local people. As skills and interest grow, the trust takes on a broader and more far-reaching role.

**FURTHER INFORMATION**

☞ Methods:
*Activity week.*
*Architecture centre.*
*Award scheme.*
*Community design centre.*
*Development trust.*
*Environment shop.*

# Urban conservation

An initiative to improve the state of historic buildings in an area by raising awareness and stimulating a wide range of local activity.

months

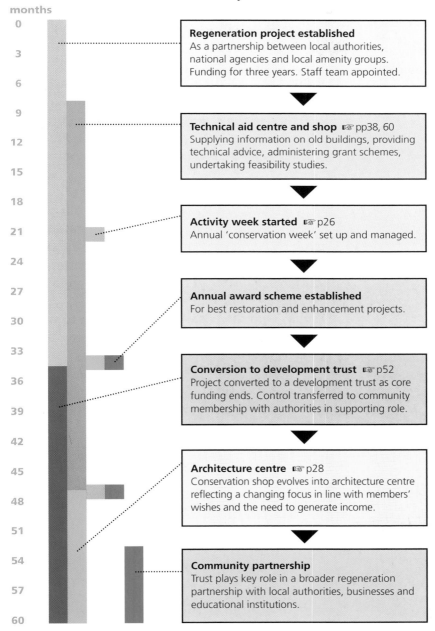

**Regeneration project established**
As a partnership between local authorities, national agencies and local amenity groups. Funding for three years. Staff team appointed.

**Technical aid centre and shop** ☞ pp38, 60
Supplying information on old buildings, providing technical advice, administering grant schemes, undertaking feasibility studies.

**Activity week started** ☞ p26
Annual 'conservation week' set up and managed.

**Annual award scheme established**
For best restoration and enhancement projects.

**Conversion to development trust** ☞ p52
Project converted to a development trust as core funding ends. Control transferred to community membership with authorities in supporting role.

**Architecture centre** ☞ p28
Conservation shop evolves into architecture centre reflecting a changing focus in line with members' wishes and the need to generate income.

**Community partnership**
Trust plays key role in a broader regeneration partnership with local authorities, businesses and educational institutions.

# Village revival

This scenario covers a village developing initiatives to preserve and build on its local character.

With changes in traditional agricultural practices, many villages suffer from either development pressure or loss of population. Often political control is exercised many miles away and local people feel powerless to do anything about it.

In this scenario parish mapping is used to generate interest and understanding. Villagers then decide to develop a local design statement to guide new development and a countryside design summary is prepared to make better links with the character of the surrounding region.

Finally, with the experience of learning to work together, a number of project groups are established to develop new facilities.

---

**FURTHER INFORMATION**

☞ Methods:
 *Community profiling.*
 *Local design statement.*
 *Mapping. Photo*
 *survey. Review session.*

# Village revival

**A village community takes steps to protect the traditional character and develop new facilities.**

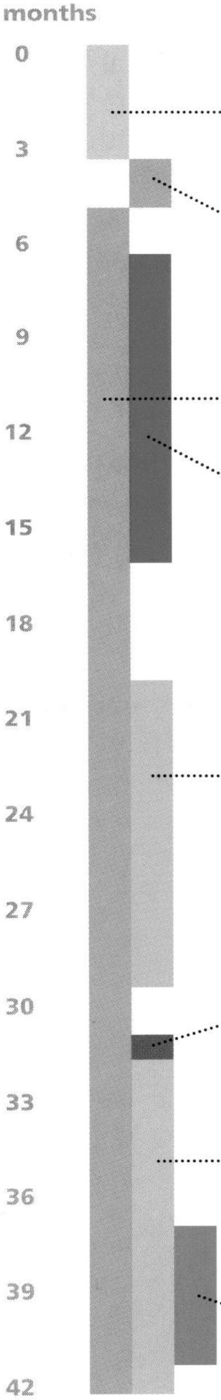

months

**Community profiling** ☞p42
Parish mapping ☞p76 or other methods used to generate information and interest.

▼

**Community planning forum** ☞p40
Evening session in a local hall with exhibition of parish maps to discuss next steps. Decision to produce a local design statement.
Steering group formed.

▼

**Local design statement** ☞p74
Produced using mapping ☞p76 and photo surveys ☞p94. Statement adopted by authorities.

▼

**Countryside design summary**
Produced by regional authorities. ☞Glossary

▼

**Review session** ☞p110
To determine future initiatives needed.

▼

**Project groups**
Established to pursue further initiatives including a community centre and transport initiative.

▼

**Local design statement revised**

# Whole settlement strategy

**FURTHER INFORMATION**

☞ Methods: *Future search conference. Interactive display. Open house event.* Useful checklists: *Community plan content.*

✉ Hertfordshire County Council.

⌂ Community Visions Pack.

A whole settlement strategy creates a vision for a village, town or city as a whole and sets out ways to achieve it: How does the place work? What is good about it? What is bad? What needs changing? How can we plan for a sustainable future?

A conventional approach would be for a local authority to engage town planning or development consultants to produce a plan which would then be put out to consultation, modified and adopted.

This scenario shows one way in which community participation can be incorporated into the development of such a strategy from the outset. This is a requirement set by the United Nations in its 'Agenda 21'. It also improves the likelihood that the strategy will be approved of and implemented. Whole settlement strategies can form the basis for more detailed Community Plans.

# Whole settlement strategy

A local authority initiates a strategy to improve a town's sustainability, involving local people and service providers in its creation.

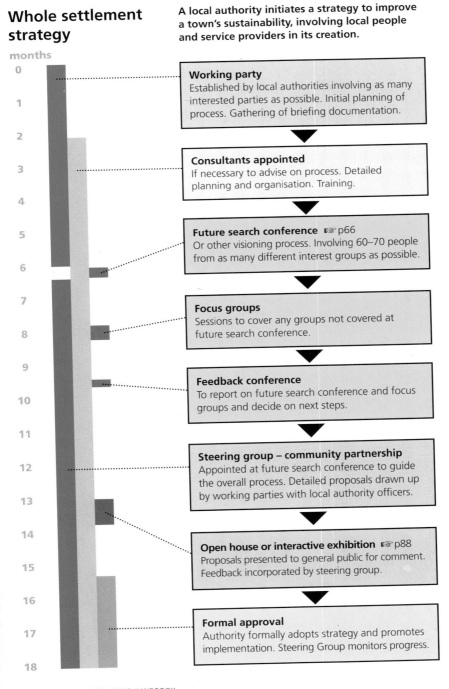

**months**

**Working party**
Established by local authorities involving as many interested parties as possible. Initial planning of process. Gathering of briefing documentation.

**Consultants appointed**
If necessary to advise on process. Detailed planning and organisation. Training.

**Future search conference** ☞p66
Or other visioning process. Involving 60–70 people from as many different interest groups as possible.

**Focus groups**
Sessions to cover any groups not covered at future search conference.

**Feedback conference**
To report on future search conference and focus groups and decide on next steps.

**Steering group – community partnership**
Appointed at future search conference to guide the overall process. Detailed proposals drawn up by working parties with local authority officers.

**Open house or interactive exhibition** ☞p88
Proposals presented to general public for comment. Feedback incorporated by steering group.

**Formal approval**
Authority formally adopts strategy and promotes implementation. Steering Group monitors progress.

Meals? ........................................

Hotels? ........................................

15. What **briefing material** should be made available or prepared?

........................................................................................................

16. Who will make sure that the results of the event are used and built on **afterwards**?

........................................................................................................

## MONEY

17. How much will it **cost** (roughly)?

| | |
|---|---|
| Admin | £...... |
| Venues | £...... |
| Publicity | £...... |
| Catering | £...... |
| Equipment | £...... |
| Photography | £...... |
| Travel | £...... |
| Accommodation | £...... |
| Report printing | £...... |
| Follow-up activity | £...... |
| Other | £...... |
| **Total** | £...... |

18. Who might **sponsor** it (or do things free)?

........................................................

........................................................

........................................................

........................................................

........................................................

........................................................

........................................................

........................................................

........................................................

........................................................

........................................................

## IMMEDIATE NEXT STEPS

19. **Who** does **what** now?

........................................................................................................

........................................................................................................

........................................................................................................

## OTHER THOUGHTS AND IDEAS

20........................................................................................................

........................................................................................................

........................................................................................................

........................................................................................................

Name and contact details (optional)

........................................................................................................

........................................................................................................

........................................................................................................

Date..............

# Action planner

For use at workshops or meetings.

Workshop title/theme ___Getting around___

Date and time ___4 October 2001, 4pm___

Convenor ___Mary___

| Topic | Action needed | By whom | When | Help needed | Priority (1-5) |
|-------|---------------|---------|------|-------------|----------------|
| Traffic | Pedestrian plan | Environment forum | July | Traffic engineers | 2 |
| Cycle racks | Install | Traders | May | Welding | 4 |
| Bus timetable | Display at all stops | Bus company | June | - | 3 |
| etc | etc | etc | etc | etc | etc |

# Progress monitor

For summarising the outcome of community planning activity and planning the next steps.

Compile and circulate for comment to a range of participants to get a full picture.

Example used: ___Developing a community plan___

| Topic | Action taken | By whom | Outcome | Next step | By whom |
|-------|--------------|---------|---------|-----------|---------|
| Controlled parking | Input into design of questionnaire | Forum | New zones in place. | - | - |
| Waste recycling | Schools promotion | Forum | Higher recycling rates noted | Resident promotion | Residents associations |
| Cycle routes | Working party set up | Cycle club | Cycleway plan being developed | Publicise for comment | Radio Libraries |
| District plan | Consultation | All voluntary organisations | Revisions made | Repeat next year | Planners |
| Station | Owner contacted. | Planning officer | Nothing | Invite to design workshop | Jenny |
| etc | etc | etc | etc | etc | etc |

# Evaluation form

For evaluating most kinds of community planning activity. Can provide insights on impacts, participants' perceptions and improvements needed. Customise to suit. Circulate to a range of participants or use as a basis for an interview or workshop agenda. Repeating the exercise at intervals may be worthwhile as the impact of activity will often not become clear for many years.

Name _____     Organisation (if any) _____
Address _____     Position (if any) _____

Title of activity _____     Date/s of activity _____
Nature of activity _____     Date of evaluation _____

1  Your role in activity _____

2  How did you become involved? _____

3  What do you think are/were the aims? _____

4  What do you think motivated people and organisations to get involved? _____

5  What effect if any has your personal contribution in the activity made? _____

6  What effect has the activity had on the physical environment? _____

7  What effect has the activity had on the local economy? _____

8  What effect has the activity had on local organisations? _____
   (eg changed roles, new partnerships, etc)

9  What effect has the activity had on individuals? _____
   (eg locals, visitors, investors etc)

10  Was the activity worthwhile? _____ If so, why? _____

11  What improvements would you make if it was being done again? _____

12  What would be your advice to others organising a similar activity? _____

13  What additional information sources would be helpful? _____

14  Any other comments? _____

Thank you for your time.
Please return this form to: _____

# Useful checklists

## Equipment and supplies

**An overall checklist of items which may be helpful for those planning activities in compiling their own lists. Checklists for some specific methods are provided on the methods pages.**

Having the right equipment and supplies can make the difference between success and failure. Different events and activities obviously require different equipment and supplies. Some require very little, if anything.

- ☐ Banners and directional signs with fixings
- ☐ Base maps and plans of the area at different scales (1:200 and 1:400 most commonly used)
- ☐ Base model with movable parts
- ☐ Bell or whistle (to announce meetings etc)
- ☐ Blackboard and chalk
- ☐ Blackout curtains
- ☐ Blu-tack
- ☐ Box files
- ☐ Cameras:
  35mm or digital with wide-angle, telephoto, flash and close-up facility
  Polaroid (for instant prints)
- ☐ Cardboard or polystyrene (for modelmaking)
- ☐ Catering gear (cups, plates, cutlery, napkins, urn, kettle etc.)
- ☐ Chairs (stackable?) and stools
- ☐ Chalk (different colours)
- ☐ Clipboards
- ☐ Clock with alarm (for timing speakers)
- ☐ Cocktail sticks (for use with model)
- ☐ Compasses
- ☐ Computer equipment:
  laptop
  laser printer and toner
  scanner if possible
  DTP and word processing software
  disks
- ☐ Correction fluid
- ☐ Cutting knives, mats, metal edge and spare blades

- ☐ Desks
- ☐ Dictating and transcribing equipment
- ☐ Drawing boards or drawing tables
- ☐ Drinks facility and fridge
- ☐ Easels and pads (24"x 30")
- ☐ Erasers
- ☐ Exhibition facilities
- ☐ Extension cables
- ☐ Filing trays
- ☐ Film:
  colour slides for presentations
  colour or black & white prints for reports
- ☐ Film projector and screen
- ☐ Flat-bed photo-stand with colour corrected lamps (for shooting drawings and plans) and spare bulbs
- ☐ Flipcharts (with non-squeaky pens)
- ☐ Food and drink
- ☐ Hole punches
- ☐ Layout pads (grid marked with non-repro blue ink)
- ☐ Light box (for sorting slides)
- ☐ Lighting, including desk lighting
- ☐ Lock-up for valuable equipment
- ☐ Name badges (or blank sticky labels)
- ☐ Overhead or opaque projectors with transparency film and markers (handy for sketching and for presentations)
- ☐ Paper:
  A4 & A2 sketch pads
  A4 writing pads (lined)
  tracing (white and yellow)
  A5 note pads
  flipchart pads
  butcher paper (long strips)
- ☐ Paperclips
- ☐ Paper trimmer or guillotine
- ☐ Pencils: normal; coloured
- ☐ Pens:
  felt-tips in bright colours and grey tones (different sizes);
  fibre-tipped with medium and fine tips
  ball points (black and red)
  technical drawing
  highlighters
- ☐ Photocopier with enlarging/reducing

facility (with rapid repair service)
- [ ] Photocopier paper, toner etc
- [ ] Pin board or pin-up wall
- [ ] Pins – different colours:
  drawing pins
  stick pins
- [ ] Plan storage system
- [ ] Pocket notebooks (for shirt pockets)
- [ ] Pointer stick for presentations (1 metre)
- [ ] Post-its (different sizes and colours)
- [ ] Power outlets
- [ ] Pritt-sticks
- [ ] Public address system with microphones
  on stands and roving
- [ ] Ring binders (A4)
- [ ] Rubber bands
- [ ] Rubber cement
- [ ] Rubbish bags
- [ ] Rulers and scale rulers
- [ ] Scissors
- [ ] Screen for copying photographs
- [ ] Shelving and filing space
- [ ] Slide projectors (carousel type) with
  screens, blackout drapes, spare carousel
  trays, spare fuses, spare bulbs, extension
  cord, remote buttons with extra long cord
  and pointer torch
- [ ] Spraymount adhesive
- [ ] Staples and staple extractors
- [ ] Sticky dots (many colours)
- [ ] Tables
- [ ] Tape:
  masking tape
  magic tape
  heavy duty tape
- [ ] Tape recorder and cassettes
- [ ] Telephones and fax machines
- [ ] Toilet paper
- [ ] T-squares, triangles and circle templates
- [ ] Velcro pads
- [ ] Video camera and cassettes
- [ ] Video play-back equipment (if relevant)
- [ ] Waste bins and garbage bags
- [ ] ................................................................
- [ ] ................................................................
- [ ] ................................................................

# Who to involve

**A checklist of people and organisations who might need to be involved in any community planning initiative. Customise your own list.**

- [ ] Allotment holders
- [ ] Archaeological groups
- [ ] Archaeologists
- [ ] Architects
- [ ] Builders
- [ ] Businesses
- [ ] Chambers of commerce
- [ ] Charities
- [ ] Children
- [ ] Churches
- [ ] Civic societies and groups
- [ ] Colleges
- [ ] Community associations
- [ ] Community-based organisations (CBOs)
- [ ] Community leaders
- [ ] Community woodland groups
- [ ] Companies
- [ ] Conservation groups
- [ ] Countryside management officers
- [ ] Craftspeople
- [ ] Designers
- [ ] Developers
- [ ] Disability groups
- [ ] Ecologists
- [ ] Economists
- [ ] Engineers
- [ ] Environmental groups
- [ ] Ethnic groups
- [ ] Estate agents
- [ ] Farmers
- [ ] Financial institutions
- [ ] Footpath and access groups
- [ ] Funding agencies
- [ ] Health workers
- [ ] Homeless people
- [ ] Industrialists
- [ ] Journalists
- [ ] Land managers
- [ ] Landowners
- [ ] Landscape architects
- [ ] Lawyers
- [ ] Local authorities

- [ ] Local history groups
- [ ] Media groups and organisations
- [ ] Migrants
- [ ] Minority groups
- [ ] Mothers' unions
- [ ] Museums (especially local history)
- [ ] Non-governmental organisations (NGOs)
- [ ] Parent–teacher organisations
- [ ] Parish councils
- [ ] Photographers
- [ ] Planners
- [ ] Playgroups
- [ ] Police
- [ ] Postmen and women
- [ ] Professional institutions and groups
- [ ] Property owners
- [ ] Public works departments
- [ ] Publicans
- [ ] Ramblers
- [ ] Religious groups
- [ ] Residents groups and associations
- [ ] Rural community councils
- [ ] Schools
- [ ] Senior citizens
- [ ] Shopkeepers
- [ ] Sports groups
- [ ] Squatters and squatters' groups
- [ ] Statutory agencies
- [ ] Street cleaners
- [ ] Student groups
- [ ] Surveyors
- [ ] Teachers
- [ ] Tenant groups and associations
- [ ] Town managers
- [ ] Traders
- [ ] Transport groups
- [ ] Transport operators
- [ ] Transport planners
- [ ] Universities
- [ ] Urban designers
- [ ] Utility providers
- [ ] Village hall committees
- [ ] Wildlife groups
- [ ] Women's groups
- [ ] Women's institutes
- [ ] Workforces
- [ ] Young people
- [ ] Youth clubs, guides and scouts
- [ ] ..........................................................

# Neighbourhood skills survey

A checklist of skills for finding out what talent exists in a community. Use it to compile your own survey form. Illustrate it if you want. Then distribute it round the neighbourhood or, better still, knock on doors and help people fill it in.

Keen beginner
Experienced

- [ ] Acting
- [ ] Artwork
- [ ] Babysitting
- [ ] Bicycle repairs
- [ ] Book keeping
- [ ] Building
- [ ] Campaigning
- [ ] Car mechanics
- [ ] Catering
- [ ] Chatting
- [ ] Child minding
- [ ] Community planning
- [ ] Computer operating
- [ ] Computer repairs
- [ ] Decorating
- [ ] Disc jockey
- [ ] Drawing
- [ ] Dress making
- [ ] Driving a bus
- [ ] Driving a car
- [ ] Driving a truck
- [ ] Electrical work
- [ ] Embroidery
- [ ] Facilitating workshops
- [ ] First aid
- [ ] Fundraising
- [ ] Gardening
- [ ] Graphic design
- [ ] Hut erection
- [ ] Journalism
- [ ] Keeping people informed
- [ ] Knitting
- [ ] Landscaping
- [ ] Letter writing
- [ ] Managing
- [ ] Motorbike repairs

- [ ] Negotiation
- [ ] Nursing
- [ ] Organising events
- [ ] Photography
- [ ] Playing music
- [ ] Plumbing
- [ ] Pottery
- [ ] Public speaking
- [ ] Publicity
- [ ] Roofing
- [ ] Running a bar
- [ ] Running a cafe
- [ ] Sports (please specify)
- [ ] Sculpting
- [ ] Site clearing
- [ ] Teaching
- [ ] Translating (specify languages)
- [ ] Typing
- [ ] Video work
- [ ] Woodwork
- [ ] Writing and editing
- [ ] Youth work
- [ ] ....................................
- [ ] ....................................
- [ ] ....................................
- [ ] ....................................

# Community plan content

**A checklist of items that might be considered in a community plan or masterplan. Customise and structure your own list.**

☐ Accessibility
☐ Action plans – for various time periods
☐ Advice services
☐ Air quality
☐ Alcohol abuse
☐ Allotments
☐ Animals and birds
☐ Anti-social behaviour
☐ Archaeology
☐ Architecture
☐ Arts – visual and performing
☐ Bad neighbour uses
☐ Boating facilities
☐ Building scale and character
☐ Building skills
☐ Building use
☐ Burial sites
☐ Buses
☐ Cafes
☐ Carnivals and celebrations
☐ Character of the area
☐ Childcare facilities
☐ Churches
☐ Cinemas
☐ Clubs and societies
☐ Colour – of buildings and townscape
☐ Community care facilities
☐ Community centres
☐ Community participation strategies
☐ Community trusts
☐ Conservation of buildings
☐ Conservation of landscape
☐ Crafts
☐ Crime – causes and deterrents
☐ Culture
☐ Cycle facilities
☐ Dance venues
☐ Densities of development
☐ Development opportunities
☐ Disability facilities
☐ Disabled access
☐ Disaster management

☐ Dogs and other pets
☐ Drainage
☐ Drug abuse
☐ Economic generators
☐ Education facilities
☐ Electricity supplies
☐ Employment
☐ Energy
☐ Enterprise
☐ Entertainment facilities
☐ Environmental art
☐ Erosion
☐ Events
☐ Farming
☐ Flooding
☐ Fly-posting
☐ Fly-tipping
☐ Friendliness
☐ Fumes
☐ Fund-raising
☐ Gardens
☐ Gas supplies
☐ Graffiti
☐ Health
☐ Historic connections
☐ Homework clubs
☐ Human resources
☐ Image
☐ Implementation mechanisms
☐ Indoor sports
☐ Infill sites
☐ Information availability
☐ Information technology
☐ Innovation
☐ Internet access
☐ Lakes and ponds
☐ Land and property use
☐ Land and property values
☐ Landmarks
☐ Libraries and other learning facilities
☐ Licensing
☐ Lighting - streets and buildings
☐ Links and alleyways
☐ Litter
☐ Litter bins
☐ Leisure facilities
☐ Local authorities
☐ Local exchange trading
☐ Local organisations and institutions

☐ Local produce
☐ Local shops
☐ Low income support systems
☐ Maintenance and management systems
☐ Market gardens
☐ Markets – indoor and outdoor
☐ Men's facilities
☐ Minority groups
☐ Mixed uses
☐ Music venues
☐ Noise
☐ Older people facilities
☐ Open spaces
☐ Parks and public gardens
☐ Paths
☐ Pedestrians
☐ Planning procedures
☐ Play facilities
☐ Policing
☐ Pollution
☐ Poverty and wealth
☐ Power supplies
☐ Principles of development
☐ Public art
☐ Public squares
☐ Pubs
☐ Quality of design
☐ Quality of life
☐ Quality of local services
☐ Railings
☐ Railways and station locations
☐ Recycling waste material
☐ Refuse collection
☐ Religions
☐ Resource centres
☐ Restaurants
☐ Rivers and streams
☐ Road building and maintenance
☐ Safety
☐ Schools
☐ School use out of hours
☐ Sense of identity
☐ Sense of place
☐ Sense of safety
☐ Sewage disposal
☐ Shopping facilities
☐ Smell
☐ Social inclusion and mix
☐ Social services

☐ Special needs facilities
☐ Sports facilities – pitches, courts
☐ Sports opportunities
☐ Street cleaning
☐ Street lighting
☐ Street signs and numbering
☐ Street trees
☐ Streetscape
☐ Sustainability
☐ Targets for action
☐ Temporary uses
☐ Timescales
☐ Tourism
☐ Townscape
☐ Traffic
☐ Traffic calming
☐ Traffic routes
☐ Transport options
☐ Vacant buildings
☐ Vacant land
☐ Vernacular architecture
☐ Views
☐ Visitors
☐ Voluntary organisations
☐ Voluntary services
☐ Water features
☐ Water supplies
☐ Women's facilities
☐ Youth clubs
☐ Youth services
☐ ..................................................
☐ ..................................................
☐ ..................................................
☐ ..................................................

# Initiatives needed

**A checklist of general policy initiatives that may help make community planning more effective. Customise to suit your country, place and circumstances.**

☐ **Build locally**
Locally-based building activity should be encouraged so that the economic benefits of development stay within the community. Provision for the employment of local labour and training of local people in building skills should be considered for inclusion in any building contract.

☐ **Career incentives**
Community planning expertise should be recognised and encouraged with more effective and systematic training programmes and career opportunities.

☐ **Centres of activity and information**
New centres, or networks of centres, on community planning should be established at national and regional level to disseminate good practice, provide advice, and evaluate and follow up on events and activities.

☐ **Community development briefs**
Development briefs should be produced with communities for all major sites and should preferably become mandatory as a basis for land valuation and acquisition.

☐ **Culture of participation**
A general culture of participation should be encouraged so that participation in planning becomes natural and inevitable.

☐ **Delegated planning powers**
Planning powers should be delegated to the lowest possible tiers of government, with regional government retaining powers to intervene only in the event of local corruption or for major strategic issues.

☐ **Derelict land and buildings**
Derelict land and buildings (both public and private) should be made available for community-led initiatives and be made the subject of punitive taxes to encourage their productive use.

☐ **Educating enablers**
The curricula of architecture and planning schools should include relevant training for professional enablers. Live project units – urban design studios – should be set up at all schools, to undertake community projects.

☐ **Environmental education**
Environmental education programmes for the public should be expanded so that people learn how the built environment works and how they can take part in improving it. Environmental education should form part of primary and secondary school curricula, and comprehensive networks of urban and rural studies centres should be established. There should be special emphasis on local vernacular architecture and building techniques.

☐ **Freedom of information**
Land ownership should be public information and always kept up to date. When property in public or social ownership is sold, there should be public debate on its use beforehand, and it should not automatically be sold to the highest bidder.

☐ **Good practice information**
More good practice guidance needs to be produced, made available and kept up to date. Specific items include:

☐ Catalogues of information already available;
☐ Detailed how-to-do-it information on methods;
☐ Toolkits of sample documents and formats;

- ☐ Contact data for people and organisations with relevant experience.
- ☐ Well presented case studies in print and on film.
- ☐ Training packs and programmes.

☐ **Gradual development**
Planning policies should generally encourage incremental, evolutionary development with large development sites broken down into smaller packages.

☐ **Information**
Information systems should be established to make data about successful examples of community planning and development widely available. Programmes should be established to encourage more exchange of experience between the various groups involved in the process – public, private, professional and voluntary. Methods should be devised for exchanging information internationally so that relevant lessons may be learned in the shortest possible space of time.

☐ **Lobbying for resources**
Multi-agency co-ordination, resources and leadership are needed to lobby for increased resources for participatory planning activity at local level and supporting services at national or regional level.

☐ **Marketing**
The importance and effectiveness of community planning should be more forcefully marketed.

☐ **Percentage for participation**
All significant developments should include in their budgets a specific amount of funding for effective participation at all stages.

☐ **Planners out in the community**
More professional planners should be physically located in multidisciplinary offices in the communities they serve. In urban areas no one should be more than a few minutes' walk from such an office. Architecture centres, community design centres and neighbourhood planning offices should all be promoted.

☐ **Planning applications**
Proposals by property owners for development should be encouraged or required to include visual details and policy statements. It should also be possible to view proposals nearby, ie in a local shop or cafe, rather than having to travel to remote government offices. Ideally, proposals should be displayed visually at the site in question.

☐ **Planning decisions**
All relevant social and environmental issues should be considered in planning appeals, public inquiries and local planning decisions. The recommendations of public inquiry inspectors should not be overturned by central government except for overriding reasons, such as national security. Community groups should be given access to the necessary resources to present their case effectively.

☐ **Practitioner listing service**
Registers of experienced community planning and community architecture practitioners should be established to help local authorities, developers and community groups obtain the best expertise available.

☐ **Professional payment**
Recommended professional fee scales should be adjusted to take account of the extra time needed to involve end-users.

☐ **Public funding**
Accountability procedures for the receipt of public funds should be redefined to encourage community initiatives and provide voluntary organisations with consistent, long-term funding, to facilitate forward planning.

☐ **Public sector enablers**
Central and local government should learn to trust community organisations and actively assist them in their formation and growth. There should be a fundamental policy shift from 'providing' to 'enabling'.

☐ **Public participation statements**
Developers of significant projects should be required to produce a 'public participation statement' identifying those affected and setting out how they will be involved in the development process. This should be an integral part of planning application procedures.

☐ **Quantify benefits**
Funding needs to be allocated to systematic analysis and quantifying of the benefits of community planning approaches.

☐ **Research**
Far more resources should be devoted to research on the built environment by government and the development industry to avoid making the same mistakes over and over again. Research and development programmes should be undertaken on the long-term cost effectiveness of different approaches and the results widely disseminated. Special attention should be directed towards the development of techniques in participatory planning and design.

☐ **Review statutory procedures**
Planning, development and management procedures need to be constantly reviewed to ensure they incorporate the best participatory practice available. This might cover:

☐ Preparing local plans;
☐ Preparing development briefs;
☐ Planning application procedures;
☐ Public inquiry procedures;
☐ Urban management procedures.

☐ **Simplify language**
Planning legislation should be re-written in straightforward language.

☐ **Technical aid**
Networks of community-controlled, publicly-funded multi-disciplinary technical aid facilities should be established and maintained.

☐ **Voluntary sector empowered**
Voluntary organisations – representing geographical communities and communities of interest – should willingly demand and accept more responsibility for the creation and management of the environment and should strengthen and restructure themselves in order to become more effective as developers and property managers. Special emphasis should be put on encouraging the formation of housing cooperatives, special project groups, development trusts, neighbourhood forums and development partnerships.

☐ ....................................................................
....................................................................
....................................................................
....................................................................

☐ ....................................................................
....................................................................
....................................................................
....................................................................

**180**

# Glossary

Common and not-so-common terms and concepts used in community planning simply explained.

Includes some methods not covered elsewhere, with cross-references to sources of further information.

➡ Refer to glossary item with similar meaning.

☞ See also *glossary item* or *page reference*.

**A-Z** Item covered more fully in the Methods A–Z.

⊘ Publication or film with further information (listing on page 203).

✉ Organisation with further information (listing on page 209).

## Editorial note

*In compiling this book I have had to make many decisions on terminology. Different people have used the same term to mean different things and different terms to mean the same thing. I have tried to use the simplest and most explanatory term wherever possible and avoid jargon. But do not get hung up on terminology. If your 'design workshop' is more likely to be successful if you call it an 'interactive planning meeting', that is what you should call it. Generally, though, using simple and direct language is likely to be most successful in sustaining interest and enthusiasm.*

## Action group
Informal organisation set up to get something achieved, usually through visible and public protest.

## Action minutes
Record of a meeting in the form of a list of steps required, who should take them and when.

## Action plan
Proposals for action. Usually in the form of a list of steps required, who should take them and when. ☞ *p170.*

## Action planning
An approach to planning and urban design involving the organisation of carefully structured collaborative events which produce proposals for action. ☞ *Action planning event.* Term also used to mean developing an action plan. ☞ *Action plan.*

## Action planning event
Carefully structured collaborative event at which all sections of the local community work closely with independent specialists from all relevant disciplines to produce proposals for action. ☞ **A-Z** *p24.*

## Activity mapping
Plotting on a map or plan how people use places as an aid to understanding how best to improve them. ☞ *Mapping.*

## Activity week
Week of activities designed to promote interest in, and debate on, a chosen theme: eg Architecture week; Urban design week; Environment week. ☞ **A-Z** *p26.*

## Activity year
Year of activities designed to promote interest in, and debate on, a chosen theme: eg Glasgow 1999; UK City of Architecture and Design.

## Adaptable model
Flexible model of an area or building which allows people to test out alternative design options. ☞ *Models.*

## Adventure playground
Playground that encourages children to construct and manage their own environment.

## Advocacy planning
Professional planners working on behalf of the disadvantaged. Term popular in the United States in the early 1970s.

## Agenda
Plan for a meeting. List of items to be discussed.

## Alternative plan
Plan for a site or neighbourhood putting forward a different approach to the prevailing plan. ☞ *Community plan.*

## Amenity trust
Charitable organisation established to manage a public amenity. ☞ *Development trust.*

## Appraisal
➡ *Community appraisal.*

## Appreciative inquiry
Group working process which builds on potentials, solutions and benefits to create change. ⊘ *The Thin Book of Appreciative Inquiry.* ✉ *Appreciative Inquiry Group.*

## Appropriate technology
Construction materials and techniques geared to local social and economic needs, possibilities and sources of materials. Sometimes referred to as *user-friendly technology*.

## Archetypes
Places with certain easily identifiable qualities. Concept sometimes used in briefing and design workshops to get people to describe the kind of places they aspire to; for instance, a certain part of a certain city or a certain building.

## Architects in schools
Environmental education programme involving architects working with children in schools.  ✉ Royal Institute of British Architects.

## Architecture centre
Place aimed at helping people understand, and engage in, the design of the local built environment. ☞ **A-Z** *p28.*

## Architecture week
Week of activities designed to promote interest in, and debate on, architecture. Usually includes opening interesting buildings to the public.
☞ *Activity week.*

## Architecture workshop
Workshop session on architecture. Term also sometimes used to describe an architecture or community design centre.
☞ *Architecture centre. Community design centre.*

## Art centre
Place providing a focus for the arts and local artists.

## Art house
Building used as a base for local artists producing and exhibiting work with and about the local community. Used as a regeneration technique for developing local pride and talent.  ☞ *Art centre.*

## Art workshop
Session where local residents work with artists designing and making artworks to improve their environment. ☞ **A-Z** *p30.*

## Asset base
Capital assets of property or cash which underpin the operations of an organisation, for instance by generating revenue from rents.

## Assistance team
➡ *Design assistance team.*

## Award scheme
Programme set up to promote good practice by presenting awards for excellence or effort.
☞ **A-Z** *p32.*

## Awareness raising day
Day of activities designed to promote interest in a community planning issue, normally held prior to a planning day or other intensive activity.

## Awareness walk
➡ *Reconnaissance trip.*

## Balanced incremental development
Development process undertaken in stages that lead on from one another. Allows schemes to evolve organically.

## Barefoot architect
Architect who works in villages helping people construct their homes. Term used in Asia.
☞ *Community architect.*

## Before and after
Photos, drawings or computer simulations showing a place before and after development has taken place from the same viewpoint. One of the most effective ways of helping people understand proposals.
☞ *example p20.*

## Best fit slide rule
A visual discussion tool designed to examine alternative street infill solutions and their consequences. An elevation of a street is drawn or assembled with photos and alternative designs inserted.
➲ *Participatory design.*

## Block models
Physical models where buildings are made out of wooden blocks.
☞ *Models.*

## Blu-tack®
Registered brand name for re-usable adhesive 'gum' for fastening paper etc to a surface.

## Bottom-up
Term used to refer to initiatives led by the community, as opposed to 'top down' initiatives led by the authorities.

## Brainstorming
Vigorous discussion to generate ideas in which all possibilities are considered. Widely used first step in generating solutions to problems.

## Briefing workshop
Working participatory sessions held at an early stage in a project or action planning event to establish a project agenda or brief. ☞ **A-Z** *p34.*

**Building cooperative**
Cooperative building contractor. All members usually receive equal rates and decisions are made collectively.

**Business planning**
Testing the viability of a project or organisation by predicting income and expenditure over a period of time.

**Business planning for real**
Computer-based simulation which helps new or existing organisations 'play through' the choices they will face in developing a business plan. Groups assemble a list of projects they would like to undertake. These are fed into a computer and the cost implications printed out. *Good practice guide to community planning and development.*

**Business planning workshop**
Session where participants work in small groups to determine project priorities and programme targets. Normally a draft business plan is prepared as a basis for discussion which is then amended until an agreed cash flow is arrived at.

**Buzz group**
Small group of people who work through an issue. Similar to a *focus group* or *workshop*.

**Capability**
The quality of being capable; the ability to do something.

**Capacity and vulnerability analysis (CVA)**
➡ *Vulnerability and capacity analysis.*

**Capacity building**
The development of awareness, knowledge, skills and operational capability by certain actors, normally the community, to achieve their purpose.
☞ *Empowerment.*

**Capacity building workshop**
Event organised primarily to establish partnerships between the public, private and voluntary sectors on development issues.

**Case study**
Description of a project. Used for helping others understand how it worked, or failed to work.

**Chairperson**
Individual who controls a meeting, deciding who can speak when. ☞ *Facilitator.*

**Champion**
Individual who believes in an idea and will promote it through thick and thin. Important ingredient for most projects. ☞ *Moving spirits.*

**Charity**
Organisation which acts in the interests of society rather than in pursuit of profit. May receive tax breaks and other benefits.

**Charrette**
➡ *Design charrette.*

**Chart**
Large sheet of paper used for writing or drawing on, usually attached to walls or placed on an easel. Essential tool of participative working.
☞ *Flipchart.*

**Choice catalogue**
Menu of items, usually visually illustrated, showing a range of design choices available.
☞ **A-Z** *p36.*

**Choices method**
Visioning process based on four steps:
1. Meetings throughout the community to brainstorm ideas for making life better.
2. Consolidation of ideas into goals and vision statements.
3. A 'vision fair' where people vote on which visions they would like to pursue and make personal commitment pledges.
4. Setting up of action groups to carry out chosen ideas.
⊘ *Chattanooga. Participation Works!*

**Citizens jury**
Informal inquiry method where a group of around 16 people, selected to be representative of the community, spend a few days examining an issue, listening to witnesses and producing a report.
⊘ *Participation Works!*

**City farm**
Working farm in an urban area, normally run by a voluntary committee of local people. Primary role is educational rather than food production.

**Civic forum**
➡ *Forum.*

**Civil society**
The arena of organised citizen activity outside of the state and market sectors. People coming together to define, articulate, and act on their concerns through various forms of organisation and expression.

**Client**
Individual or organisation that commissions buildings or other projects. ☞ *User-client.*

## Cohousing
Housing with shared living components. Ranges from sharing of gardens to sharing of workshops, laundry rooms and even kitchens.
⟳ *Cohousing.*

## Committee
Group of people elected or delegated to make decisions, usually in meetings.
☞ *Workshop.*

## Community
Used in many ways. Usually refers to those living within a small, loosely defined geographical area. Yet any group of individuals who share interests may also be described as a community. Also sometimes used to describe a physical area rather than a group of people.
☞ *following entries on community.*

## Community action
A process by which the deprived define for themselves their needs, and determine forms of action to meet them, usually outside the prevailing political framework.

## Community action planning
➡ *Microplanning workshop.*
☞ *Action planning.*

## Community appraisal
Survey of the community by the community to identify needs and opportunities. Usually based on a self-completion questionnaire devised by the community and delivered to every household.
⟳ *Village Appraisals Software for Windows.*
☞ *Community profiling.*

## Community architect
Architect who practises *community architecture.* Will often live and work in the neighbourhood he or she is designing for.
☞ *Community architecture.*

## Community architecture
Architecture carried out with the active participation of the end users. Similarly *community design*, *community planning* and so on.

## Community art
Visual and performance art addressed to the needs of a local community. Often related to environmental issues.
☞ *Art workshop.*

## Community-based organisation (CBO)
Voluntary organisation operating at a local level to represent a local community or interest group. Term increasingly used at international level. Similar in meaning to *community group.*
☞ *Community group. Non-governmental organisation.*

## Community build
Building construction carried out by members of the local community, often voluntarily or as part of a training course.
☞ *Self-build.*

## Community building
Building conceived, managed and sometimes built, by the local community for community use. Phrase also used to describe the activity of building a community; physically, socially and economically.

## Community business
Trading organisation owned and controlled by the local community which aims to create self-supporting and viable jobs for local people and to use profits to create more employment, provide local services or support local charitable work.

## Community consultation
Finding out what local people want. ☞ *Consultation.*

## Community design
Design carried out with the active participation of the end users. Similarly *community architecture*, *community planning* and so on.

## Community design centre
Place providing free or subsidised architectural, planning and design services to people who cannot afford to pay for them. Also known as a *community technical aid centre.* ☞ **A-Z** *p38.*
☞ *Community technical aid centre.*

## Community design house
Local office used by a *community designer* or *community architect.* Term used in Japan. ☞ *Community design centre.*

## Community designer
Practitioner of *community design.* Person who designs places *with* people rather than *for* people.

## Community development
Promotion of self-managed, non-profit-orientated projects to serve community needs.

**Community development corporation**
Non-profit-orientated company undertaking development for community benefit. American concept similar to the UK's *development trust*.
☞ *Development trust*.

**Community development trust**
➡ *Development trust*.

**Community driven**
Term used to reflect key role of the community in an initiative.

**Community enterprise**
Enterprise for the benefit of the community rather than private profit by people within the community.

**Community forest**
Woodland area developed and managed by and for the communities living in and around it. Programme established in England by the Countryside Agency and Forestry Commission.
✉ Countryside Agency.

**Community garden**
Publicly accessible garden or small park created and managed by a voluntary group.

**Community group**
Voluntary organisation operating at local level.
☞ *Community-based organisation*.

**Community indicators**
Measures devised and used by communities for understanding and drawing attention to important issues and trends. Useful for building an agenda for education and action.
⊘ *Communities Count!*

**Community landscape**
Landscape architecture or design carried out with the active participation of the end users.

**Community learning and education centre**
Focal point for information and education at community level.

**Community mapping**
Making maps as a communal activity. ☞ *Mapping*.

**Community newspaper**
Information source controlled by the local community. Also *community newsletter*; similar on a smaller scale.

**Community plan**
Plan for the future of a community devised by the local community. Sets out proposals for the way in which a community wants to develop and respond to changes in the future. No set format. Will usually contain statements of principle, physical design proposals and targets.
☞ *checklist p176*.

**Community planning**
Planning carried out with the active participation of the end users. Similarly *community architecture*, *community design* and so on.

**Community planning council**
Umbrella organisation at neighbourhood level with powers to deal with planning matters. Concept developed and recommended by the UK's Royal Town Planning Institute in 1982. Councils would be made up of representatives from various sectional voluntary interests. ☞ *Forum*.

**Community planning day**
➡ *Planning day*.

**Community planning forum**
Multipurpose session lasting several hours designed to secure information, generate ideas and create interaction between interest groups.
☞ A-Z *p40*.

**Community planning weekend**
➡ *Planning weekend*.

**Community politics**
Style of political action through which people are enabled to control their own destinies. Identified with an on-going political movement which seeks to create a participatory democracy.

**Community profiling**
Way of reaching an understanding of the needs and resources of a community with the active involvement of the community. Similar approach as *participatory appraisal*. ☞ A-Z *p42*.

**Community project**
Facility for the local community, created and managed by a voluntary committee, elected or unelected, from that community.

**Community projects fund**
➡ *Feasibility fund*.

**Community safety plan**
Plan drawn up by the local community to reduce crime and disorder.

GLOSSARY

### Community technical aid

Multi-disciplinary expert assistance to community groups enabling them to play an active role in the development of land and buildings. The term 'technical aid' is used to cover the diverse range of skills likely to be needed including architecture, planning, landscaping, engineering, surveying, ecology, environmental education, financial planning, management, administration and graphics.

### Community technical aid centre

Place staffed by multidisciplinary group of experts who work for voluntary groups, helping them to undertake any project involving the development of buildings and land. Will provide whatever assistance is needed – design, planning, organisation, decision-making, management – from conception to completion. Similar to a *community design centre*.
☞ *Community design centre.*

### Community trust

Independent fundraising and grant-making charity which funds initiatives in the local community.

### Community visioning

Thinking collectively about what the future could be. Term used to describe group working processes which help a community to develop imaginative shared visions for the future of a site, area or organisation. Approach often adopted by local authorities as part of their Agenda 21 processes.
✉ *New Economics Foundation.*
☞ *Future search conference.*

### Community woodland
➡ *Community forest.*

### Computer aided design

Way of visually simulating designs in three dimensions on computer.

### Consensus building

Procedure for helping people with different views to come together interactively on a dispute, project, plan or issue, to work towards agreeing a sensible solution or way forward which is mutually satisfactory.

### Consultation

Seeking people's views (but not necessarily involving them in decision-making).

### Co-operative

An enterprise conducted for the mutual benefit of its members. This might be a business that is democratic, each member having one vote irrespective of capital or labour input. Any economic surplus belongs to the members – after providing for reserves for the development of the business.
☞ *Housing co-operative.*

### Co-ownership

Tenure arrangement in which property is partly owned by the occupier, the remaining portion being gradually purchased during the period of occupation.

### Core costs

Expenditure essential to keep an organisation going. As opposed to project costs. Includes such things as staff wages, rent, heating.

### Countryside design summary

Simple description of the design relationship between the landscape, settlement patterns and buildings. Usually produced by the planning authority for a region, often combined with the production of local design statements for neighbourhoods within the region.
☞ *Local design statement.*
✉ Countryside Agency.

### Critical mass event

Umbrella term for organisation development techniques involving large-scale events often lasting several days and often involving hundreds of people. Mostly used for organisational change but may also be appropriate for community planning. Labels given to specific types of event – structured in different ways and promoted by different people – include *future search conference, large-scale interactive process, conference model, real-time strategic change, participative work redesign* and *open space workshops.*
☞ *Future search conference. Open space workshop.*

### Daily routine chart

Diagram showing people's daily activities and time taken to accomplish each of them. Usually produced by groups of women, men and children separately. Useful to deepen the analysis on seasonal calendars and highlight divisions of labour and responsibilities.
☞ *Community profiling. Seasonal calendars.*

**186**

## Design assistance team (DAT)

Multidisciplinary team which visits an area and produces recommendations for action, usually after facilitating an action planning event. Similar terms in use include *Urban design assistance team (UDAT)* and *Housing assistance team (HAT)* (where only housing involved). ☞ **A-Z** *p44.*

## Design charrette

Intensive design session, often including 'all-nighter', originally just for architecture students but more recently including the public and professionals. Term originated at the Paris Ecole des Beaux-Arts at the turn of the century. Projects were collected at designated times on a cart ('charrette') where students would be found putting finishing touches to their schemes. Term now widely used in the USA to describe any intensive, group brainstorming effort. *Charrette* often used without the '*Design*' in front. Similar to design workshop.
☞ *Design workshop.*

## Design day

Day when architects and local people brainstorm for design solutions to particular building problems, usually in teams. Term also used to describe day when local residents can drop in and talk through design ideas with professionals
⊘ *Building Homes People Want.*
☞ *Drop-in office.*

## Design fest

Action planning event where multidisciplinary design teams develop and present their ideas in public. ☞ **A-Z** *p46*

## Design game

Method for devising building and landscape layouts with residents using coloured cut-outs of possible design features on plans. ☞ **A-Z** *p48.*

## Design guide

Document setting out general urban design principles which should be adopted by any development in an area.
☞ *Local design statement.*

## Design meeting

Meeting for developing designs. Usually organised on a regular basis during the design stage of a project. Users and professionals will be present. The users, or clients, set the agenda but the meeting is normally conducted by the professionals. Various techniques will be used to present information and make decisions: showing slides, models, drawings, catalogues. Normal arrangement is for participants to sit round a table.

## Design simulation

Playing at designing to get people used to the various roles in the design process.

## Design surgery

Where architects, planners or other professionals work through design issues with individuals, for instance occupants in a new housing scheme.

## Design workshop

Hands-on session allowing groups to work creatively developing planning and design options.
☞ **A-Z** *p50.*
☞ *Design charrette.*

## Designing for real

Term used to describe the use of adaptable models to develop detailed design proposals for a building or site. Participants explore options by moving parts of the model around: ie, parts of a building or whole buildings. Similar concept to Planning for Real but on a smaller scale.
☞ *Planning for Real*

## Development officer

Individual who gets a project or organisation up and running.

## Development partnership

Arrangement for collaboration by two or more parties to facilitate development, usually between the public and private sectors. ☞ *Partnership.*

## Development planning for real

Adaptation of *Planning for Real* specially devised for developing countries.
☞ *Planning for Real.*

## Development trust

Independent, not-for-profit organisation controlled by local people which facilitates and undertakes physical development in an area. It will have significant community involvement or control, will bring together a wide range of skills and interests, and will aim to sustain its operations at least in part by generating revenue.
☞ **A-Z** *p52.* ☞ *Community development corporation.*

## Diagramming

Creating diagrams in groups.
☞ *Diagrams.*

**Diagrams**
Visual representations of information which help explain current issues or future proposals. ☞ **A-Z** *p54*.

**Direct action**
Exertion of political pressure by tactics other than voting at elections. Usually used to refer to strikes, squatting or occupations.

**Direct observation**
Noting of events, objects, processes and relationships; particularly useful for issues hard to verbalise.

**Disabling**
Non-participatory form of service which renders the user unable to have a say in the process.

**Disaster**
Serious disruption of the functioning of society, causing widespread human, material, or environmental losses which exceed the ability of the affected society to cope using its own resources (UNDP 91).

**Disaster management**
All aspects of planning for,.and responding to, disasters.

**Disaster mitigation**
Reducing the impact of disasters on society by reducing the hazards and/or society's vulnerability to them.
☞ *Mitigation*.

**Disaster preparedness**
The ability to predict, respond and cope with the effects of a disaster.

**Disaster relief**
Extraordinary measures necessary for coping with a disaster.

**Discussion method**
Structure for effective communication which allows everyone in a group to participate.
☞ *Technology of participation*.

**Drop-in office**
Working office open to the public. Set up by architects or urban designers working in a neighbourhood to encourage local involvement in the design process. May be permanent or temporary (on an *open day* for instance).

**Economic audit**
Audit of local economy, usually undertaken by independent professional economist.

**Elevation montage**
Display technique for helping people to understand and make changes to streetscapes.
☞ **A-Z** *p58*.

**Empowerment**
Development of confidence and skills in individuals or communities leading to their being able to take more control over their own destinies.
☞ *Capacity building*.

**Enabler**
Professional or other person with technical expertise or in a position of authority who uses it to help people to do things for themselves. The term can also be used to refer to organisations which behave likewise.

**Enabling**
Professional and other services that consciously encourage or allow users to participate.
☞ *Enabler*.

**Enquiry by design**
Intensive action planning workshop process involving urban designers and local stakeholders. Devised for developing plans for new urban villages.
✉ Urban Villages Forum.

**Enspirited envisioning**
Way of developing individual and shared visions of the future through personal and group development.
➔ *Participation works!*

**Enterprise agency**
Non-profit-making company whose prime objective is to respond through practical action to the economic and training needs of its local community. A principal activity is providing free advice and counselling to support the setting up and development of viable small businesses. Mostly public sector-led in partnership with the private sector but there are many exceptions.

**Enterprise trust**
➡ *Enterprise agency*

**Environment forum**
Non-statutory body for discussing and co-ordinating environmental issues in an area. ☞ *Forum*.

**Environment shop**
Shop selling items and providing information which helps people improve their environment. Similarly *architecture shop, conservation shop* etc.
☞ **A-Z** *p60*.

**Environment week**
Week of activities designed to promote interest in, and debate on, the environment.
☞ *Activity week*.

**Environmental capital**
Inclusive, participatory process for evaluating what environmental features and attitudes matter to local interest groups and why.
✉ Countryside Agency.

**Environmental education**
Programmes aimed at making people more aware of their environment and the forces which shape it.

**Environmental impact assessment**
Process whereby all impacts of a development are identified and their significance assessed. Increasingly a statutory requirement before planning permission is granted by a local authority.

**Envisioning**
➡ Visioning.

**Equity sharing**
➡ Co-ownership.

**Exhibition**
Displays of information. May be simply for presenting information or for getting feedback too.
☞ Interactive exhibition.

**Facilitation**
Bringing people together to decide what they wish to do, and to work together to decide how to do it.

**Facilitator**
Person who steers a process, meeting or workshop. Less dominant role than a 'chairperson'. Also known as a moderator.

**Farmers market**
Market exclusively for local food producers and countryside products.

**Feasibility fund**
Revolving fund providing grants to community groups for paying professional fees for the preparation of feasibility studies for community projects. Also known as a community projects fund. ☞ **A-Z** p62.

**Feasibility study**
Examination of the viability of an idea, usually resulting in a report. ☞ example p63.

**Fence method**
Prioritising procedure using a line with a fence in the middle to establish people's views on conflicting alternatives.
☞ example p105.

**Festival market**
Market for bric-a-brac and crafts.

**Field workshop**
Workshop programme on location. Term used to describe events lasting several days involving a range of community profiling, risk assessment and plan-making activities. ☞ **A-Z** p64.

**Fish bowl**
Workshop technique where participants sit around, and observe, a planning team working on a problem without taking part themselves.
⊘ Community Participation in Practice.

**Five Ws plus H**
What, When, Why, Who, Where and How. Useful checklist in planning any activity.

**Flipchart**
Large pad of paper on an easel. Standard equipment for participatory workshops as it allows notetaking to be visible.

**Flipcharter**
Person who records points made at a workshop or plenary session on a flipchart or large sheet of paper pinned on a wall in full view of the participants. ☞ Flipchart.

**Fly-posting**
Pasting up posters in public places, usually without permission from building owners or authorities.

**Focus group**
Small group of people who work through an issue in workshop sessions. Membership may be carefully selected or entirely random.

**Forum**
Non-statutory body for discussing and coordinating activity and acting as a pressure group for change.
☞ Environment forum. Neighbourhood forum.
Term also used to describe a one-off open meeting aiming to create interaction.
☞ Community planning forum. Public forum.

**Full-scale simulation**
Acting out a scenario to test a design idea using full-scale mock-ups. Particularly useful for helping people design new building forms.
☞ Design simulation. Mock-up.

**Future search conference**
Highly structured two and a half day process allowing a community or organisation to create a shared vision for its future. Ideally 64 people take part; eight tables of eight.
☞ **A-Z** p66.

### Futures workshop
Term used for a workshop devised to discuss options for the future. Various formats are possible. ☞ *Briefing workshop. Design workshop.*

### Gallery walk
Report back process where workshop flipchart sheets are pinned up at a plenary session and the reporter 'walks' past the sheets, using them as a prompt to summarise what took place.

### Gaming
The use of games to simulate real situations. ☞ **A-Z** *p68.* ☞ *Role play. Simulation.*

### Giving evidence
Formal presentation of information, for instance to a public inquiry or local authority committee.

### Group interview
Pre-arranged discussion with an invited group to analyse topics or issues against a checklist of points or local concerns. ☞ *Interview.*

### Group modelling
Use of physical models as a basis for working in groups to learn, explore and make decisions about the environment. ☞ *Models.*

### Guided visualisation
Group process using mental visualisation techniques for establishing a community's aspirations.
➔ *Participation Works!*

### Habitat
The social and economic, as well as physical, shelter essential for well-being.

### Hands-on exhibition.
➡ *Interactive exhibition.*

### Hazard
Phenomenon that poses a threat to people, structures or economic assets and which may cause a disaster. It could be either human-made or naturally occurring.

### Hazard analysis
Identification of types of hazard faced by a community, their intensity, frequency and location.

### Heritage centre
Place aimed at helping people understand, and engage in, the historic local built environment. Key elements: old photos, old artefacts, leaflets, books, information sheets, maps, postcards, models, trails.
☞ *Architecture centre. Local heritage initiative.*

### Historic buildings trust
Charitable organisation set up to preserve historic buildings.

### Historical profile
Key events and trends in a community's development, usually displayed visually.
☞ *Community profiling.*

### Historical profiling
Construction of historical profile in groups. Information about past events is gathered to explain the present and predict possible future scenarios. One approach involves people describing and explaining their life history with respect to particular issues. Information is marked up on maps or charts to build a comprehensive time-line of events and issues that mould and affect a community.

### Homeowners file
File of book-keeping schedules designed to help families to control the construction and management of their homes.

### Homesteading
Programme in which property owners (usually local authorities) offer substandard property for sale at low cost to householders who will work on them in their own time, doing basic repairs and renovation to standards monitored by the original owners.

### Housing association
Association run by an elected management committee which uses government money to provide housing in areas and for people which the government believes to be a high priority. Building society money is also increasingly used to fund housing associations.

### Housing co-operative
Organisation which owns or manages housing and which is owned and managed by the occupants of that housing. Often referred to as a *housing co-op.* ☞ *Co-operative. Secondary co-operative.*

### Human capital
Ability of individuals to do productive work; includes physical and mental health, strength, stamina, knowledge, skills, motivation and a constructive and co-operative attitude.
☞ *Social capital.*

### Icebreaker
Group activity aimed at making people feel comfortable with each other. Often held at the start of action planning events.

## Ideas competition
Competition for generating options for improving a neighbourhood, building or site aimed at stimulating creative thinking and generating interest.
☞ **A-Z** *p70.*

## Illustrated questionnaire
Questionnaire with pictures to find out people's design preferences.
☞ *Choice catalogue. Questionnaire survey.*

## Imagine
Method for establishing positive initiatives based on a structured approach to imagining the future.
⊘ *Participation Works!*

## Imaging day
Day when people visualise the future with the assistance of a skilled artist.

## Immediate report writing
Writing reports in the field or at an event rather doing it later in the office.

## Informal walk
Walking in a group without a definite route, stopping to chat and discuss issues as they arise.
☞ *Community profiling.*

## Interactive display
Visual display which allows people to participate by making additions or alterations. Also known as a *hands-on display.* ☞ **A-Z** *p72.*

## Interactive exhibition
Exhibition which allows people to participate by making additions or alterations. Also known as a *hands-on exhibition.* ☞ *Interactive display. Open house event.*

## Interview
Recorded conversation, usually with prepared questions, with individuals or groups. Useful for information gathering. More flexible and interactive than a questionnaire.
☞ *Group interview. Key informant interview. Semi-structured interview.*

## Jigsaw display
Exhibit where groups prepare different parts which are then assembled as a whole.

## Key informant
Person with special knowledge.

## Key informant interview
Informal discussion based on a pre-determined set of questions with people who have special knowledge.
☞ *Interview.*

## KISS
Stands for 'Keep It Simple, Stupid'. Useful reminder in a complex field.

## Ladder of participation
Useful and popular analogy for likening the degree of citizen participation in any activity to a series of rungs on a ladder. First put forward in 1969 (by Sherry Arnstein) with 8 rungs:
1. Citizen control.
2. Delegated power.
3. Partnership.
4. Placation.
5. Consultation.
6. Informing.
7. Therapy.
8. Manipulation.
This has been modified in many different ways by many people since. ☞ *page 10.*
⊘ *The Guide to Effective Participation.*

## Landscape character assessment
Process for describing an area's sense of place, features and attributes. Useful foundation for making planning and land management decisions for an area.
☞ *Local character workshop.*
✉ Countryside Agency.

## Large group interventions
➡ *Critical mass event.*

## Launch
Event to promote the start of an initiative or project. Useful for generating interest and involvement.

## Leaflet
Sheet of paper providing information, usually produced in large quantities. Standard publicity technique.

## Linkage diagram
Shows flows, connections and causality. ☞ *Diagrams.*

## Livability
Somewhat loose measure of the quality of life where needs that are justifiable according to natural justice are met.

## Living over the shop scheme
Programme to encourage people to occupy vacant premises over shops, usually by offering grant aid. Town centre regeneration method.

## Lobbying
Influencing decision-makers through individual and group face-to-face persuasion or letter writing.

## Local
Pertaining to a particular rural or urban place or area.

**Local authority**
Organisation governing local area. For instance; borough council, county council, town council, village council.

**Local character workshop**
Workshop designed to help people identify what makes an area special. Usually undertaken as part of preparing a local design statement or landscape character assessment. Involves mapping and photo surveys.
☞ *Landscape character assessment. Local design statement.*

**Local design statement**
Published statement produced by a community identifying the distinctive character of the place. The aim is for it to be used by planning authorities to ensure that future development and change is sympathetic and has community support.
☞ **A-Z** *p74.*

**Local environmental resource centre**
Resource centre focusing on local environmental issues.
☞ *Resource centre.*

**Local heritage initiative**
Process for helping people record and care for their local landscape, landmarks and traditions.
✉ *Countryside Agency.*

**Local people**
People who live in a particular rural or urban place or area.

**Local regeneration agency**
Organisation set up to undertake regeneration work in an area.

**Local resource centre**
Place providing information and support for people at a community level.
☞ *Resource centre.*

**Local support team**
Locally-based team providing expertise for an activity or event.

**Local sustainability model**
Process allowing a community to assess its present position and test the likely effect of projects.
➔ *Participation Works!*

**Logical framework analysis**
Method for thoroughly testing the effectiveness of any project proposal. Assesses objectives, purposes, inputs, assumptions, outputs, effects and inputs. Much used by international funding agencies.

**Low-cost housing**
Housing affordable by people on low incomes.

**Maintenance manual**
Instructions on how to maintain a building or open space. Important for helping users to keep places in good order.

**Managed workspace**
Communally managed building for individual, and independent, enterprises sharing common support facilities and services. Sometimes known as a *working community.*

**Management committee**
Governing body of a project or organisation. Similar to board of directors in a company.

**Mapping**
Physical plotting of various characteristics of an area in two dimensions. May be done individually or communally.
☞ *Activity mapping. Community mapping. Mental mapping. Mind map. Parish mapping.* ☞ **A-Z** *p76.*

**Market**
Place for buying and selling goods and services. An important regeneration tool. Types of market include: street market, covered market, farmers market, festival market.

**Masterplan**
Overall planning framework for the future of a settlement. May be highly detailed or schematic. Used to provide a vision and structure to guide development.

**Matrix**
Diagram in the form of a grid allowing comparison of two variables. Used for assessing options. ☞ *Diagrams.*

**Mediation**
Voluntary process of helping people resolve their differences with the assistance of a neutral person.

**Meeting**
Event where people come together to discuss and decide. May be formal or informal, public or private.

**Mental mapping**
Production of maps by individuals or communities showing how they perceive their neighbourhood (as opposed to geographically accurate maps). ☞ *Mapping.*

**Micro-finance**
Banking system which provides small loans to poor people without collateral.

**Microplanning workshop**
Intensive planning procedure developed specifically for upgrading settlements in developing countries involving a minimum of preparation, materials and training. Also referred to as *community action planning*. ☞ **A-Z** *p78*.

**Mind map**
Diagram showing people's perceptions of trends and linkages. Not a geographical map. Used in future search conferences. ☞ *Diagrams. Future search conference*.

**Mini visioning**
Basic and succinct visioning workshops. ☞ *Visioning*.

**Mission statement**
Written explanation of the purpose of a project, event or organisation. Usually brief and to the point. Useful for avoiding misunderstanding, particularly in partnerships.

**Mitigation**
Measures taken to minimise the impact of a disaster. By modifying the hazard itself or by reducing vulnerability to it. Ranges from physical measures such as flood defenses, to raising people's living standards so they no longer need to inhabit areas at risk. Mitigation can take place before, during and after a disaster.

**Mobile unit**
Caravan or mobile home converted into an office/studio as a base for undertaking community planning activity on location. ☞ **A-Z** *p80*.

**Mock-up**
Full-size representation of a change or development, usually on its proposed site, prior to finalising the design.

**Modelling**
Making models. Usually refers to making models as a group process. Similar to mapping but in three dimensions instead of two. ☞ *Mapping. Models*.

**Models**
Physical three-dimensional constructions simulating a building or neighbourhood. ☞ **A-Z** *p82*.

**Moderator**
➡ *Facilitator*.

**Moving spirits**
People in a community who want to improve things for the better and who are prepared to give time and thought to something they think might help. Also referred to as *movers and shakers* or *social entrepreneurs*. ☞ *Champion*.

**Mutual aid**
Where people help each other without any formal organisation.

**Neighbourhood council**
Elected body at neighbourhood level with certain statutory powers. Urban equivalent of a parish council and effectively a mini local authority.

**Neighbourhood forum**
Non-statutory body for discussing a neighbourhood's affairs and acting as a pressure group for improvements. Members may be publicly elected – usually in categories (eg residents, traders, churches, etc.) – or be nominated by organisations entitled to be represented under the constitution. May be effectively a non-statutory *neighbourhood council* although procedural practice varies considerably.

**Neighbourhood planning office**
Local office established to co-ordinate community planning activity. ☞ **A-Z** *p84*.

**Neighbourhood skills survey**
Survey to establish what skills and abilities people have in a neighbourhood. Used to find out what a community can do for itself and to generate interest. Sometimes referred to as a neighbourhood *talent* survey. ☞ *Useful checklists p175*. ☞ *Resource survey*.

**Neighbourhood talent survey**
➡ *Neighbourhood skills survey*.

**Networking**
Exchanging experience with people engaged in similar activities. Usually in an informal manner.

**Newspaper supplement**
Special insert or section of a newspaper. Can be used to cover local design issues. ☞ **A-Z** *p86*.

### Non-governmental organisation (NGO)
Voluntary and non-profit-distributing organisation. The difference between an NGO and a CBO (community-based organisation) is that an NGO is normally organised and funded from outside the local community in which it operates.
☞ *Community-based organisation.*

### Notetaker
Person who records points made at a workshop or plenary session with a view to writing up a record and/or making a presentation of the results.

### Off-setting biases
Being self-critically aware of biases in behaviour and learning, and deliberately countering them.

### Open design competition
Competition open to everyone. Contrasts with *limited* or *closed* competitions to which entry is restricted.
☞ *Ideas competition.*

### Open day
Day when a project or organisation encourages people to come and find out what it is doing and how it works. Often used to generate interest and momentum.

### Open house event
Event designed to allow those promoting development initiatives to present them to a wider public and secure reactions in an informal manner. Halfway between an exhibition and a workshop.
☞ **A-Z** *p88.*

### Open space technology
Framework within which open space workshops are held.
☞ *Open space workshop.*

### Open space workshop
Workshop process for generating commitment to action in communities or organisations. Features include starting without an agenda.
☞ **A-Z** *p90.*

### Opinion survey
Survey to find out what people think about an issue. ☞ *Survey.*

### Outcomes
Results of projects or programmes, usually unmeasurable (eg, people are happier). ☞ *Outputs.*

### Outputs
Measurable results of projects or programmes (eg, number of trees planted). ☞ *Outcomes.*

### Outreach
Taking consultation to the people rather than expecting them to come to you.

### Outsiders
Non-local people. Usually refers to professionals and facilitators.

### Ownership
Term often used to refer to a sense of responsibility for an initiative or project. eg, 'People will have *ownership* of an idea or a project if they have been involved in creating it'.

### Pair-wise ranking
Rapid and simple way of selecting the most important issues or problems facing a community. Brainstorming generates a preliminary list. A group of people then vote on the significance of every item against each other item using a matrix.

### Paradigm
A coherent and mutually supporting pattern of concepts, values, methods and action, amenable or claiming to be amenable, to wide application.

### Parish mapping
Arts based way in which a community can explore and express what they value in their place through the creation of maps out of a wide variety of materials. ☞ *Mapping.*
✉ *Common Ground.*

### Participation
Act of being involved in something.

### Participationitis
When everything has to be checked by everyone. Too much participation.

### Participation training
Short courses or workshop sessions on participation approaches. May be aimed at professionals or community activists.

### Participatory appraisal
An approach to gaining a rapid in-depth understanding of a community, or certain aspects of a community, based on the participation of that community and a range of visual techniques. Allows people to share and record aspects of their own situation, conditions of life, knowledge, perceptions, aspirations, preferences and develop plans for action. Not restricted to planning issues. Many terms used to imply similar concept including participatory learning and action.
☞ *Community profiling.*
⟁ *Whose Reality Counts?*

## Participatory building evaluation
Method for users and providers to jointly assess the effectiveness of buildings after they have been built.
*⊘ User Participation in Building Design and Management.*

## Participatory democracy
Process which involves people directly in decision-making which affects them, rather than through formally elected representatives such as councillors or MPs as in representative democracy.

## Participatory design
Design processes which involve the users of the item or places being designed.

## Participatory editing
Method of involving large numbers of people in producing reports and other material. ☞ **A-Z** *p92*.

## Participatory monitoring and evaluation (PME)
Monitoring and evaluation undertaken with the participation of those who took part in the activity being monitored and evaluated.

## Participatory rapid appraisal (PRA)
➡ *Participatory appraisal.*

## Participatory theatre
The use of physical movement and creativity to explore people's experience and develop a common vision.
*⊘ Participation Works!*

## Partnership
Agreement between two or more individuals or organisations to work together to achieve common aims.
*⊘ Managing Partnerships.*

## Partnership agreement
Formal document setting out the terms and conditions of a partnership arrangement.
☞ *Partnership.*

## Pattern language
Method devised to enable untrained people to design their own buildings and cities in accordance with well-tried principles of good design.
*⊘ A Pattern Language.*

## People's organisation
➡ *Community-based organisation.*

## People's wall
Wall covered with large sheets of paper where visitors to a design fest or workshop can write and draw. ☞ *Public wall.*

## Percent for participation
Campaign to get a percentage of total development costs spent on participation. Started by the Royal Institute of British Architects' Community Architecture Group.
✉ *Community Architecture Group.*

## Permaculture
Approach to designing sustainable environments based on ecological principles of co-operation with nature.

## Permaculture design course
Courses aimed at making groups self-reliant and sustainable and helping them to take initiatives. Introductory courses last a weekend. Main courses are 2 weeks or a series of weekends.
✉ *Permaculture Association.*
*⊘ Permaculture Teachers Handbook.*

## Photo survey
Survey of locality using cameras. ☞ **A-Z** *p94*.

## Pile sorting
Method of categorising by sorting cards or other items into piles. Used in group sessions.

## Planning aid scheme
The provision of free and independent information and advice on town planning to groups and individuals who cannot afford consultancy fees. ☞ **A-Z** *p96*.

## Planning assistance kit
Series of worksheets designed to assist community organisations in physical planning, implementation and management of their environment.

## Planning assistance team
Similar to a *design assistance team.*
☞ *Design assistance team.*

## Planning day
Day when interested parties work intensively together developing urban design options for a site or neighbourhood. ☞ **A-Z** *p98*.

## Planning department
Section of local authority dealing with planning issues.

## Planning for Real ®
Registered brand name for a method for community involvement in planning and development focusing on the construction and use of flexible cardboard models and priority cards. ☞ **A-Z** *p100*.

### Planning weekend
Sophisticated and highly structured action planning procedure in which professionals work with local people over a long weekend to produce proposals for action. The term *community planning weekend* is also used (often with the word 'community' being added during the process). Terms *planning week* and *community planning week* have also been used for slightly longer events. ☞ **A-Z** *p102.*

### Plenary session
Meeting of all participants at an event (for instance after a number of separate workshop groups).

### Popular planning
Planning from the bottom up. Term used by the Greater London Council in the 1980s.

### Post-it note ®
Or simply 'Post-it'. Registered brand name for a sheet of paper with a sticky edge. Come in pads. Great technical aid to collective working as, unlike cards, they can be stuck on vertical surfaces and moved around to create groups.

### Preparedness
Measures taken in anticipation of a disaster aimed at minimising loss of life, disruption and damage if the disaster occurs. Includes formulating contingency plans, developing warning systems, maintenance of relief supplies and an efficient emergency relief distribution system. ☞ *Disaster.*

### Prioritising
Deciding what needs doing when. Ranking of problems to be dealt with or projects to be undertaken. Term usually used to refer to group prioritising processes. ☞ **A-Z** *p104.*

### Priority Estates Project
Experimental UK government programme to give council tenants a chance to exercise more control over their homes and neighbourhoods by establishing estate-based management systems. Set up in 1979. ✉ PEP.

### Priority search
Survey technique based on a computerised questionnaire package which analyses responses to structured questions.

### Problem tree
Visual way of analysing the inter-relationships among community issues and problems. A process of asking why is used to arrive at consensus about root causes and related effects. A symbolic tree is drawn with the trunk representing problems, the roots representing causes and branches representing the effects. ☞ *example page 43.*

### Process design
Activity of designing the process.

### Process planning session
Event organised to allow people to determine the most appropriate process for their particular purposes. ☞ **A-Z** *p106.*

### Public forum
Public meeting with an emphasis on debate and discussion rather than speeches and a question and answer session. Participants will normally sit in a circle or a horseshoe arrangement. ☞ *Forum. Public meeting.*

### Public meeting
Advertised, open access event at which issues are presented and commented on and at which decisions may be made. Term normally used to refer to fairly formal events with the audience sitting in rows facing a speaker or panel of speakers with a chairperson who controls the proceedings. ☞ *Public forum. Workshop.*

### Public wall
Area of wall space or display boards where members of the public can make their views known by putting up drawings or text and making comments on material already there. ☞ *People's wall.*

### Publicity
Raising awareness of a situation through use of posters, leaflets and so on.

### Questionnaire survey
Survey which involves collection of information in the form of written responses to a standard set of questions. Often a starting point for participation processes. Frequently used with other methods. ☞ *Survey.*

### Rapporteur
➡ *Reporter.*
French term often used even at English speaking events.

**Reconnaissance trip**
Direct inspection of area under consideration by mixed team of locals and technical experts. ☞ **A-Z** *p108*.

**Referendum**
Public vote on an issue of special importance. May be used for strategic planning issues (for instance in the Netherlands).

**Regional/urban design assistance team (R/UDAT)**
Name originally given to the planning weekend programme started by the American Institute of Architects in 1967. A *generic R/UDAT* uses the same process to look at problems common to many communities. A *mini R/UDAT* uses a similar process with a student team.
☞ *Design assistance team.*
☞ *Planning weekend.*

**Reporter**
Person who reports to a plenary session on the outcome of a workshop.

**Residents' choice catalogue**
➡ *Choice catalogue.*

**Residents' tool loan service**
Service lending out tools and equipment to make it easier for residents to carry out building work on their environment.

**Resource assessment**
Identification of resources and capacities within a community.
☞ *Resource survey.*

**Resource centre**
Place designed to provide community groups with the facilities they need to make the most of their energies and enthusiasm. No two centres are exactly alike but will provide some or all of the following: information, office equipment, professional advice and support, meeting facilities, equipment for meetings and fund raising, training courses and opportunities for groups to meet and share ideas.
☞ *Neighbourhood planning office.*

**Resource survey**
Survey to identify local resources which may be mobilised. Will include people, organisations, finance, equipment and so on.
☞ *Neighbourhood skills survey.*

**Risk assessment**
Examination of risks from disasters existing in any community. The basis for risk reduction. Comprises three components: Hazard analysis; vulnerability analysis; resource assessment. ☞ **A-Z** *p112*.

**Roadshow**
Series of linked public workshops, exhibitions and public forums to explore the potential for improving the built environment and provide a catalyst for action.
☞ **A-Z** *p114*.

**Role play**
Adopting the role of others and acting out scenarios. Used to help people understand the views and aspirations of others.
☞ *Gaming.*

**Round table workshop**
Workshop process for engaging the main stakeholders in generating a vision and strategy for an area. Often used for consensus building between previously antagonistic parties.
⊘ *Participation Works!*
✉ Urbed.

**Rural rapid appraisal (RRA)**
➡ *Participatory appraisal.*
Similar approach in rural areas.

**Scoping**
Preliminary exploration of a subject or project.

**Search conference**
Conference or workshop for key interested parties organised as a first stage in a consultation process on a project. May include briefings, role play, reconnaissance, interactive displays, workshops and plenary sessions. Term much used in Australia. Similar to *planning day* or *community planning forum*.
⊘ *Community Participation in Practice.*

**Seasonal calendar**
Chart showing a community's work and social activities month by month to highlight problems or concerns about such things as livelihood, health and community relations.
☞ *Community profiling.*

**Secondary co-operative**
Organisation which provides services, such as technical aid, to a co-operative which is also owned and managed by that co-operative.
☞ *Co-operative. Housing co-operative.*

## Secondary data
Indirect information sources; files, reports, maps, photos, books and so on.

## Secondary data review
Collection and analysis of published and unpublished material such as maps, reports, census statistics and newspaper clippings. Normally done prior to field work.

## Self-build
Construction (or repair) work physically undertaken directly by future (or present) occupiers on an individual or collective basis.

## Self-help
Where people take responsibility, individually or collectively, for solving their problems.

## Self-management
Where a facility is managed by the people who use it.

## Self-sufficiency
Reduction of dependence on others, making devolution of control easier and encouraging self-reliance.

## Seminar
Meeting or workshop with educational slant.

## Semi-structured interview
Conversational open discussion with local inhabitants to understand their needs, problems and aspirations. Uses a checklist of questions as a flexible guide in contrast to a formal questionnaire. Different types include; individual, group, focus group, and key informant.  ☞ *Interview.*

## Serendipity
Making happy discoveries by accident.

## Shared presentation
Presentation by a group or several individuals.

## Shell housing
Construction system where only floors, walls, roofs and services are provided, leaving occupiers free to build their own interiors.

## Short-life housing
Use of empty property on a temporary basis, usually by a voluntary organization.

## Simulation
Acting out an event or activity as a way of gaining information and insights prior to formulating plans.
☞ **A-Z** *p116.*

## Site and services
Provision of a serviced site for self-builders. Usually by government, but increasingly also by the private sector.

## Skills survey
Assessment of skills and talent. Often done in a neighbourhood to establish what the community can do for itself and what extra help is needed. Also known as a *skills audit* or *skills inventory.*
☞ *Neighbourhood skills survey.*

## Slide show
Presentation based on projecting images from transparencies. Widely used in workshops as they can be prepared and presented by participants (more easily than video) and enable people to present visual information to groups (if the projector doesn't break down!).

## Small group discussion
➡ *Small group work*

## Small group work
People working together in small groups of 8 – 15. Term used to cover a range of similar methods such as workshops and focus groups which enable people to discuss, evaluate, learn and plan together. Group work can be formal or informal, one-off or regular, topic related or wide-ranging.

## Social architecture
Similar concept to *community architecture.* Term commonly used in the United States.
☞ *Community architecture.*

## Social audit
Tool to help an organisation understand, measure and report upon its social performance through the eyes of its stakeholders. Over time, the approach can be used to help an organisation improve its social performance.
✉ *New Economics Foundation.*

## Social capital
Ability of social structures and institutions to provide a supportive framework for individuals; includes firms, trade unions, families, communities, voluntary organisations, legal/political systems, educational institutions, health services, financial institutions and systems of property rights.
☞ *Human capital.*

## Social entrepreneur
Person who makes things happen by taking initiative in the interests of his or her community rather than for private or personal gain.

### Social survey
Survey to find out about the nature of a community. May cover aspects like age, gender, wealth, health and so on. ☞ *Survey.*

### Special projects group
Non-statutory group formed to undertake a particular project. ☞ *User group.*

### Squatting
Unlawful occupation of land or housing.

### Staffed exhibition
Exhibition where organisers are present to engage in discussion. ☞ *Interactive exhibition. Open house event.*

### Stakeholder
Person or organisation with an interest because they will be affected or may have some influence.

### Steering group
Informal group set up to pursue a project or goal. ☞ *User group.*

### Stick
Metaphor for control. 'Handing over the stick' is a much used term to mean the experts or facilitator handing over the chalk, pen or microphone to enable local people to become the analysts, planners and facilitators of their own situation.

### Storefront studio
Community design office located in a prominent shop, often temporarily for an action planning event or 'charrette'. Term used in the USA.

### Story-telling
Verbal recounting of tales which may be actual or mythical. Used to understand local values, standards, practices and relationships. Particularly valuable with children and people who are illiterate. Also the singing of local songs and reciting of poetry. Performance sets off discussion to explain local knowledge and beliefs.

### Strategic planning
Organised effort to produce decisions and actions that shape and guide what a community is, what it does, and why it does it.

### Street party
Party for the whole community held in the street. Often organised to galvanise regeneration initiatives.

### Street stall
Way of securing public comment on planning issues by setting up an interactive exhibition in a public street or square. ☞ **A-Z** *p118.*

### Street survey
Survey carried out by stopping people in a street or shopping centre. Used for securing views of people using a place (rather than necessarily living or working there). ☞ *Survey.*

### Study day
Day spent examining a particular issue. Similar to a *planning day* but less structured. Useful for simple issues. ☞ *Planning day.*

### Subsidiarity
Maximum local autonomy.

### Suggestions box
Box in which people place their written suggestions or comments on a place or proposals. Useful device in consultation allowing participants to remain anonymous if they wish.

### Supports and infill
Concept of design, management and construction which aims to distinguish between individual and collective areas of responsibility. Developed at the Stichting Architecten Research in the Netherlands.

### Surgery
➡ *Design surgery.*

### Survey
Systematic gathering of information. ☞ *Opinion survey. Questionnaire survey. Resource survey. Social survey. Street survey.*

### Sustainable community
Community that lives in harmony with its local environment and does not cause damage to distant environments or other communities – now or in the future. Quality of life and the interest of future generations are valued above immediate material consumption and economic growth.

### Sustainable development
Development that meets the needs of the present without compromising the ability of future generations to meet their own needs (Brundtland Report definition).

## Sweat equity
Where an individual or community acquires an asset by expending labour rather than money.

## SWOT analysis
Determination of the Strengths, Weaknesses, Opportunities and Threats relating to an organisation or activity.

## Table scheme display
Simple way of securing comment on design proposals by taping drawings on a table top and requesting people to vote with sticky dots.
☞ **A-Z** *p120*.

## Talent survey
➡ *Skills survey*.

## Task Force
Multidisciplinary team of students and professionals who produce in-depth proposals for a site or neighbourhood based on an intensive programme of site studies, lectures, participatory exercises and studio working, normally lasting several weeks.
☞ **A-Z** *p122*.

## Team-building
Learning to work together as a group by getting to know each other and developing shared aims, values and working practices.

## Technology of participation
A framework of practical methods that help facilitators working with groups. Term used by the Institute of Cultural Affairs. Includes Discussion method, Workshop method and Action Planning method.
✉ *Institute of Cultural Affairs*.

## Temporal snapshot
Finding out how spaces are used at different times of day and night.

## Tenant management organisation (TMO)
Organisation set up to allow housing tenants to participate in the management of their homes.

## Think tank
Brainstorming group. Increasingly used by governments and city authorities. Often for 'experts' only. May use an action planning format. Sometimes called an *expert panel* or *symposium*.

## Third wave
Revolution currently transforming society based on growth of high technology and information systems. The first wave was the agricultural revolution, the second the industrial revolution.

## Time-line
Line calibrated to show a historical sequence of events or activities. ☞ *Diagrams. Historical profiling.*

## Time money
Alternative currency which credits the time people spend helping each other. Participants earn credit for doing jobs – an hour of your time entitles you to an hour of someone else's time. Credits are deposited centrally in a 'time bank' and withdrawn when the participant needs help themselves. ✉ *New Economics Foundation*.

## Time-use analysis
Assessment of time spent on various activities, on a daily or seasonal basis.

## Top-down
Term used to refer to initiatives led by the authorities as opposed to 'bottom up' initiatives led by the community.

## Topic workshop
Workshop session on a particular topic.
☞ *Workshop*.

## Town centre manager
Person employed to improve town centres by working with all interested parties and taking initiatives.

## Town development trust
Organisation created by a local urban community to revitalise that community's physical surroundings.
☞ *Development trust*.

## Town workshop
Workshop organised on the future of a town.

## Trail
Carefully planned walk through an area designed to help people understand the problems and opportunities. Designed to be walked unaccompanied.
☞ *Reconnaissance trip*.

## Transect walk
Systematic walk along a pre-determined route through an area to gather information about such things as land-use, social and economic resources or the state of the environment. Usually done by community members with facilitators or technical experts. Information is subsequently recorded on maps and as text.
☞ *Reconnaissance trip*.

**Treasure hunt**
Trail designed with the added incentive of prizes for the correct answers to questions about things seen on route. Useful warm up to a community planning event, generating interest and getting people to look closely at the physical nature of an area. ☞ *Trail.*

**Trust**
Term used in the name of an organisation, usually implying that it has charitable objectives. Also used to mean 'have confidence in'.

**Urban aid**
Government funding intended for community development in urban areas.

**Urban community assistance team**
➡ *Design assistance team.*

**Urban design**
Discipline concerned with three-dimensional built form and the ecology of streets, neighbourhoods and cities.

**Urban design action team**
➡ *Design assistance team.*

**Urban design assistance team**
➡ *Design assistance team.*

**Urban design game**
Role-play game designed to help people to understand the planning process and the views of others by simulating future scenarios. ☞ *Gaming.*

**Urban design studio**
Unit attached to an architecture or planning school which focuses on involving local communities in live project work. ☞ **A-Z** *p124.*

**Urban design workshop**
➡ *Design workshop.*

**Urban farm**
➡ *City farm.*

**Urban laboratory**
➡ *Urban design studio.*

**Urban resource centre**
Local or regional centres aiming to co-ordinate training in cross-professional skills and disseminate best practice and innovation in regeneration and community planning.

**Urban studies centre**
Centre of environmental education, usually focusing on the immediate surroundings. ☞ *Architecture centre. Environmental education.*

**Urban village**
Mixed use development. Term used successfully to promote the idea that urban areas are more popular when they are diverse and lively rather than dominated by single uses as mostly preferred by developers and planners.

**User**
Actual or future occupier of a building or neighbourhood or beneficiary of a service. ☞ *User-client.*

**User-client**
People who are the end-users of buildings and are treated as the client, even if they are not technically responsible for paying the bills.

**User group**
Group of actual or future occupiers of a building or neighbourhood or beneficiary of a service. ☞ **A-Z** *p126.*

**Venn diagram**
Diagram using circles of different sizes to indicate roles of different organisations and the relationships between them. Used for analysing institutional and social networks. ☞ *Diagrams.*

**Vernacular architecture**
Architecture of and by the people and rooted in a particular locality.

**Video box**
Use of video to help people express and communicate ideas and opinions. Used for presentation or as a discussion tool. Particularly useful for young people. ☞ *Video soapbox.*

**Video soapbox**
Use of large screens in public locations to project people expressing ideas and opinions. ☞ **A-Z** *p128.* ☞ *Video box.*

**Village appraisal**
➡ *Community appraisal.*

**Village design day**
Day when people work intensively on developing ideas for their village. ☞ *Planning day.*

**Village design statement**
Local design statement produced by a village community. ☞ *Local design statement.*

**Vision**
An image of how things might be in the future. May be in words or pictures. Provide useful guide for developing project and programme priorities. 'Having vision' implies being imaginative. ☞ *Visioning.*

## Vision fair
Event where people vote on their favourite visions. Vision statements or images, usually from a previous workshop or brainstorm, are exhibited. People use sticky dots or other means to indicate which visions they would like to pursue. They may also make personal · pledges to take action. ☞ *Choices method. Vision.*

## Visioning
Thinking about what the future could be and creating a vision. ☞ *Community visioning. Vision.*

## Visioning conference
➡ *Future search conference.*

## Visit
Trip by a group of people planning an initiative to a community that has recently undertaken a similar initiative, to learn from their experience. May be highly structured with formal notetaking, interviews and feedback sessions, or informal. ☞ *photos p17.*

## Visual simulation
Showing how buildings or townscape will look when constructed using photomontages.

## Voluntary sector
Organizations controlled by people who are unpaid, and usually elected, but do not form part of statutory government. Range from national to local organizations. Increasingly the divisions between the public, private and voluntary sectors are becoming blurred.

## Vulnerability
Extent to which a community, structure or service is likely to be damaged or disrupted by a disaster. ☞ *Disaster.*

## Vulnerability analysis
Identification of what and who is vulnerable to disaster and the extent of that vulnerability. ☞ *Disaster.*

## Vulnerability and capacity analysis
Method based on a matrix chart for organising information about a community's vulnerability to, and capacity to withstand, the effects of extreme events such as natural disasters. ☞ *p112-113.*

## Wealth ranking
➡ *Well-being ranking.*

## Web site
Space on the Internet. Immense potential for providing sites with information, discussion groups and interactive material on community planning projects. ☞ *websites listed in Contacts section starting on p209 for some examples.*

## Well-being ranking
Assessment of well-being of different households, usually using pile-sorting technique. Also known as *wealth ranking*. ☞ *Community profiling.*

## Wheel of fortune
Graphic way for people to collectively rank competing priorities. ☞ *p105.*

## Wish poem
Poem made up by combining wishes of participants at a workshop.

## Working community
➡ *Managed workspace.*

## Working group
Small number of individuals with a specific task to complete.

## Working party
➡ *Working group.*

## Workshop
Meeting at which a small group, perhaps aided by a facilitator, explores issues, develops ideas and makes decisions. A less formal and more creative counterpart to a public meeting or committee. A *topic workshop* focuses on specific issues. A *design workshop* includes the use of participatory design techniques. ☞ *Briefing workshop. Design workshop. Public meeting. Seminar. Topic workshop.*

## Youth planning day
Day of activities designed specifically to involve young people in the planning process. ☞ *Planning day.*

# Publications and film A–Z

An annotated selection of
useful material. In
alphabetical order by title.

## Information listed

- **Title**
- Medium
  - 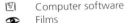 Books
  - 🖳 Computer software
  - 👁 Films
  - ☼ Packs
  - § Leaflets
  - ¶ Magazines
  - ✖ Posters & wall charts
  -  Reports & booklets
- *Subtitle*
- Author/editor/director
- Publisher
- Date of latest edition
- ISBN number
- Annotation
- Languages available other
  than English
- (Where to obtain if non-
  standard publisher and
  publisher not listed in
  *Contacts A-Z p210*).

---

### Website updates
www.wates.demon.co.uk
For latest listing.

### New material
If you know of material which
should be listed on the website
and in future editions, please
send review copies. Address
page 221.

If you have difficulties getting
hold of material, let us know.

---

**4B**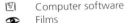
*Project development, monitoring
and evaluation in disaster
situations*, Merdi Jean Arcilla et al
(eds), Citizens' Disaster Response
Center, 1998, 971-9031-00-X.
Handy local guide with useful
methods produced in the Philippines.
(Centre for Disaster Preparedness.)

**Action Planning**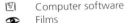
*How to use planning weekends and
urban design action teams to
improve your environment*, Nick
Wates, Prince of Wales's Institute of
Architecture, 1996, 1-898465-11-8.
Illustrated how-to-do-it handbook.
Also in Chinese, German, Czech.
(The Prince's Foundation.)

**Action Planning for Cities**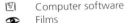
*A guide to community practice*,
Nabeel Hamdi and Reinhard
Goethert, John Wiley & Sons, 1997,
0-471-96928-1.
Well illustrated textbook on the
theory and practice of community
planning in developing countries.

**At Risk**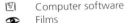
*Natural hazards, people's
vulnerability and disasters*,
Piers Blaikie, Terry Cannon, Ian
Davis and Ben Wisner, Routledge,
1994, 0-415-08477-2.
Comprehensive explanation of why
a people-first approach is essential
and how to initiate it.

**Brick by Brick**
*How to develop a community
building*, English Partnerships, 1997.
Guide for organisations wanting to
build or refurbish property for
community use.

**Building Democracy**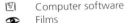
*Community architecture in the
inner cities*, Graham Towers, UCL
Press, 1995, 1-85728-089-X.
Detailed account of the development
of community architecture with
some UK case studies.

**Building Design Pack** ☼
Neighbourhood Initiatives
Foundation. Regularly updated.
Provides the materials for a group
to make an adaptable 3-dimensional
model of an existing or new building.

**Building Homes People Want**
*A guide to tenant involvement in
the design and development of
housing association homes*,
Pete Duncan and Bill Halsall,
National Housing Federation, 1994,
0-86297-272-8.
Useful guide by and for practitioners.
(NHF, 175 Gray's Inn Rd, London
WC1X 8UP, UK
Tel: +44 (0)20 7278 6571
Email: info@housing.org.uk.)

**The Change Handbook**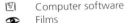
*Group methods for shaping the
future*, Peggy Holman and Tom
Devane, Berrett-Koehler, 1999,
1-57675-058-2.
Guide to 18 change strategies for
tapping human potential in
organisations and communities.

**Changing Places**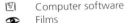
*Children's participation in
environmental planning*, Eileen
Adams & Sue Ingham, The
Children's Society, 1998,
1-899783-00-8.
Practical guide for practitioners and
teachers wishing to involve children
in planning and design.

**Chattanooga** 👁
*A community with a vision*, Anne
Macksoud, Leonardo's Children
Inc., 1993, 25 mins.
Inspiring insight into a city-wide
visioning process which has clearly
achieved extraordinary results. (New
Economics Foundation.)

**Co-design**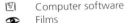
*A process of design participation*,
Stanley King et al, Van Nostrand
Reinhold, 1989, 0-442-23333-7.
Lovely, well illustrated guide to
conducting design workshops, based
on 197 case studies in the USA.

## Cohousing

*A contemporary approach to housing ourselves,* Kathryn McCamant & Charles Durrett, Habitat Press/Ten Speed Press, Berkeley, 1994, 0-89815-306-9. How to develop housing schemes with a strong shared element as pioneered in Denmark.

## Communities Count!

*A step by step guide to community sustainability indicators,* Alex MacGillivray, Candy Weston & Catherine Unsworth, New Economics Foundation, 1998. 1-899407-20-0. Handy guide to using indicators to measure trends that really matter and build an agenda for education and action.

## Community Action Planning

*Plan for Action,* SIGUS Wall Charts, 1998, 22"x 28". Wallchart providing an overview of the main steps in running a microplanning, or community action planning, field workshop. (SIGUS Wall Charts, School of Architecture and Planning, Room N52-357A, Massachusetts Institute of Technology, Cambridge, MA 02139, USA. Email: sigus@mit.edu Fax: +1 617 253 8221.)

## Community & Sustainable Development

*Participation in the future,* Diane Warburton (ed), Earthscan, 1998. 1-85383-531-5. Inspiring collection of writings on the current state of the art.

## Community Architecture

*How people are creating their own environment,* Nick Wates & Charles Knevitt, Penguin, 1987, 0-14-010428-3. Overview of movement for community participation in architecture and planning. Also in Chinese and Japanese. (Text on www.wates.demon.co.uk.)

## Community Design Primer

Randolph T Hester, Ridge Times Press, 1990, 0934203067. Good introduction to community design USA style with do-it-yourself training exercises for the would-be community designer.

## Community Participation in Practice

Wendy Sarkissian, Andrea Cook and Kelvin Walsh, Institute for Science and Technology Policy, Murdoch University. Excellent series of publications and film designed to assist community planning and design work. Comprises:
• *A Practical Guide,* 1997, 0-86905-556-9. Covers a range of useful methods, some pioneered in Australia.
• *The Workshop Checklist,* 1994, 0-869053027. How-to for workshop organisers.
• *Casebook,* 1994, 0-86905-363-9. Describes and illustrates 12 case studies from Australia.
• *Listening to all the voices,* 28 min. video. Shows and debates methods in action.
• *The Community Participation Handbook; Resources for public involvement in the planning process,* 1986, revised 1994, 0-86905-359-0. Practical and theoretical essays by a number of authors. Above items available individually or as a discounted package. (Murdoch University.)

## Community Participation Methods in Design and Planning

Henry Sanoff, Wiley, 2000, 0-471-35545-3. Detailed, well-illustrated guide for professionals and students. Combines theoretical analysis with practical design games and international case study material for a broad range of applications.

## Community Involvement in Planning and Development Processes

Department of the Environment, HMSO, 1994, 0-11-753007-7. Results of a planning research study which demonstrates the value of community participation.

## Community Planning Toolkit

Community Planning Publications, 2000. Selection of original documents from community planning activities: programmes, timetables, leaflets, reports. Useful for inspiration and saves wasting time re-inventing the wheel. (Catalogue from CPP.)

## Community Visions Pack

New Economics Foundation, 1998. Contains how-to on setting up a community visioning exercise, briefings on future search, guided visualisation and participative theatre, and case studies.

## The Connected City

*A new approach to making cities work,* Robert Cowan, Urban Initiatives, 1997, 1-902193-008. Includes checklists for preparing action plans for cities or neighbourhoods. (Urban Initiatives, 35 Heddon Street, London W1R 7LL, UK. Tel: +44 (0)20 7287 3644.)

## Creating a Design Assistance Team for Your Community

American Institute of Architects (AIA), 1996. Guidebook on the AIA's Assistance Team Programme. Particularly useful for organisations wanting to set up their own support systems.

## Development at risk?

*Natural disasters and the third world,* John Twigg (ed), UN International Decade for Natural Disaster Reduction, 1999. Clear, concise explanation of the differences within and between communities from a natural disasters perspective. (Tony Eades, RAE, 29 Great Peter Street, London SW1P 3LW, UK. Tel: +44 (0)20 7222 2688. Email: eadesa@raeng.co.uk. Or on www.gfzpotsdam.de/ewc98/.)

**Disaster Mitigation** ⚒
*A community-based approach.*
Andrew Maskrey, Oxfam, Oxford
1989. 0-85598123-7.
Seminal polemic.

**The Do-ers guide to Planning for Real Exercises** ⚒
Tony Gibson, Neighbourhood
Initiatives Foundation, 1998,
1-902556-06-2.
Nicely illustrated explanation of
Planning for Real.

**Duke Street/Bold Street Planning Weekend** ⚒
John Thompson & Partners for
English Partnerships, 1997.
Good example of a detailed report
of a community planning weekend.
(John Thompson & Partners – reports
of other planning weekends in
Europe also available.)

**Economics of Urban Villages** 📖
Tony Aldous (ed), Urban Villages
Forum, 1995. 0-9519028-1-4.
General guide on the practical
realities of developing urban
villages. (The Prince's Foundation.)

**Effective working with rural communities** 📖
James Derounian, Packard
Publishing, 1998, 1-85341-106-X.
Includes a useful chapter on
community appraisals.

**Future Search** 📖
*An action guide to finding common
ground in organisations and
communities,* Marvin R Weisboard
and Sandra Janoff, Berrett-Koehler,
1995,1-881052-12-5.
Good step-by-step guide to running
future search conferences.

**From Place to Place** 📖
*Maps and parish maps,* Sue Clifford
and Angela King (eds), Common
Ground, 1996. 1-870-364-163.
The background and experience of
parish mapping with contributions
from several authors.

**The Good, the Bad and the Ugly** 📖
*Cities in crisis,* Rod Hackney, Frederick
Muller, 1990. 0-09-173939-X.
Inspiring personal account of a
crusade to help people shape their
own environments by a pioneering
community architect.

**Good Practice Guide to Community Planning and Development** 📖
Michael Parkes, London Planning
Advisory Committee, 1995.
Detailed guide with case studies by
a seasoned practitioner.
(LPAC, Artillery House, Artillery
Row, London SW1P 1RT, UK.
Tel: +44 (0)20 7222 2244.)

**The Guide to Effective Participation** ⚒
David Wilcox, Partnership Books,
1994, 1-870298-00-4.
Overview of general participation
methods. (David Wilcox, 1/43
Bartholomew Close, London EC1, UK
Email: david@communities.org.uk.
Also on www.partnerships.org.uk.)

**The Guide to Development Trusts and Partnerships** 📖
David Wilcox, Development Trusts
Association, 1998. 0-9531469-0-3.
Handbook aimed particularly at
those setting up trusts. (Full text
also on www.partnerships.org.uk.)

**Guiding urban design series** 👁
*Three-part video on urban design,*
Tony Costello, Martin Cramton Jr,
Bruce Race and Nore Winter,
American Institute of Certified
Planners, American Planning
Association Bookstore, 1994. 312-
955-9100. Total of 6 hours videos
entitled: Community-decision
making; Understanding design
context; Design implementation.

**Here to Stay** ⚒
*A public policy framework for
community-based organisations,*
Caroline Davies (ed), Development
Trusts Association, 1997.
0-9531469-0-1.
Review of development trusts
movement in the UK and policies
necessary for developing it further.

**Housing by people** 📖
Towards autonomy in building
environments, John F C Turner,
Marion Boyars, 1976,
0-7145-2569-3.
Seminal work on housing, drawing
on experience in developing
countries to illustrate the universal
necessity for dweller control.

**Hucknall 20/20 Vision Conference** 👁
Audio Visual Arts, 1997.
Case study of a future search
conference in the UK. Useful
introduction and insight into the
process, 12 minutes (from New
Economics Foundation).

**Ideas Annuals** 📖
*Innovative ideas and examples of
successful community work
practice,* Community Links, 1997 &
1998 available.
Excellent illustrated series aimed at
community organisations.

**Imagine Chicago** 👁
David Szabo, Imagine Chicago, 1998.
Inspiring case study on a project
based on future search and
appreciative inquiry. 15 mins.
(from New Economics Foundation).

**Innovations in Public Participation** ⚒
Jane Morris (ed), IDeA, 1996.
0-7488-9599-X.
Brief but illuminating introduction
to mechanisms for increasing
citizen involvement including
citizens juries, study circles, citizens
panels, teledemocracy, focus
groups, techniques for workshops
and resolving conflicts, future
search and visioning (IDeA, Layden
House, 76-86 Turnmill Street,
London EC1M 5QU, UK.
Tel: +44 (0)20 7296 6600).

**Involving communities in urban and rural regeneration** ⚒
*A guide for practitioners,* Pieda plc,
Department of the Environment,
1995, 1-85112201-X.
Useful overview on general
approaches with handy checklists
and summaries.

### Involving Citizens in Community Decision Making
*A Guidebook,* James L Creighton, Program for Community Problem Solving, 1997.
Very clear and easy guide for local government staff in designing, developing and managing citizen participation programs, based on original version commissioned for the City of Glendale, California. (915 15th Street, NW., Suite 601, Washington DC 20005, USA.)

### Large Group Interventions
*Engaging the entire organisation for rapid change,* Barbara Benedict Bunker and Billie T Alban, Jossey-Bass, 1997, 0-7879-0324-8.
Practical guide to some of the many ways of involving everybody in improving whole systems.

### The Linz Cafe
Christopher Alexander, Oxford University Press, 1981. 0-19520-263-5.
*Beautiful account of the design and construction of an Austrian cafe based on user participation.*

### Making Cities Better
*Visions and implementation,* Ziona Strelitz, George Henderson and Robert Cowan (eds), Vision for Cities, De Montfort University, 1996. 0-9527500-0-7.
Report on a series of 20 Vision for Cities workshops in the mid 1990s. (Department of Architecture, De Montfort University, The Gateway, Leicester LE1 9BH, UK.)

### Making Places
EDAW Consultants, English Partnerships, 1998.
Guide to good practice in mixed development schemes. (The Prince's Foundation.)

### Managing Partnerships
*Tools for mobilising the public sector, business and civil society as partners in development,* Ros Tennyson, Prince of Wales Business Leaders Forum, 1998. 1-899159-84-3.
Excellent how-to on partnerships crammed with useful checklists, tips and sample documents.

### Measuring Community Development in Northern Ireland
Voluntary Activity Unit, Northern Ireland Department of Health and Social Services, 1996.
Handbook for practitioners, including set of indicators grouped into two clusters: community empowerment, and change in the quality of community life. (VAU, CDP, DHSS, Dundonald House, Upper Newtownards Road, Belfast BT4 3SF, UK.)

### Open space technology
*A user's guide,* Harrison Owen, Abbott Publishing, 1992. 0-9618205-3-5.
Step-by-step journey through the open space workshop method.

### The Oregon experiment
Christopher Alexander et al, Oxford University University Press, 1975. 0-19-501824-9.
Classic account of the planning process for the University of Oregon where the entire community of 15,000 were involved in the planning and design.

### Parish maps
Common Ground, 1996. Why and how to make a parish map, with Illustrated examples.

### Participation Works!
*Twenty-one techniques of community participation for the twenty-first century,* Julie Lewis, Catherine Unsworth and Perry Walker (eds), New Economics Foundation, 1998. 1-899407-17-0.
Useful standard summary profiles on a varied range of general participation methods.

### Participatory Action in the Countryside
*A literature review,* Diane Warburton, Countryside Agency, 1998.
Useful annotated listing.

### Participatory Design
*Theory and techniques,* Henry Sanoff (ed), North Carolina State University, 1990, 0-9622107-3-0.
Rich compendium of interesting theoretical and practical material, particularly from USA experience.

### Participatory Learning and Action
*A trainer's guide,* Jules Pretty, Irene Guijt, John Thompson and Ian Scoones, International Institute for Environment and Development, 1995, 1-899825-00-2.
Excellent handbook for trainers involved in using participatory methods.

### A Pattern Language
Christopher Alexander et al., Oxford University Press, 1977, 0-19501-919-9.
Influential book describing working method enabling untrained people to design any part of the environment themselves; homes, streets, neighbourhoods.

### The Permaculture Teachers Handbook
Andrew Goldring (ed), WWF-UK, 2000, 1-85850-168-7.
Explains how to run permaculture design courses.

### PLA Notes
Published three times a year by the Sustainable Agriculture and Rural Livelihoods Programme of the International Institute of Environment and Development. Frank exchange of experience and views on participatory learning and action, by and for practitioners in the field. ( IIED.)

### Plan, Design and Build
*21st Century Halls for England,* Alan Wilkinson, Action with Communities in Rural England (ACRE) 1997, 1-871157-48-X.
Excellent how-to-do-it on creating community centres including community involvement.

**Plan for Action** 👁
The Mount Wise Community Action Planning event, 1999. Case study. Useful introduction and insight into the process, 25 minutes (from Mount Wise Action Planning).

**Planning for Real Community Pack** ☼
Neighbourhood Initiatives Foundation. Revised 1999. Provides the materials for a group to make an adaptable 3-dimensional model of an existing or new neighbourhood.

**Planning for Real – the video** 👁
Neighbourhood Initiatives Foundation, 1997, 17 mins. Good insight into the origins and value of Planning for Real including two case studies.

**The Power in our Hands** ✍
Neighbourhood-based world-shaking, Tony Gibson, Jon Carpenter Publishing, 1996, 1-897766-28-9.
Powerful account of ordinary people doing extraordinary things all over the world.

**Projects with People** ✍
The practice of participation in rural development, Peter Oakley et al., ILO (IT Publications), 1991. 922-107-2827.
Comprehensive analysis based on international experience over several decades. Especially good on rationale, benefits and practical problems and how to overcome them. Excellent summaries and tables.

**Real Time Strategic Change** ✍
Robert Jacobs, Berrett-Kohler, 1994, 1-881052-45-1.
How-to on this participatory approach to enterprise management.

**Rising from the Ashes** ✍
Development strategies in times of disaster, Mary B Anderson and Peter J Woodrow. Intermediate Technology Publications, 1998 (reissue), 1-85339-439-4.
Explains capacities and vulnerabilities analysis and how to apply it to projects.

**Recycling Streets Workshops** §
Jack Sidener. Nicely illustrated leaflet providing a guide to staging a neighbourhood improvement workshop. (Chinese University of Hong Kong, attn. Jack Sidener. Free, send self-addressed envelope.)

**Reducing Risk** ✍
Participatory learning activities for disaster mitigation in southern Africa, Astrid von Kotze and Ailsa Holloway, University of Natal, South Africa and International Federation of Red Cross, Geneva, 1997. 0-85598-347-7.
Reference material and ideas for participatory training/learning exercises for field workers involved in community-based disaster mitigation.

**Reducing Urban Risk** ☼
CD and action planning help-cards for project facilitators on how to reduce urban risk at community level, based on research and projects in India. (Centre for Development and Emergency Practice.)

**The Scope of Social Architecture** ✍
Richard Hatch, Van Nostrand Reinhold, 1984. 0-442-26153-5.
Fascinating and detailed case studies of community architecture and planning projects from twelve countries, mostly in the developed world. Range from housing projects to replanning entire cities.

**The Self-Build Book** ✍
How to enjoy designing and building your own home, Jon Broome and Brian Richardson, Green Books,1995, 1-900322-00-5.
Clear explanation of a variety of self-build techniques including the timber frame method evolved by the architect Walter Segal.

**Small is Bankable** ✍
Community reinvestment in the UK, Ed Mayo et al., New Economics Foundation, 1998, 1-85935-047-X.
Guide to a range of community finance initiatives which can help build financially sustainable regeneration.

**Streetwise** ¶
Magazine which often covers community planning issues. Contact Places for People for an index.

**Taking Power** ✍
An agenda for community economic renewal, Ed Mayo, Stephen Thake and Tony Gibson, New Economics Foundation, 1998, 1-899407-14-6.
Provocative paper on how to build on the work of people at community level to rebuild society neighbourhood by neighbourhood.

**The Thin Book of Appreciative Inquiry** ⚒
Sue Annis Hammond, Kodiak Consulting, 1998, 0-9665373-1-9. Handy introduction to this technique. (Appreciative Inquiry Group.)

**Tenant Participation in Housing Design** ⚒
A guide for action, Royal Institute of British Architects and the Institute of Housing, RIBA Publications, 1988. 0-947877-02-9.
Simple, practical advice aimed mainly at development professionals and housing managers.

### Unleashing the Potential 🔨
*Bringing residents to the centre of regeneration,* Marilyn Taylor, Joseph Rowntree Foundation, 1995. 1-85935-014-3.
Draws lessons from 33 studies from the Foundation's Action on Estates programme. Covers many different aspects of community involvement and ways of developing a more central role for residents in the regeneration of estates. Useful for principles and examples.

### Urban Design in Action 📖
*The history, theory and development of the American Institute of Architects' Regional/Urban Design Assistance Teams Program (R/UDAT),* Peter Batchelor and David Lewis, North Carolina State University School of Design and the American Institute of Architects, 1985. 0-913962-80-5. Classic work on the development of action planning in the USA.

### Urban Projects Manual 📖
*A guide to preparing upgrading and new development projects accessible to low income groups,* Forbes Davidson and Geoff Payne (eds), Liverpool University Press, 1986, revised 1999, 0-85323-484-1. Well illustrated guide based on field experience, mainly in Egypt.

### Urban Villages 📖
*A concept for creating mixed-use urban development on a sustainable scale,* Urban Villages Forum, 1997. 0-9519028-0-6. Housebuilders, funders, planners and developers make the case for a more people-friendly approach to mixed-use sustainable development (The Prince's Foundation.)

### User Participation in Building Design and Management 📖
David Kernohan, John Gray, John Daish, Butterworth-Heinneman, 1996, 0-7506-2888-X. Useful how-to-do-it on participatory evaluations of buildings after they have been erected. Well-thought through process. Good drawings.

### Village Appraisals Software for Windows 💻
Questionnaire generation and analysis programme for undertaking village, parish or community appraisals. Easy to use. IBM compatible. £50. (from Countryside & Community Unit, Cheltenham & Gloucester College of Higher Education, Francis Close Hall, Swindon Road, Cheltenham GL50 4AZ, UK. Tel: 01242-544083).

### Village design ☀
*Making local character count in new development,* Countryside Commission UK, 1996, CCP 501 (Part 1).
Excellent guidance pack explaining how to produce village design statements. Contains handbooks plus two examples.
(CC Postal Sales, PO Box 124, Walgrave, Northampton NN6 9TL, UK. Tel: +1 (0)1604 781848.)

### Village views 👁
*Making local character count in new development,* Eye to Eye for the Countryside Commission UK, 1996, CCV 05.
Useful introduction to local design statements based on the UK village context. 10 mins.
(CC Postal Sales, PO Box 124, Walgrave, Northampton NN6 9TL, UK. Tel: +44 (0)1604 781848.)

### A Vision of Britain 📖
*A personal view of architecture,* HRH The Prince of Wales, Doubleday, 1989. 0-385-26903-X. Inspiring statement of the Prince's influential approach to architecture including Ten Principles for creating humane environments.

### Viterbo; Santa Maria in Gradi 📖
Brian Hanson and Liam O'Connor (eds), Union Printing Edizioni, Viterbo, 1994. 1-898465-09-6. Fully illustrated account of an urban design task force in Italy. Also in Italian. (The Prince's Foundation.)

### The Weller Way 📖
*The story of the Weller Streets housing cooperative,* Alan McDonald for the Weller Streets, Faber and Faber, 1986, 0-571-13963-9. Lively blow-by-blow narrative of how 61 working-class families battled tirelessly to build Liverpool's first new-build housing co-operative.

### The What, How and Why of Neighbourhood Community Development 🔨
Christine Flecknoe and Neil McLellan, Community Matters, 1994. Explains what community development is, the values it reflects and what it can achieve in a neighbourhood, and offers simple models for evaluating those achievements. Excellent, short, easy to read.

### When we build again 📖
*Let's have housing that works,* Colin Ward, Pluto Press, 1985. 0-74530-022-7. Very readable summary on how paternalistic government housing policies should be transformed to enable people to house themselves.

### Whose Reality Counts? 📖
*Putting the first last,* Robert Chambers, Intermediate Technology Publications, 1997, 1-85339-386-X. State of the art treatise on Participatory Rapid Appraisal (PRA).

### Your Place and Mine 🔨
*Reinventing planning.* Town & Country Planning Association, 1999. 0-902797-33-6. Proposals for restructuring the planning system incorporating a community planning approach.

### Youth Planning Charrettes 📖
*A manual for planners, teachers and youth advocates,* Bruce Race and Carolyn Torma, American Planning Association,1998. Written as a resource for planners and educators working with young people. Gives advice on how to design an informed and interactive process.

**Groundwork**
85/87 Cornwall Street, Birmingham
B3 3BY, UK
**t** +44 (0)121 236 8565 **f** 236 7356
**e** info@groundwork.org.uk
**w** www.groundwork.org.uk
UK network of local trusts working
through partnership to improve the
quality of life in deprived areas.
Sister organisations in Japan and USA.
Useful publications and videos.

**Habitat Budapest Office**
VATI Magyar Regionalis Fejlesztesi
Urbanisztikai KHT, Gellerthegy u.30-
32, 1016 Budapest PF 2011253,
Hungary
**t** +361 375 5691 **f** 356 8003
Contact: Nora Horcher.
Useful regional contact point.

**Habitat International Coalition**
PO Box 34519, Groote-Schuur
7937, Cape Town, South Africa
**t** +27 21 696 2205 **f** 696 2203
**e** hic@mweb.co.za
**w** http://home.mweb.co.za/hi/hic/
Global forum for NGOs concerned
with human settlements.

**Hackney Building Exploratory**
Queensbridge Building, Albion
Drive, London E8 4ET, UK
**t/f** +44 (0)20 7275 8555
**e** building.exploratory@virgin.net
Architecture centre developing
innovatory display techniques.

**Hastings Trust**
35 Robertson Street, Hastings TN34
1HT, UK
**t** +44 (0)1424 446373 **f** 434206
**e** post@htgate.demon.co.uk
**w** www.hastingstrust.co.uk
Local development trust. Building
an international database on Tools
for Community Regeneration.

**Hertfordshire County Council**
Environment Department, County
Hall, Pegs Lane, Hertford SG13
8DN, UK
**t** +44 (0) 1992 555231 **f** 555251
Contact: David Hughes.
Experience of using future search to
develop whole settlement strategies.

**HUD USER**
P.O. Box 6091, Rockville, MD
20849, USA
**t** +1 800 245 2691 **f** 301 519 5767
**e** huduser@aspensys.com
**w** www.huduser.org/
Government department for USA.
Information and publications.

**Imagine Chicago**
35 East Wacker Drive, Suite 1522,
Chicago, Illinois 60601, USA
**t** +1 312 444 1913 **f** 444 9243
**e** bbrowne@teacher.depaul.edu
**w** www.imaginechicago.org
Contact: Bliss Brown.
Innovative project helping people
develop their imagination as city
creators, based on future search
and appreciative inquiry methods.
Resource materials available.

**Institute of Cultural Affairs**
Rue Amedee Lynen 8, B-1210
Brussels, Belgium
**t** +32 (0)2 219 00 87 **f** 219 04 06
**e** icai@linkline.be
**w** www.icaworld.org
Global network of private, non-
profit organisations concerned with
the human factor in world
development. Runs courses based
on its Technology of Participation
(ToP) methodology.

**Institute of Development
Studies, Brighton**
University of Sussex, Brighton BN1
9RE, UK
**t** +44 (0)1273 877263 **f** 621202
**e** participation@ids.ac.uk
**w** www.ids.ac.uk/ids/particip
A Participation Group produces
regular newsletter and website on
participatory approaches with
useful bibliographies, contacts and
listings of events around the world.

**Intermediate Technology
Publications**
103-105 Southampton Row,
London WC1B 4HH, UK
**t** +44 (0)20 7436 9761 **f** 7436 2013
**e** orders@itpubs.org.uk
**w** www.oneworld.org/itdg/
publications.html
Publishing arm of the Intermediate
Technology Development Group.
Material on all aspects of development
and appropriate technology
including community participation.

**The International Association of
Public Participation Practitioners**
IAP3 Headquarters, PO Box 82317,
Portland, Oregon 97282, USA
**t** 503 236 6630 **f** 233 0772
**w** www.journalism.wisc.edu/cpn/se
ctions/affiliates/iap3.html
Non-projit corporation aiming to
allow practitioners throughout the
world to exchange good practice.

**International Institute for
Environment and Development**
3 Endsleigh Street, London WC1H
0DD, UK
**t** +44 (0)20 7388 2117 **f** 7388 2826
**e** mailbox@iied.org **w** www.iied.org
Independent organisation
promoting sustainable world
development. Its Resource Centre
for Participatory Learning and
Action has over 2000 documents
covering most participatory
approaches, focusing primarily on
Africa, Asia and South America.

**Isabel Val de Flor**
Architecture, Urbanisme, Ecologie
Urbaine, 91 Route de Carrieres,
78400 Chatou, France
**t/f** +33 (0) 39 52 96 08
Architect and urbanist promoting
community participation and
ecology. Useful regional contact.

**Jigso**
1 North Parade, Aberystwyth,
Ceredigion SY23 2JH, Wales, UK
**t** +44 (0)1970 623255 **f** 639033
**e** post@jigso.org **w** www.jigso.org
Information on community
participation methods for Wales.
Useful publications and info sheets.
Good web site.

### John Thompson & Partners
77 Cowcross Street, London EC1M 6EJ, UK
**t** +44 (0)20 7251 5135 **f** 7251 5136
**e** jtplon@jtp.co.uk
**w** www.jtp.co.uk
Contact: John Thompson.
Architects, urban designers and community planners with much experience of participatory and action planning methods in the UK and Europe.

### Kala Karthikeyan, Community Educator
C 1/1, Humayun Road, New Delhi 110003, India
**t** +91 11 4632818 & 4632919
**e** karthi@bol.net.in
Useful regional contact point.

### Kobe University
Department of Architecture and Civil Engineering, Rokkodai Nada, Kobe 657-0013, Japan
**t/f** +81 (0)78 803 6039
**e** shiozaki@kobe-u.ac.jp
Contact: Yoshimitsu Shiozaki.
Research and practical experience in community architecture and planning in Japan including disaster reconstruction.

### The Local Futures Group
5 Southampton Place, London WC1A 2DA, UK
**e** mark.hepworth@lfg.co.uk
**w** www.lfg.co.uk
Contacts: Mark Hepworth, Ian Christie.
Specialises in regeneration based on 'joined up' policies and private–public partnerships. Relationship marketing for companies through focus groups, workshops and use of local knowledge databases. Futures analysis of social, economic, political and cultural trends.

### Massachusetts Institute of Technology
Department of Architecture, 77 Mass Avenue, Cambridge, Mass 02130, USA
**t** +1 617 253 7904 **f** 522 0613
**e** wampler@mit.edu
Contact: Professor Jan Wampler.
Academic and practical expertise in many countries. Useful publications.

### MATCH (MAnaging The CHange)
Entwicklungsberatung
Horstweg 10, D-14059 Berlin, Germany
**t** + 49 30 326 5012 **f** 326 5214.
**e** avz@matchconsult.de
**w** www.matchconsult.de
Contact: Andreas von Zadow.
Development companions for sustainable development in cities, communities and organisations.

### Max Lock Centre
University of Westminster, 35 Marylebone Road, London NW1 5LS, UK
**t** +44 (0)20 7911 5000 **f** 7911 5171
**e** maxlockc@wmin.ac.uk
**w** www.wmin.ac.uk/~maxlockc/krttp.html.
Research unit based on the civic diagnosis and participatory ideals of the Max Lock Group, supplemented with the archives of John Turner.

### Medvode Community
Mayor and City Planning Dept., Cesta Komandanta Staneta 12, si–1215 Medvode, Slovenia
**t** +386 (0)61 613 600 **f** 611 686
e obcina@medvode.si
w http://welcome.to/Medvode
Contact: Mayor Stanislav Zagar
Useful regional contact point.

### Mount Wise Action Planning
Estate Management Office, 102 Pembroke Street, Plymouth PL1 4JT, UK
**t** +44 (0) 1752 607277.
Active local group. Supply video and report on action planning.

### Murdoch University
Institute for Science and Technology Policy, Murdoch, Perth, Western Australia 6150
**t** +618 9360 2913 **f** 9360 6421
**e** istp@central.murdoch.edu.au
**w** wwwistp.murdoch.edu.au/
Useful research and publications.

### National Tenants Resource Centre
Trafford Hall, Ince Lane, Wimbolds Trafford, Chester CH2 4JP, UK
**t** +44 (0)1244 300 246 **f** 300 818
Training centre for tenants and other community organisations.

### Neighbourhood Initiatives Foundation
The Poplars, Lightmoor, Telford TF4 3QN, UK
**t** +44 (0)1952 590777 **f** 591771
**e** nif@cableinet.co.uk
**w** www.nif.co.uk
Charity specialising in community participation, training and development, often using 'Planning for Real' which is a registered trademark of the Foundation. Has membership scheme, regular newsletter, training courses and useful publications and packs.

### Neighbourhood Planning for Community Revitalisation
330 Humphrey Center, 301-19th Ave South, Minneapolis, MN 55455, USA
**t** 612.625-1551
**e** nelson@freenet.msp.mn.us
**w** www.freenet.msp.mn.us/org/npcr/
University project providing technical assistance and applied research to local community-based organisations.

### New Economics Foundation
Cinamon House, 6-8 Cole Street, London SE1 4YH, UK
**t** +44 (0)20 7407 7447 **f** 7407 6473
**e** info@neweconomics.org
**w** www.neweconomics.org
Contact: Perry Walker/Julie Lewis, Centre for Participation.
Promotes community visioning, indicators, community finance and social audit. Coordinates UK Participation Network.

### Nishikawa Tetsuya
Hosei University Graduate School of Architecture, 7-16-6 Yanaka Taitoh-ku, Tokyo 110-0001, Japan
**t** +81 (0)3 5685 1995 **f** 5685 1995
Contact: Yanaka Gakko.
Experience of community-based development, planning and design.

## North Carolina State University

School of Design, Campus Box 7701, Brooks Hall, Pullen Road, Raleigh, North Carolina 27695-7701, USA
**t** +1 919 515 2205  **f** 515 7330
**e** henry_sanoff@ncsu.edu
**w** www4.ncsu.edu/unity/users/s/sanoff/www/henry.html
Contact: Henry Sanoff.
Expertise in participatory design. Useful publications available.

## North-South Research Network

**w** www.eca.ac.uk/planning/cehs.htm
**e** cehs@eca.ac.uk
Internet-based network of institutions based in the UK involved in human settlements research in the developing world. Includes this handbook with update information and feedback facilities. Hosted by Centre for Environment & Human Settlements, Edinburgh, Scotland (see separate entry).

## Novosibirsk State Academy of Architecture and Fine Arts

Krasny Prospect 38, Novosibirsk-99 630099, Russia
**t** +7 383 2 225 830  **f** 222 905
**e** zhurin@online.nsk.ru
Contact: Nikolai P Zhurin.
Useful regional contact point.

## OKO-Stadt – Universite de Dortmund

Faculty of Spatial Planning, Paul-Lincke-Ufer 30, D10999 Berlin, Germany
**t**. +49 (0) 30 611 8511  **f** 611 2320
**e** oekocity@aol.com
Contact: Prof. Dr. Ekhart Hahn
Private office dealing with model projects and research on urban and spatial ecology.

## Open Society Fund

A. Jaksto st. 9, 2600 Vilnius, Lithuania
**t** +370 2 62 90 50  **f** 22 14 19
**e** sarunas@osf.lt
Contact: Sarunas Liekis.
Useful regional contact point.

## Participatory Design Conference

**e** pdc@cpsr.org
**w** www.cpsr.org/conferences/pdc98/background.html
Network based on a biannual conference in North America.

## PEP

2 Albert Mews, Albert Road, London N4 3RD, UK
**t** +44 (0)20 7281 0438  **f** 7281 3587
**e** admin@pepltd.demon.co.uk
**w** www.pep.org.uk
Non-profit consultancy and training on locally-based housing services and resident involvement. Useful publications and information sheets.

## Permaculture Association

BCM Permaculture Association, London WC1N 3XX, UK
**t** +44 (0)7041 390170
**e** office@permaculture.org.uk
**w** www.permaculture.org.uk
Can provide details of Permaculture design courses and local contacts.

## Places for People

c/o ETP, 9 South Road, Brighton, BN1 6SB, UK
**t/f** +44 (0)1273 542660
**e** streetwise@pobox.com
**w** http://pobox.com/~streetwise
Network of the UK National Association for Urban Studies. Publishes *Streetwise* magazine and useful newsletter.

## Planners Network

Pratt GCPE, 200 Willoughby Ave, Brooklyn, NY 11205, USA
**t** +1 718 636 3461
**e** pn@plannersnetwork.org
**w** www.plannersnetwork.org
Association of progressive planners. Useful publications, papers, contacts.

## Post-war Reconstruction and Development Unit

University of York, The King's Manor, York YO1 2EP, UK
**t** +44 (0)1904 433959  **f** 433949
**e** iaas1@york.ac.uk
**w** www.york.ac.uk/depts/prdu
Contact: Sultan Barakat.
Community planning expertise in post-war situations.

## The Prince of Wales Business Leaders Forum

15-16 Cornwall Terrace, Regent's Park, London NW1 4QP, UK
**t** +44 (0)20 7467 3600  **f** 7467 3610
**e** info@pwblf.org.uk.
Contact: Ros Tennyson, Learning Programmes.
Organises partnership capacity-building events worldwide with focus on the developing world.

## The Prince's Foundation

19-22 Charlotte Road, Shoreditch, London EC2A 3SG, UK
**t** +44 (0)20 7916 7380  **f** 7916 7381
**e** info@princes-foundation.org
**w** www.princes-foundation.org
Unites and extends HRH The Prince of Wales's initiatives in architecture, building and urban regeneration. Encourages a more holistic and humane approach to the planning and design of communities.

## Public Participation Campaign

c/o Friends of the Earth, 26-28 Underwood Street, London N1 7JQ, UK
**t** +44 (0)20 7566 1687  **f** 7566 1689
**e** maryt@foe.co.uk
**w** www.participate.org
Contact: Mary Taylor, Co-ordinator.
Campaign by European non-governmental organisations for transparency and participation in decision-making on the environment. Publishes newsletter, *Participate*, from: Mara Silina, FoE Europe, 29 Rue Blanche, B-1060, Brussels, Belgium
**t** +32 2 542 0180  **f** 537 55 96
**e** mara.silina@foeeurope.org
Eastern European contact point: Svitlana Kravchenko
**t** +380 44 229 3690  **f** 229-3645
**e** skravchenko@gluk.kiev.ua

## Rajyoga Education and Research Foundation National Coordinating Office

25 New Rohtak Road, Karol Bagh, New Delhi, India
**t** +91 11 752 8516  **f** 777 0463
**e** bkshanti@vsnl.com
Contact: Asha Puri.
Useful regional contact point.

## Rod Hackney Associates
St Peters House, Windmill Street,
Macclesfield, Cheshire SK11 7HS, UK
**t** +44 (0)1625 431792 **f** 616929
**e** mail@stpeter.demon.co.uk
Experienced community architecture
and planning practice.

## Roger Evans Associates
59-63 High Street, Kidlington,
Oxford OX5 2DN, UK
**t** +44 (0)1865 377030 **f** 377050
**e** urbandesign@rogerevans.com
Urban design practice with
community planning expertise.

## Royal Institute of British Architects
66 Portland Place, London W1N
4AD, UK
**t** +44 (0)20 7580 5533 **f** 7225 1541
**e** admin@inst.riba.org
**w** www.riba.org
Runs Architects in Schools
programme. Can supply a Schedule
of Services for Community
Architecture. Clients Advisory
Service provides lists of local
community architects. Bookshop
and library have useful publications.

## Royal Town Planning Institute
26 Portland Place, London W1, UK
**t** +1 (0)20 7636 9107 **f** 7323 1582
**e** online@rtpi.org.uk
**w** www.rtpi.org.uk
Promotes public participation in
planning through environmental
education, awards schemes,
publications and a planning
aidscheme.

## Rural Development Network & RuralNet
National Rural Enterprise Centre,
Stoneleigh Park, Warwickshire CV8
2RR, UK
**t** +44 (0)24 7669 6986 **f** 7669 6538
**e** ruralnet@ruralnet.org.uk
**w** www.ruralnet.org.uk/
Provides support for grass-roots
rural development organisations.
See also **InfoRurale**
**w** www.nrec.org.uk/inforurale/.
Internet 'gateway site' with links to
rural development resources.

## Samara State Academy of Architecture and Engineering
Nikitinskaya Square 5/28-19,
443030 Samara, Russia
**t** +7 846 2 362 119 **f** 321 965
**e** academy@icc.ssaba.samara.ru
Contact: Elena Akhmedova
Useful regional contact point.

## Sarkissian Associates Planners
11 Laurel Street, Highgate Hill,
Queensland Australia 4101
**t** + 617 3846 3693 v**f** 3846 2719
**e** sarki_w@arch.usyd.edu.au
Contact: Wendy Sarkissian.
Experienced practitioners and
academics. Useful regional contact.

## Sheep Network
#204 Mejiro House K, 3-25-10
Mejiro, Toshima-ku, Tokyo ZIP171,
Japan
**t** +81 3 3565 4781 **f** 3565 4061
Contact: Mariko Saigö.
Expertise in community architecture
and planning. Regional contact.

## Shelter Forum, Kenya
PO Box 39493, Nairobi, Kenya
**t** +254 2 442108 **f** 445166.
**e** <elijah@itdg.or.ke>
Contact: Elijah Agevi.
Coalition of NGOs in East Africa
with research and training
programmes about community
involvement in urban upgrading.

## Shoevegas Arts and Media
Top floor, 24-28 Hatton Wall,
London EC1N 8JH, UK
**t** +1 (0)20 7916 6969 **f** 7916 9977
**e** studio@shoevegas.com
**w** www.shoevegas.com
Multimedia group. Experience with
creating electronic maps.

## Society for Development Studies
Opp. Pillanji, Sarojini Nagar, New
Delhi 110023, India
**t** +91 11 6875862 **f** 6875862
**e** sds@giasdl01.vsnl.net.in
**w** www.sdsindia.org
Contact: Vinay D. Lall, Director.
Research, training and consultancy
institution. Useful regional contact
point.

## Sofia University of Architecture, Civil Engineering and Geodesy
1 Smirnensky Blvd, Sofia 1421,
Bulgaria
**t** +359 2 668 449 **f** 656 809
**e** st_popv_far@bcace%.uacg.acad.bg
Contact: Stefan Popov.
Useful regional contact point.

## SOFTECH Energie, Tecnologia, Ambiente
via Cernaia 1, 1-10121 Torino, Italy
**t** +39 (0) 11 562 2289 **f** 540 219
**e** softech@softech-team.it
Contact: Roberto Pagani.
Consultancy integrating technology,
economy, public administration and
citizen participation in regeneration.

## South Bank University
Faculty of the Built Environment,
202 Wandsworth Road, London
SW8 2JZ, UK
**t** +44 (0)20 7815 7283 **f** 7815 7366
**e** nick.hall@sbu.ac.uk
Contact: Nick Hall.
Community-based disaster
management research. Courses on
tenant participation.

## Sustainable Strategies & Solutions, Inc.
1535 NE 90th Street, Seattle, WA
98115-3142, USA
**t** +1 (206) 979-9842 **f** 524-2524
**e** J_Gary_Lawrence@msn.com
Contact: J. Gary Lawrence.
Helps public, private and civic
organizations achieve their
individual and shared objectives
through incorporation of
sustainable development theory
and practice.

## Tallinn College of Engineering
Tallinn, Estonia.
**t** +372 2 645 0588 **f** 645 0956
**e** info@joan.ee
Contacts: Aleksander Skolimowsk,
Kristi Aija.
Useful regional contact point.

## Tamagawa, Community Design
House, 2-11-10 Tamagawa Den-en
chofu, Setagaya-ku, Tokyo, Japan
**t** +81 3 3721 8699 **f** 3721-8699
**e** itoxx24@ibm.net
Contact: Yasuyoshi Hayashi.
Experienced practitioners.

**Tenants Participatory Advisory Service**
Brunswick House, Broad Street, Salford M6 5BZ, UK
**t** +44 (0)161 745 7903  **f** 745 9259
**e** info@tpas.org.uk
**w** www.tpas.org.uk
Provides information, advice, training, consultancy, seminars and conferences on involving tenants in their housing management.

**Tirana Polytechnical University**
Faculty of Engineering, Architecture Dept., Rruga Udhamed Gvolle, shavsha No. 54, Tirana, Albania
**t** +355 42 332 52
Contact: Nardiola Hoxa
Useful regional contact point.

**Tokyo La-Npo**
1-6, Akazuthumi 4 Chome, Setagayaku, Tokyo 156, Japan
**t** +81 (0)3 3324 4440  **f** 3324 3444
**e** BYA17344@nifty.ne.jp
Contact: Misako Arai.
Supports local community planning activity in Japan.

**Town & Country Planning Association**
17 Carlton House Terrace, London SW1Y 5AS, UK
**t** +44 (0)20 7930 8903
**e** tcpa@tcpa.org.uk
**w** www.tcpa.org.uk
Campaign group for reforming the planning system. Useful publications.

**United Nations Centre for Human Settlements (Habitat)**
Pob 30030, Nairobi, Kenya
**t** +254 2 624 231  **f** 624 265/66
**e** selman.erguden@unchs.org
**w** www.unchs.org
Contact: Selman Erguden
Focal point for social development.

**United Nations Development Programme, Turkey**
Zeki Pasa, Apt 12-6, Macka Caddesi, MackA, Istanbul, Turkey
**t** +90 212 248 3612  **f** 296 1951
Contact: Uner Kirdar (Secretary for UN Habitat 2 conference, 1996).
Useful regional contact point.

**Urban Design Group**
6 Ashbrook Courtyard, Westbrook Street, Blewbury, Oxfordshire OX11 9QA, UK
**t** +44 (0)1235 851415 **f** 851410
**e** admin@udg.org.uk
**w** rudi.herts.ac.uk
Contact: Susie Turnbull.
National voluntary organisation that helps set urban design agenda. Its Public Participation Programme promotes good practice through research and publications. Register of experienced professionals and good practice guidance on web site including information relating to this handbook.

**Urban Design Alliance**
**w** www.towns.org.uk/ppo/udal
Inter-professional campaign group promoting urban design.

**Urban Villages Forum**
19-22 Charlotte Road, Shoreditch, London EC2A 3SG, UK
**t** +44 (0)20 7916 7380  **f** 7916 7381
**e** info@princes-foundation.org
**w** www.princes-foundation.org
Contact: David Warburton.
Campaigning organisation promoting urban villages; the planning and development of integrated, sustainable communities. Provide support for action planning events. Maintains list of experienced professionals. Useful publications.

**URBED**
19 Store Street, London WC1E 7DH, UK
**t** +44 (0)20 7436 8050  **f** 7436 8083
**e** urbed@urbed.co.uk
**w** www.urbed.co.uk
Contact: Nicholas Falk.
Urban regeneration consultants with long experience of community planning. Expertise in round table workshops.

**Vista Consulting**
16 Old Birmingham Road, Lickey End, Broomsgrove B60 1DE, UK
**t** +44 (0)1527 837930  **f** 837940
**e** vistaanne@aol.com
Contact: Ann Brooks
Information and consultancy on critical mass events such as real time strategic change.

**Wikima**
23 Leamington Road Villas, London W11 1HS, UK
**t/f** +44 (0)20 7229 7320
**e** romys@compuserve.com
Contact: Romy Shovelton.
Information and consultancy on open space technology. Useful publications and videos.

**Wilkinson Hindle Hallsall Lloyd**
98-100 Duke Street, Liverpool L1 5AG, UK
**t** +44 (0) 151 708 8944  **f** 709 1737
Architecture practice with expertise in housing cooperatives, choice catalogues and design meetings.

**Wordsearch**
5 Old Street, London EC1 9HL, UK
**t** 0171 549 5400  **f** 336 8660
**e** studio@wordsearch.co.uk
**w** www.wordsearch.co.uk
Contact: Lee Mallett.
Communications consultancy with expertise in public participation in urban design.

**Yale Urban Design Workshop**
Center for Urban Design Research, Box 208242, New Haven, Connecticut 06520, USA
**t** +1 203-432-2288  **f** 432 7175
**e** udw@yale.edu
**w** www.architecture.yale.edu/re/udw/FrontDoor/
Contacts: Alan Plattus, Michael Haverland.
Well established urban design studio at Yale University working with surrounding local communities.

# Credits and thanks

This handbook is the product of three related initiatives:

**Tools for Community Design Programme**
Supported by The Prince's Foundation (and formerly The Prince of Wales's Institute of Architecture), this initiative promotes good practice through the production of high quality, universally applicable, how-to-do-it information using participatory editing techniques.

**Urban Design Group Public Participation Programme (UDGPPP)**
Funded by the Department of the Environment, Transport and the Regions (DETR) for England, this action research programme assisted and evaluated 12 public participation events and 10 seminars in England during 1996 and 1997 to establish good practice principles.

**Action Planning in Developing Countries Research Project**
Funded by the UK's Department for International Development (DFID), this project examined practice in countries in many parts of the world during 1998 and 1999 to establish methods most appropriate for developing countries.

The book has benefited from close collaboration with other related initiatives. These include:

**Community-based Disaster Mitigation**
A research project funded by the European Community and based at London's South Bank University.

**Tools for Community Regeneration**
A project to develop a database of community regeneration based at Hastings Trust, UK.

An advisory group of individuals from the above initiatives – listed on the imprint page – has been particularly helpful in guiding the book's evolution.

Many **people** have helped with the work. Special thanks are due to all those who sent in material, participated in editing workshops, provided inspiration or commented on drafts. They include:

| | |
|---|---|
| Jon Aldenton | Ripin Kalra |
| Anthea Atha | Joan Kean |
| Debbie Bartlett | Sonia Khan |
| Stephen Batey | Sally King |
| Roger Bellers | Charles Knevitt |
| Dianah Bennett | Anne Kramer |
| John Billingham | Alison Lammas |
| Jeff Bishop | Birgit Laue |
| Peter Blake | Akan Leander |
| Jeremy Brook | David Lewis |
| Charles Campion | Julie Lewis |
| Jeremy Caulton | Arnold Linden |
| June Cannon | Melanie Louise |
| Emma Collier | David Lunts |
| Tony Costello | Caroline Lwin |
| Robert Cowan | Frances MacDermott |
| Simon Croxton | Lee Mallett |
| Robin Deane | Tony Meadows |
| James Derounian | Frances MacDermott |
| Stephanie Donaldson | Jo McCaren |
| Roger Evans | Nim Moorthy |
| Yanaka Gakko | Babar Mumtaz |
| Flora Gathorne-Hardy | Michael Mutter |
| Joanna Gent | Mary Myers |
| Christine Goldschmidt | Jenneth Parker |
| Suzanne Gorman | Michael Parkes |
| Andrew Goldring | Geoffrey Payne |
| Peter Greenhalf | Alan Plattus |
| Virginia Griffin | Jules Pretty |
| Felicity Gu | Richard Pullen |
| Susan Guy | Debbie Radcliffe |
| Rod Hackney | Renate Ruether-Greaves |
| Nick Hall | Peter Richards |
| Nabeel Hamdi | Alex Rook |
| Brian Hanson | Jon Rowland |
| Lorraine Hart | David Sanderson |
| Yasuyoshi Hayashi | Henry Sanoff |
| Michael Hebbert | Yoshimitsu Shiozaki |
| Mandy Heslop | Romy Shovelton |
| David Hughes | Jack Sidener |
| Paul Jenkins | Jonathan Sinclair Wilson |
| Richard John | Miriam Solly |
| Sam Jones-Hill | Steve Smith |

Ian Taylor
Ros Tennyson
Simon Thomas
John Thompson
Stephen Thwaites
Catherine Tranmer
Susie Turnbull
John F C Turner
John Twigg
Pat Wakely
Perry Walker
Diane Warburton

Colin Ward
Margaret Wilkinson
Diane Warburton
Mae Wates
Max Wates
Dick Watson
Nicholas Wilkinson
Adele Wilter
Julie Witham
John Worthington
Charles Zucker

**Organisations** which have provided assistance include:

Architecture Foundation
Ball State University
*Building Design*
Centre for Community Visions
Centre for Disaster Preparedness
Countryside Commission
CLAWS 2
Chinese University of Hong Kong
Edinburgh World Heritage Trust
Free Form Arts Trust
Hackney Building Exploratory
Hertfordshire County Council
Neighbourhood Initiatives Foundation
Planning Aid UK
RUDI
Roger Evans Associates
Shoevegas

*Apologies for any omissions.*

## Book evolution

The production of this book has been guided by the belief that participatory editing and testing of good practice guidance is one of the most effective ways of achieving widespread improvement of practice and knowledge transfer.

The process adopted has been as follows:

1 **Title and format**
Overall concept established by the author, designer and supporting organisations.
2 **Publicity**
Call for information leaflet distributed widely.
3 **Pilot projects, seminars and research**
Monitoring and evaluation of pilot projects, participation in seminars and workshops, desk research.
4 **Sample material published**
Ten methods and four scenarios published in *Urban Design Quarterly*, July 1998. Over 1,000 copies distributed. Also available on Urban Design Group web site.
5 **Editing workshops**
Held at the South Bank University in London, November 1998, and in the Philippines, January 1999.
6 **Consultation draft**
Circulated to over 60 practitioners. Over 35 responses received.
7 **Final draft**
Circulated to main supporting organisations and advisors.

Feedback received at each stage has been invaluable in developing the book, although the editor takes full responsibility for all views expressed.

It is planned to continue the process with further editions, translations and adaptations tailored to specific local contexts.

# Photocredits

**Location, date, and photographer or source of photos and illustrations. Many thanks to all those who have allowed their material to be used.**

Photos not credited are by Nick Wates.

Cover: Yellamanchilli, Adrapradesh, India, 96, Nick Hall; Berlin, John Thompson & Partners, 96; Hong Kong, 98, Jack Sidener; Hackney Building Exploratory, London, UK, 99.
ii       Duke Street, Liverpool, UK, 97.
12      Wakefield, UK, 97.
14      Woodberry Down, London, UK, 97.
15      Liverpool, UK, 97.
16      Punjab, Pakistan, 92, Jules Pretty. Hastings, UK, 97.
17      Honduras, 94, Jules Pretty. Runcorn, UK, 79, CDS Liverpool.
19      Pruitt Igoe, USA.
20      Sri Lanka, 92, Jules Pretty. Wenceslas Square, Prague, Czech Republic, 96, John Thompson & Partners.
21      Trans Nzoia, Kenya, 93, John Thompson. Hastings, UK, 90.
22      Hong Kong, 98, Jack Sidener.
25      Prague, Czech Republic, 96, John Thompson & Partners.
26      Hastings, UK, 90.
28-9   Hackney Building Exploratory, London, UK, 99.
30      Town Quay, Barking, UK, 98, Free Form Arts Trust.
31      Caldmore Green, Walsall, UK, 98, Free Form Arts Trust.
33      *Leeds Evening Post*, 9.8.94 *The Times*, 23.8.94 & 29.12.94. *West Cumbrian News & Star,* 15.11.94.
34      Blairs College, Aberdeen, UK, 94, John Thompson & Partners. Holy Trinity Brompton, London, UK, 97 (2). Wornington Green, London, UK, 89, John Thompson & Partners.
35      Sidon, Lebanon, 97, John Thompson & Partners. Liverpool, UK, 97.
37      West Cork, Ireland, 87 (6).
39      Setagaya Community Design Centre, Tokyo, Japan, 95.
41      Richmond Virginia, USA, 96.
42      Fiji, 95, Jules Pretty.
44      Duke Street, Liverpool, 97.
47      Hong Kong, 98, Jack Sidener.
48-9   London, UK, Alexandra Rook, CLAWS (2). Tokyo, 98, Henry Sanoff.
50      Brixton, London, UK, 93. Duke Street, Liverpool, UK, 97 (2).
54      Kiambu, Kenya, 93, Jules Pretty. Anon.

55      Sri Lanka, 92, John Thompson. Kiambu, Tamil Nadu, India, 91, Irene Guijt. Burkina Faso, Africa, 92, Jules Pretty.
56      Hastings, 99, Greenhalf Photography.
57      Shoreditch, London, 98, ShoeVegas.
58      Birmingham, UK, 94.
59      Kingswood, UK, 96, Roger Evans Associates.
61      New Town, Edinburgh, 96, Edinburgh World Heritage Trust. Hastings, UK, 90.
64      Yellamanchilli, Adrapradesh, India, 96, Nick Hall. Yellamanchilli, 96, Roger Bellers. Igbalangao, Panay Island, Philippines, 95, Nick Hall. Yellamanchilli, 96, Nick Hall.
66-7   Reproduced from *Future Search.*
68      Tower Hamlets, London, UK, 99, Architecture Foundation.
69      Ball State University, Indiana, USA, 95, Tony Costelllo.
71      George Street, Hastings, UK, 89.
72-3   East Street, Farnham, UK, 97 (4). Bath, UK, 97.
75      Kent, UK, 97, Debbie Bartlett.
76      Igbalangao, Panay Island, Philippines, 95, Nick Hall.
77      Easton, Bristol, UK, 93, Vizability Arts. West Bengal, India, 90, Robert Chambers.
78      Bangaladesh, 94, Nabeel Hamdi.
80      London, 70s, Town & Country Planning Association.
81      Ball State University, Indiana, USA, 85, S.Talley.
82      The Prince of Wales's Institute of Architecture, London, UK, 97.
83      Oxpens Initiative, Oxford, UK, 97, Roger Evans Associates. Birmingham, UK, 94. Stockport, UK, 88, Community Technical Aid Centre Manchester. Forge Project, Cinderford, UK, 93.
84      Hackney, London, UK, 82, Hunt Thompson Associates. MUDStudio, Ball State University, Indiana, USA, 94, Anthony Costello (2).
85      Lea View, Hackney, London, UK, 82, Hunt Thompson Associates. St Leonards-on-sea, UK, 90.
86      *Madison Courier*, USA, 86.
87      *The Daily Clintonian*, USA, 81.
88-9   East Street, Farnham, UK, 97.
91      The Prince of Wales's Institute of Architecture, London, UK, 97.
94      Hastings, UK, 99, Greenhalf Photography.
95      Igbalangao, Panay Island, Philippines, 95, Nick Hall. Kent, UK, 96, Debbie Bartlett.
96      Leaflets: Planning Aid for London,

South Wales Planning Aid.
99      Oxpens Quarter, Oxford, UK, 97.
101    Queens Park, Bedford,UK, 95, unknown. London, UK, 97.
102    Duke Street, Liverpool, UK. 97. Ore Valley, Hastings, UK, 97.
106    Ore Valley, Hastings, UK, 97.
107    East Street, Farnham, UK, 96.
108    Mount Wise, Plymouth, UK (map). Pittsburgh, USA, 88, John Thompson & Partners. Poundbury, UK, 89. Panay Island, Philippines, 95.
109    Calvay Coop, Glasgow, 85. Wakefield, UK, 97.
110-1  Mount Wise, Plymouth, UK, 99.
115    Muncie Design Studio, Ball State University, USA, 97, Tony Costello.
117    Igbalangao, Panay Island, Philippines, 95, Nick Hall.
119    Bath, UK, 97.
120-1  Farnham, UK, 97.
123    El Cerrito, California, USA, 98. Richard Ivey. Viterbo, Italy, 94. Richard Ivey (2).
124-5  Yale University, USA, 96.
126    Shoreham, UK, 97. Lightmoor, UK, 90, Tony Gibson, NIF.
128    *Building Design* 9.4.98 (3 + drawing). Hammersmith, London, 98, Architecture Foundation.
130    Yunnan, China, 97, Jules Pretty.
132    Lostwithiel, Cornwall, UK, 85, CAG
134    Krakow, Poland, 96.
136    Kobe, Japan, 95.
138    North Shields, UK, 87, Freeform.
140    Hesketh Street, Liverpool, UK, 84, *Architects' Journal.*
142    Wakefield, UK, 97.
144    Children's drawing, Nishikawa Tetsuya, Tokyo, Japan, 98.
146    Mount Wise, Plymouth, UK 97.
148    Model of Krakow, Poland, 96.
150    Shoreham, UK, 98.
152    Remaking Cities, Pittsburgh, USA, 98.
154    Unknown, John F C Turner.
156    Farnham, UK, 97.
158    Krakow, Poland, 96.
160    Crowhurst, UK, Peter Smith, Picturemaps, Hastings.
162    Hitchen Vision, Hertfordshire County Council, UK, 96.
164    Sidon, Lebanon, 97, John Thompson & Partners.
173    Drawings by Jack Sidener.
175    Drawing by Tony Costello, 98.
177    Drawing by Tony Costello, 98.
180    Drawing by Tony Costello, 98.
222    Planning Aid Conference, South Bank University, London, UK, 98.
224    John Thompson & Partners
230    Greenhalf Photography, 99.

# Feedback on this book

**Further editions of this handbook are planned as well as translations and adaptations. So feedback would be most useful and welcome.**

## Ways you can help

- **Comments**
  Send any comments on the book, good or bad. Quotes suitable for publicity especially welcome!

- **Changes**
  Send specific amendments, preferably marked up in coloured ink on the book or photocopies of pages.

- **Additions**
  Send details of material that should be covered: extra principles, methods, scenarios, glossary items, books, films, contacts etc. It would help greatly if these could be in the same format as the book.

- **Illustrations**.
  Good photos or drawings are always welcome (be sure to specify clearly if you want them back).

- **Hold an editing workshop**.
  Organise an editing workshop and send in the results. See next page for a sample format.

- **Help with a translation or adaptation**.
  Translators, editors, local publishers needed. Why not use the framework and incorporate your own photos and local examples.

Please complete the form on page 223 or make contact in any way convenient: post, email, fax or telephone.

## All communication to:

Handbook Editor, Community Planning Publications
7 Tackleway, Hastings TN34 3DE, United Kingdom
Tel: +44 (0)1424 447888  Fax: +44 (0)1424 441514
Email: info@wates.demon.co.uk
Check the Community Planning Handbook Website for the latest information: www.wates.demon.co.uk

Dear Editor,

Your handbook is great. But in the next edition, please include:

1. A page on the .......................... method (info enclosed).

2. Scenario for .......................... based on our project here (details enclosed).

3. A really good video called .......................... (also enclosed)

Let me know when it comes out.

yours ever

PS. Check out www.................... if you haven't already. Some useful info there.

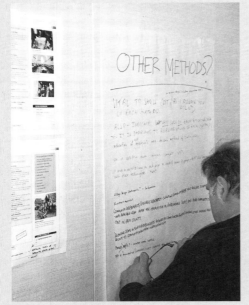

**Editing workshop**
*Blown up photocopies of book pages pinned on the wall allow people to write in comments and amendments. Blank sheets stimulate people to think about additional material that could be included in the next edition.*

## Exhibition material
Display pages of *The Community Planning Handbook* are available from Community Planning Publications, in colour or black and white, and at various sizes. Enquire for details.

# Editing workshop format

For helping make improvements to this handbook. Also useful for stimulating debate on community planning generally. Can be run as independent sessions or as part of a conference or other programme. Participants should ideally have had time to look through the book beforehand but this is not essential.

**1   Setting up**
Display some or all of the pages on a wall, preferably blown up to A3 size on a photocopier. Arrange in sections – 'Principles', 'Methods', 'Scenarios' etc – with large headings above. Insert blank pages in each section with headings 'Other principles', 'Other methods', etc. Have a supply of coloured felt tips.  (2 hours)

**2   Introduction**
Welcome participants. Explain purpose of event and structure of book display. (10 mins)

**3   Participatory editing**
Participants examine the display individually or in small groups and write comments directly on the pages or blank sheets. Informal discussion encouraged. (20 - 60 mins depending on whether people have looked through the book beforehand)

**4   General discussion**
On implications for local activity, initiatives needed etc. (20-40 mins)

**5   Send in results**
Mail or fax originals or copies of sheets plus any notes of the discussion to:
Handbook Editor,
Community Planning Publications,
7 Tackleway, Hastings TN34 3DE, UK
Fax: +44 (0)1424 441514

**Running time: 60–100mins**
**Ideal numbers: 5–20**

# Feedback Form

Please complete and return the form below if you want to be notified of future editions or can offer any help or advice. Feel free to use additional sheets, enclose material or communicate in a different way altogether.

Name _____

Organisation (if any) _____

Contact details (address, tel, fax, email, web)
_____
_____

Comments on this edition (good and bad)
_____
_____
_____

Suggestions for a revised edition (suggestions adopted will be acknowledged)
_____
_____
_____

I/we can supply information/photos/drawings covering the following methods/case studies/ publications/films etc. (all material used will be acknowledged)
_____
_____
_____
_____

Please let me/us know when the revised
English language edition is available   ☐ yes   ☐ no

I/we would be interested to have translations or adaptations in the following languages
_____

I/we could help with work on translations or adaptations   ☐ yes   ☐ no

I am happy for you to pass my details on
to other community planning networks   ☐ yes   ☐ no

Date _____

**Return to**: Handbook Editor, Community Planning Publications
7 Tackleway, Hastings TN34 3DE, UK
Fax: +44 (0)1424 441514  Email: info@wates.demon.co.uk

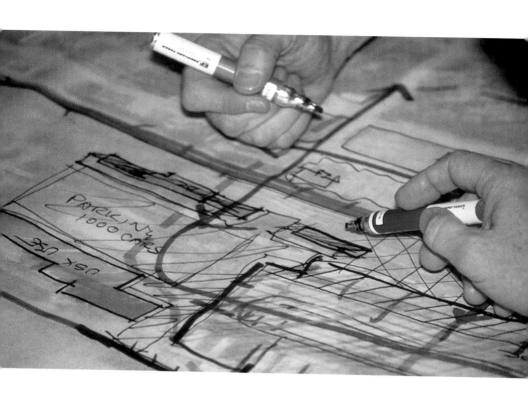